Congress on Display, Congress at Work

Congress on Display, Congress at Work

Edited by

WILLIAM T. BIANCO

Ann Arbor

THE UNIVERSITY OF MICHIGAN PRESS

Published in the United States of America by
The University of Michigan Press
Manufactured in the United States of America
∞ Printed on acid-free paper

2003   2002   2001   2000   4   3   2   1

A CIP catalog record for this book is available from the British Library.

Library of Congress Cataloging-in-Publication Data

Congress on display, Congress at work / edited by William T. Bianco.
     p. cm.
   Includes bibliographical references and index.
   ISBN 0-472-11118-3 (cloth : alk. paper) — ISBN 0-472-08711-8
(pbk. : alk. paper)
   1. United States. Congress.   I. Bianco, William T., 1960–

JK1021 .C557   2000
328.73—dc21   00-033802

For Dick Fenno,
who taught us all

Contents

Preface

This book is the product of a conference held at the University of Rochester in October 1997 in honor of Richard F. Fenno's 40th anniversary as a university professor. It honors a man whose contributions to legislative studies, to political science, to the Rochester political science department, and to his students are so large as to defy superlatives.

The essays in this book span the field of legislative studies, ranging from Aldrich and Shepsle's theory of legislative institutions to Castle and Fett's analysis of party switching by southern politicians to Balla and Wright's work on congressional control over the bureaucracy. All of them have their roots somewhere in Dick Fenno's research program. His characterization of legislators as rational actors, his expectation that congressional rules, procedures, and institutions reflect the preferences and constraints faced by members of Congress, and his insistence on seeing politics as politicians do are a constant throughout this volume.

As with any edited work, this one owes its fruition to the efforts of many individuals and institutions. Many thanks are owed to the Department of Political Science at the University of Rochester, especially Pamm Ferguson, Bruce Jacobs, and Harold Stanley for their work in organizing the conference, and to the University of Rochester for providing the necessary funding.

As for myself, I'd like to thank the more senior Rochester graduates for cheerfully deferring to my judgments about this volume's format, content, and deadlines. Chuck Myers of the University of Michigan Press also deserves thanks for finding this book a home. James Honaker provided able research assistance. And Regina Smyth supplied her usual and much-appreciated sage advice and wise counsel.

My final acknowledgment is to Dick Fenno. His career is a demonstration of the qualities that define a first-rate scholar: focus, persistence, insight, and grace. After an amazing 40-year run, with awards and accomplishments enough for an entire subfield, he remains hard at work, soaking and poking away. He is an academic's academic.

As a final demonstration of the position that Dick holds in all of our hearts, I defer to another scholar, Chuck Jones. During my first year as a graduate student at Rochester, Jones gave the Cutler Lecture. Before beginning his

x   Preface

discussion of the Carter presidency, Jones explained to the nonacademics in the audience what a top-notch political science department they had at Rochester. When he got to Dick Fenno, he offered an analogy. The way congressional scholars see it, he said, Dick Fenno sits at the right hand of God. In fact, he continued, when students of Congress die and go to heaven, which is their reward for trying to make sense of the legislative process, they'll walk through the gates, look up at the dais, and ask, "Who's that guy sitting next to Dick Fenno?"

Jones was entirely right. Dick Fenno has changed the way that we think about Congress and how we think Congress should be studied. For these accomplishments, and for all the other lessons he has taught us along the way, this book is gratefully dedicated to him.

Richard Fenno's Conventional Wisdom

William T. Bianco

In this essay I examine how Richard Fenno's seminal works, *Congressmen in Committees* and *Home Style,* underlie and motivate studies of the legislative process. To paraphrase *Home Style,* my goal is to describe these works as they are seen through the eyes of legislative scholars. Along the way, I will show how the chapters in this book fit into this literature, both in their citations of Fenno's work and in their attempts to extend Fenno's insights, hypotheses, and findings.

At one level, gauging Dick Fenno's influence on legislative scholarship is easy: it is all pervasive. It is hard to imagine a graduate reading list in American politics or legislative studies that does not include most of Fenno's publications. A look at citation indexes reinforces this image. Stewart (1998) finds that *Home Style* and *Congressmen in Committees* were, respectively, the second and third most cited works in articles on congressional politics published between 1991 and 1997 in the *American Political Science Review, American Journal of Political Science,* and *Legislative Studies Quarterly.*

Fenno's work has also profoundly influenced how scholars teach courses on Congress and the legislative process. I suspect that virtually every course has a lecture on the relationship between member goals and strategic premises, as described in *Congressmen in Committees,* or works through *Home Style*'s litany of allocation of resources, presentation of self, and explanations of Washington activity. Long after they were written, Fenno's books remain popular choices for undergraduate courses. In fact, Maisel's (1984) review of texts for legislative politics courses noted that anyone who wanted his or her new texts to be widely adopted would be wise to "change their name to Fenno" (1). All in all, these results suggest that congressional scholars would not go too far wrong if they simply followed the lead of Austen-Smith and Wright (1994) and listed one or more of Fenno's books in their reference section, even if they do not actually cite the works in the main text.

The goal in this essay is to identify elements of Fenno's research that have become conventional wisdom or stylized fact in the field of legislative studies. The data consist of a citation search on Journal Storage (JSTOR) to capture all mentions of *Home Style* and *Congressmen in Committees* in articles published in three journals: *American Political Science Review, American Journal of Political Science,* and *Journal of Politics.* The search examined citations made after 1978, the year *Home Style* was published.[1]

The search revealed five interesting concentrations. *Congressmen in Committees* stands out for its description of members of Congress as rational, purposive actors and for its statement that congressional committees both mat- ter and differ. *Home Style* is noted for its focus on legislators' careers in their districts and for the distinctions it draws among geographic, reelection, and primary constituencies. Both books are also cited for their use of participant- observation techniques.

Making the World Safe for Purposive Behavior

An easy finalist for Dick Fenno's most important contribution to the conven- tional wisdom on Congress and legislatures is his characterization in *Con- gressmen in Committees* of House members and Senators as purposive, goal- directed, rational actors:

> A member of the House is a congressman first and a committee member second. As a congressman he holds certain personal political goals. As a committee member he will work to further these same goals through com- mittee membership. Committee membership, in other words, is not an end in itself for the individuals. Each member of each committee wants his committee service to bring him some benefit in terms of goals he holds as an individual congressman. And he will act on his committee in ways cal- culated to achieve these goals.
>
> Of all the goals espoused by members of the House, three are basic. They are: re-election, influence within the House, and good public policy. A fourth one, a career beyond the House, will be treated peripherally. (A fifth, private gain, will not be treated at all.) (Fenno 1973, 1)

This passage from *Committees* appears in papers ranging from various analyses of committees (e.g., Maltzman 1995; Shipan 1992) to pork barrel politics (Evans 1994), bill sponsorship in the Senate (Schiller 1995), elite response to referenda (Gerber 1996), legislative agenda setting (Mouw and Mackuen 1992), and presidential nomination campaigns (Gurian 1993).

Purposive behavior assumptions also play a central role in all of the papers in this volume. For example, Balla and Wright's analysis of congres- sional advisory committees begins by assuming that members of Congress are motivated by goals such as reelection and policy. Advisory committees have the important task of supplying members with information about how these goals can best be achieved—and whether the bureaucracy is helping or hinder- ing these pursuits. Along the same lines, Diana Evans's paper on how party leaders use distributive legislation to win support for other proposals rests on the assumption that legislators hold both reelection and policy goals and that they are willing to trade off one in favor of the other. Castle and Fett show that party switching, in which members of Congress change their party affiliation, can be traced to goals such as reelection and the desire to enact good public policy.

In addition, all of this volume's analyses of the post-1994 Republican majority in the House (by DeGregorio, Forgette, Sinclair, and Marshall et al.) assume that both party leaders and their followers make strategic, purposive choices. Sinclair, in particular, uses principal-agent theory to assess the leadership styles of former Speaker Gingrich and his Democratic predecessors. Her results suggest that the observed stylistic differences were more a response to context than a revolutionary shift from one model of leadership to another.

Fenno as Exemplar

Fenno was not the first congressional scholar to make purposive behavior assumptions. Even so, his effort was notable for three reasons. To begin, it was one of the first uses of the assumption by a scholar whose research was clearly part of legislative studies rather than positive theory—and a scholar whose previous work had relied on theories of norms and roles (Searing 1991). By working to "dismantle purposive roles to investigate personal political goals" (Searing 1991, 1248), Fenno's endorsement of purposive behavior made it much harder for traditionally oriented scholars to dismiss the approach.

The use of purposive behavior assumptions in *Congressmen in Committees* was also significant because of the book's strong empirical component. Rather than discussing Congress in the abstract, Fenno showed how the assumption helped to explain important real-world outcomes, including committee assignments, committee organization, and policy outputs. His approach put meat on the purposive behavior bones. The point was not how an imaginary legislator would pursue reelection, good public policy, or internal influence. Rather, Fenno emphasized the problems and opportunities facing members of Congress in the postwar, prereform era and how they solved the former in pursuit of the latter.

Fenno's description of purposive behavior was also notable for its richness. His members of Congress are motivated by several goals. Moreover, different motives might drive behavior in different contexts. This characterization served as a recommendation and corrective to both the pro– and anti–rational choice camps in legislative studies and in the discipline at large. Scholars who were critical of the approach were reminded that they could not conflate rational choice with simple operationalizations of this assumption, such as the notion that legislators are single-minded seekers of reelection.

For positive theorists, "Fenno's admonition" (Browne 1992, 1190) was a warning that scholars cannot ignore the "richness of legislators' motivations"

(Herrick, Moore, and Hibbing 1994, 215). The value of more complicated (and more realistic) specifications of motivations is evident in many contemporary works, such as Lindsay's (1991) study of voting on the Strategic Defense Initiative, Sinclair's (1992a) work on congressional leadership, and Sullivan's (1990) analysis of presidential influence in Congress. Similar evidence has been found in analyses of legislatures in other countries, including Shamir's (1991) analysis of Israeli political elites, as well as in analyses of the historical Congress (Bianco, Spence, and Wilkerson 1996).

Moving Beyond Fenno's Specification

Fenno's characterization of members of Congress as rational actors has become a well-cited referent in the legislative politics literature—a statement of what most if not all scholars accept to be true. In effect, what Fenno did was make purposive behavior assumptions safe for other scholars who work in legislative politics and in other subfields.

In this volume, the Aldrich-Shepsle paper illustrates how Fenno's assumptions about purposive behavior continue to motivate inquiry. Aldrich and Shepsle focus on the evolution of congressional institutions, including the growth of House committees under Henry Clay, the emergence of majoritarian rules of procedure under Thomas Reed, the fight to eliminate the Rules Committee as a veto point in House proceedings, and the evolution of cloture in the Senate.

Aldrich and Shepsle argue that scholars must move beyond descriptions (however detailed) of these events to explanations of why they occurred. The solution, they argue, is to begin as Fenno did, by assuming that members of Congress are rational actors who choose institutions that are consistent with their goals. The essential message of this paper is that purposive behavior assumptions do not amount to wholesale simplifications of real-world calculations and processes, as many critics have claimed. Rather, as the authors' discussion of Clay's speakership suggests, these assumptions provide us with a framework with which to characterize the nature of these complexities and their impact on behavior and outcomes.

This paper is also notable for its attempt to wrestle with the complexities inherent in applying a rational choice model to the real world. If we accept Fenno's notion that legislators can be motivated by a number of very different goals (or some combination), it may be difficult to establish a particular legislator's motivations in some situation. Likewise, legislators may have different, even incompatible, ideas of what ends will be achieved by changes in congressional institutions. A rational choice model of institution selection must account for all of these complexities while remaining tractable and solvable.

Specifying How "Committees Matter, Committees Differ"

Congressmen in Committees has also stimulated researchers to identify and explain differences in the internal organization and operation of congressional committees. As Fenno stated in his introduction,

> This book rests on a simple assumption and conveys a simple theme. The assumption is that congressional committees matter. The theme is that congressional committees differ. Both are commonplace. But this book has been written because those who think committees matter and those who think committees differ have not yet fully accommodated one to the other—not intellectually and not in practice. (Fenno 1973, xiii)

In essence, Fenno argues that the established picture of congressional committees (e.g., committees are experts in their jurisdictions, floor legislators defer to committee recommendations, and committee chairs are powerful) had been stated as though it applied equally to all committees. His goal was to demonstrate that committees in both the House and the Senate differed on these and other dimensions.

More specifically, Fenno shows that 1960s-era congressional committees differed with respect to the committee members' goals and the committee's environment (actors off the committee who care about what the committee does and who can influence whether members achieve their goals). This variation in turn caused committees to differ with respect to their strategic premises (members' general rules or guidelines for decision making), decision-making processes (the amount of partisanship, degree of specialization, and role of the committee chair), and, ultimately, the committee's outputs or substantive policy decisions.

Fenno's conclusions about specific committees appear frequently in contemporary research as a source of information about how a particular committee operates. Examples include Schiller's (1995) work on bill sponsorship in the Senate, Cook's (1988) analysis of members' media strategies, Wright's (1990) and Kolman's (1997) study of committee-level lobbying, Wooley's (1993) paper on regulatory politics, and Hall and Evans's (1990) model of subcommittee politics. More generally, Schickler and Rich (1997) use *Committees* to underlie their analysis of procedural coalitions in the House. These works implicitly accept Fenno's characterization of the factors that drive committee membership, organization, and outputs and the expectation that committees will differ with respect to these factors.

Scholars also use *Committees* to justify a variety of assumptions about the committee assignment process (Munger 1988; Schiller 1995; Stewart 1992). Krehbiel and Rivers (1988) and Schiller (1995) posit that assignments are largely driven by self-selection. However, as Dion (1992) suggests, members are often co-opted onto certain committees. These citations confirm Fenno's message that committee assignments are made for a variety of reasons and that there is no one model of what requests are made or how requests are translated into assignments (see, e.g., Sinclair 1988).

Looking for Variation

One of the enduring consequences of *Congressmen in Committees* is work by many scholars to characterize the internal workings of congressional committees and, more importantly, to fit their descriptions inside a general framework. Rather than setting out "a single statement asserting the uniqueness of each committee," this research moves toward a set of "limited comparisons" (Fenno 1973, xiv): how committees differ and why these differences matter.

One line of research focuses on how anticipation of floor preferences constrains committee decisions—and why this effect might vary across committees (e.g., Dion 1992; Krehbiel and Rivers 1988; Squire 1988), including the impact of the Rules Committee (Dion and Huber 1996, 1997; Krehbiel 1997). Others have analyzed the internal workings of committees and refined Fenno's conclusions about the presence or absence of reciprocity and specialization norms at the congressional level (Hall and Evans 1990; Shipan 1992) and in city council committees (Pelissero and Kreps 1997). Alder and Lapinski (1997) offer a more general analysis of the link between constituency characteristics and committee composition.

A livelier debate has arisen around the question of whether congressional committees are designed to supply information and expertise to the parent chamber or whether they are a distributional mechanism by which members acquire disproportionate influence in jurisdictions they regard as important. Notwithstanding Fenno's admonitions, the distributional rationale was a well-cited, widely accepted general explanation well into the late 1980s (see Talbert, Jones, and Baumgartner 1995 for a useful summary). However, Gilligan and Krehbiel's (1989, 1990) informational rationale for committees has provided a compelling alternate hypothesis.

At present, the literature on why committees exist is very much a work in progress. Recent works have emphasized Fenno's expectation that committees can serve a variety of purposes. Most notably, Maltzman (1995) uses a wider range of committees and statistical analysis to show that committee outputs vary with member goals and the committee's policy environment. Hall and Grofman (1990) generate similar results in their analysis of subcommittee organization and behavior.

Although these results extend Fenno's work in important ways, they leave fundamental questions unaddressed. For example, many scholars have attempted to link member goals and committee structure; they suggest that committees dominated by reelection-oriented members will provide distributive benefits, whereas committees populated by influence-oriented members will supply information and expertise. This assumption implies that a committee's internal workings are essentially plastic and can be freely altered to suit member goals (Squire 1988).

However, it is not clear whether there is a natural mapping between member goals and committee jurisdictions. What we see as a committee dominated by influence seekers might just as easily be a committee dominated by a different set of members whose primary interest is reelection. Thus, conclusions about the role a given committee plays in the contemporary House must also consider whether the committee could be organized to fulfill a different role.

Home Styles and the Career in the District

In *Home Style,* Fenno presents a theory of how members of the House of Representatives win and hold their districts, a theory based not in the things members do in Washington but in their activities in their district. As he notes in the introduction,

> When we talk with our national legislators about their constituencies, we typically talk to them in Washington and, perforce, in the Washington context. But this is a context far removed from the one in which their constituency relationships are created, nurtured, and changed. . . . Asking constituency-related questions on Capitol Hill, when the House member is far from the constituency itself, could well introduce a distortion of perspective. Researchers might tend to conceive of a separation between the representative "here in Washington" and his constituency "back home," whereas the representative may picture himself or herself as part of the constituency—me-*in*-the constituency, rather than me-*and*-the constituency. (Fenno 1978, xiii)

In essence, Fenno argues that legislators generate political support by engaging in a range of activities that he labels a home style. Members allocate their time and energy between home and Washington. They work to present themselves as qualified, accessible, and empathic. And they strive to construct (or act consistent with) politically beneficial explanations of their activities in Washington.

Fenno was certainly not the first scholar to argue that legislators spend much time making sure that their constituents are happy. *Home Style* was and is an important book because it gives students of congressional elections a much more detailed picture of how legislators win reelection and how legislators' actions are linked to the preferences of their constituents.

In particular, *Home Style* shifted the focus of representation studies away from Washington and toward the district. The point is not that actions taken in Washington are politically inconsequential. They are critical. However, Fenno argues that a representative's actions in the district often mediate constituent evaluations of both the representative's behavior in office and the Congress itself.

For example, by being accessible to constituents and presenting themselves in a way that suggests agreement with constituent interests, legislators gain voting leeway—the ability to vote as their personal policy preferences dictate rather than as their constituents demand. *Home Style* tells us that attempts to predict or explain legislators' behaviors in Washington must begin with an understanding of their behaviors in their districts and how these actions influence what constituents think about the representatives' motivations and character.

Even so, it would be a misreading of *Home Style* to conclude that constituents are easily led or that legislators who are sufficiently attentive to their districts can act as free agents. A sizable fraction of a legislator's home style is composed of actions that reflect rather than shape constituent expectations. Fenno notes that legislators take care to avoid any attempts at educating their constituents or otherwise indicating that constituents might not be seeing the full picture with regard to a policy matter. Moreover, legislators "run for Congress by running against it" (Fenno 1978, 168); they respond to the electorate's distrust of Washington by making the same arguments and then suggesting that their reelection is necessary to protect district interests against a rapacious government.

Using the Concept

Over the past 20 years, the term *home style* has become shorthand in the literature on congressional elections to describe the complex, intertwined relationship between legislators and their constituents. Overby et al. (1992) refer to *Home Style* as setting out the "authoritative statement" (998) of this reciprocal linkage; Calvert, McCubbins, and Weingast (1989) cite the book as the modern statement of the theory of representation. A legislator's home style is seen as a crucial variable in explaining his or her electoral success (Brown and Woods 1991; Cox and Katz 1996).

Scholars have also taken Fenno's concept both on the road and across time, finding evidence of home styles in Western European democracies (Powell and Whitten 1993), in Costa Rica (Taylor 1992), in local politics (Cohen and Dawson 1993), and in historical American politics (Bianco, Spence, and Wilkerson 1996; McDonagh 1989).

Congressional scholars have been less successful at refining the details of home style. In effect, the term has become a label for a series of ill-understood though obviously crucial interactions. More progress has been made in identifying the kinds of constituent perceptions that incumbents would like to engender than in describing how incumbents shape these beliefs. And although scholars agree that the ability to construct a successful home style varies across members (e.g., Abramowitz 1991; Swain 1994), there is little consensus about the factors that cause this variation.

Consider allocations. How does an incumbent's allocation of resources influence constituent perceptions? Parker and Parker (1993) argue that personal contact is crucial for building trust between representatives and their constituents. However, *Home Style* provides no evidence that electoral safety is related to objective indicators such as the number of trips home or number of days in the district (see also Abramowitz 1991; Wooley 1993).

Presentation of self has proved even more difficult to characterize. Larson (1990) and McCurley and Mondak (1995) show that perceptions of an incumbent's competence and honesty are correlated with positive voter evaluations. (For similar results, see Franklin 1991.) Sellers (1997) presents empirical evidence for the electoral importance of consistency in an incumbent's presentations.

These findings are important, but they do not fully specify how incumbents influence their constituents' perceptions, both positively and negatively. Moreover, how constituents respond to presentations appears to be complex, conditional, and poorly understood.

Consider the 1992 House Bank scandal (Alford et al. 1994; Groseclose and Krehbiel 1994; Jacobson and Dimock 1994). Although legislators with numerous overdrafts were more likely to be defeated or retire, many survived and prospered despite their supposed malfeasance. The point is not that constituents who were angered by check bouncing were assuaged by other more positive aspects of their incumbents' behaviors. Rather, it appears that some incumbents had reputations that caused their constituents to overlook their banking foibles entirely.

Another example comes from research on how incumbents dissociate themselves from Congress. Many scholars (e.g., Durr, Gilmour, and Wolbrecht 1997; McAdams and Johannes 1988; Powell and Whitten 1993; Radcliff 1988) accept and reinforce Fenno's conclusion that the strategy of running for Congress by running against it is "ubiquitous, addictive, cost-free, and foolproof" (Fenno 1978, 168). However, other research suggests limits on this conjecture. Born (1991) shows that voters' judgments about Congress are a strong predictor of their evaluations of their representatives. Analyses of the House Bank scandal show that under certain conditions, an incumbent's behavior can tie him or her to a wider, institution-level scandal (Alford et al. 1994). A similar conclusion is suggested by the Republicans' success during the 1994 elections at holding

Democratic incumbents responsible for congressional failures and foibles (for details, see the papers by Sinclair and DeGregorio in this volume).

These concerns are echoed in the literature on explanations, in which there is considerable disagreement over what the concept describes. One line of research assumes that explanations are actual statements made by an incumbent with the goal of manipulating voter evaluations (Austen-Smith 1992; Lau, Smith, and Fiske 1991; McGraw 1991; McGraw, Best, and Timpone 1995). Other scholars see explanations as capturing the calculations incumbents make when they consider the political consequences of different actions (Cameron, Cover, and Segal 1990). Analyses based on interviews with members of Congress support the latter characterization (Bianco 1994), although the jury remains out.

Bianco's paper in this volume offers a game-theoretic analysis of these issues. The analysis predicts an asymmetry in how voters respond to an incumbent's efforts as a function of their initial impressions. Voters who believe initially that an incumbent shares their interests are more likely to listen to new information that he or she presents, less likely to discount presentations that might be strategic, and more likely to be sensitive to search costs. Thus, claiming affinity with constituents ("I am one of you") is more useful as a means of reinforcing favorable impressions than of turning opponents into supporters. Moreover, an incumbent's ability to deliver information to voters, thereby lowering their search costs, is also more useful as a reinforcement strategy than as a means of converting opponents.

The Constituency versus the Reelection Constituency: Operationalizing "Concentric Circles"

Home Style's second major contribution to the field was its specification of how legislators organize perceptions of their districts. According to Fenno, legislators do not see their districts as an undifferentiated mass of people. Rather, their perceptions are best described in terms of four concentric circles (Fenno 1978, chap. 1):

- Geographical Constituency, a description of the district in terms of its size, location, demographics, and range of significant interests.
- Reelection Constituency, the people in the district that the representative sees as likely supporters in an election.
- Primary Constituency, a representative's strong supporters, the people who are likely to vote for him or her regardless of the identity of the opponent.
- Personal Constituency, a representative's "close political advisors and confidants." (1978, 24)

In effect, this specification is part of Fenno's answer to the questions posed in his introduction:

> What does a representative see when he or she sees a constituency? And, as a natural followup, What consequences do these perceptions have for his or her behavior? The key problem is perception. And the key assumption is that the rest of us cannot understand the representative-constituency relationship until we can see the constituency through the eyes of the representative. (1978, xiii)

The expectation is that these perceptions govern a legislator's political calculations and decisions. For example, how will a legislator evaluate the impact a particular law will have on his or her district? The answer lies in the legislator's beliefs about the geographic constituency. Does the legislator feel electorally safe or vulnerable? This question is really an inquiry about the size of the legislator's primary and reelection constituencies and not about the composition of the geographic constituency.

Implicit in Fenno's characterization is the idea that legislators' responsiveness to their constituents is not unbiased. When calculating the political consequences of different actions, legislators do not weigh each voter's possible reactions equally. Rather, their focus is on the evaluations formed by members of their reelection and primary constituencies. Which group will be given priority is not obvious. One possibility is that voters in the primary constituency will be given the greatest weight. Even though these voters probably cannot reelect the incumbents by themselves, the reliability of their support makes them a valuable asset—an asset that incumbents are loath to jeopardize. Alternatively, incumbents may worry more about the reactions of their reelection constituency, on the grounds that support from primary constituency members is a given, whereas voters in the reelection constituency might switch to challengers if they disapprove of their incumbent's behaviors.

Fenno's description of the constituency also suggests that incumbents' political calculations assign a low weight to demands made by voters who are not members of their reelection, primary, or personal constituencies. The reason is not that these voters are thought to be inattentive or that incumbents are not mindful of how these voters will react. Rather, Fenno's incumbents appear to believe that a high percentage of these voters are unshakable in their opposition. Thus, their opposition is a given in the incumbents' calculations.

Fenno's description of how incumbents view their districts has two important implications for the study of representation. For one thing, it suggests that incumbents do not focus on the median voter in their district à la Downs. Rather, their responsiveness to constituent demands is biased in the direction of their reelection and primary constituencies. Or, in Downsian terms, the focus is on some voter or group of voters who lie some distance from the district median.

Moreover, Fenno's description implies that the pursuit of reelection does not lead incumbents to take actions that maximize the vote they receive in the next election. The observed attentiveness to the primary and reelection constituencies suggests that incumbents work hard to build floors under their expected vote. Put another way, vote maximization does not maximize incumbents' probability of reelection. A better tactic is to take actions that reduce the variance of incumbents' expected votes and raise their minimum values.

The importance of reducing variance in future election returns also explains why incumbents persist in aggressive campaigning even after they have won reelection with large margins (Green and Krasno 1988). These efforts are directed at expanding the primary constituency, even at the cost of reducing incumbents' expected votes.

Measuring Reelection and Primary Constituencies

Fenno's description of how members see their districts is a perennial citation in analyses of congressional elections. Scholars agree that "the constituency is a complex object" (Jackson and Kingdon 1992, 807) that cannot be adequately described by a single summary measure (see also Hall and Grofman 1990). Moreover, as Grier and Munger (1993) note, it is accepted that the composition of a legislator's reelection or primary constituency may be hard to predict on the basis of district demographics. Districts may well contain more than one viable reelection constituency (Kiewiet and McCubbins 1988; Lindsay 1990, 1991). This possibility may explain why some states are represented by pairs of senators who have significantly different ideological dispositions and voting records (see, e.g., Segal, Cameron, and Cover 1992).

Although scholars have accepted that simple measures of the constituency are flawed, there is no consensus on what the right measure would look like. Some scholars (e.g., Cohen and Dawson 1993; Verba et al. 1993; West 1988) suggest that the reelection and primary constituencies can be described in terms of elites, activists, and other organized groups. Sullivan (1988) argues for a definition based on "basic district interests and electoral cleavages" (573), a theme echoed in Kerr and Miller's (1997) analysis of Latino representation. Roberts (1990) suggests that in districts that have a dominant industry or corporation, voters with some connection to this enterprise are likely to be members of any reelection constituency that a successful incumbent might construct.

The problem with these definitions is that they do not offer systematic criteria for determining which elites, groups, interests, or cleavages are large enough or important enough to make their support necessary to an incumbent's success. Moreover, the search for such criteria may be misguided. Given that districts may contain several viable reelection constituencies, the question of whether any of these candidates are necessary components of a reelection or primary constituency remains open.

Attempts to characterize reelection and primary constituencies in empirical terms raise similar questions. Grenzke (1989) uses political action committee contributions as an indicator of which groups belong to an incumbent's reelection constituency. Similarly, Hall and Wayman (1990) offer a definition based in part on who contributes to an incumbent's campaign. McDonagh's (1989) analysis of voting on the Nineteenth Amendment defines constituent pressures using actual votes on referenda from the Progressive era. None of these definitions offers a compelling, complete description. Scholars are left with plausible but inadequate measures, such as defining a legislator's reelection constituency in terms of who voted for him or her in the last election or electoral safety in terms of an incumbent's previous margin of victory.

Clearly, students of congressional elections, as well as those who study representation more generally, need a better way to operationalize Fenno's description of how legislators view their districts. Although this description by itself offers new insights into how representation works in contemporary American politics, our inability to build on Fenno's insights is a singular failure, one with important implications for how we interpret election results. To describe one example, Fleisher (1993) finds no evidence that the evolution of the two-party system in the South, coupled with increased participation by African-Americans, liberalized the primary and reelection constituencies of southern Democratic members of the House. However, using a different definition of these constituencies, Whitby and Gilliam (1991) make precisely the opposite argument. Thus, conclusions about how and why the Republicans managed to capture southern congressional seats from the Democrats await a better characterization, operationalization, and measurement of the reelection and primary constituencies.

The Virtues of Participant Observation

Dick Fenno's research is also well cited for its use of participant observation as a means of developing and testing hypotheses about politics. As he notes in *Home Style,*

> Research based on participant–observation is likely to have an exploratory emphasis. Someone doing this kind of research is quite likely to have no crystallized idea of what he or she is looking for or what ques-

tions to ask when he or she starts. Researchers typically become interested in some observable set of activities and decide to go have a firsthand
look at them. They fully expect that an open-minded exposure to events
in the milieu and to the perspectives of those with whom they interact
will produce ideas that might never have occurred to them otherwise.
Only after prolonged, unstructured soaking is the problem formulated.
(1978, 250)

I knew intellectually that activity in Washington to some uncertain degree
reflects what people are saying, thinking, and doing out in the country;
but I felt I did not know what went on "out there." I wanted to acquire, at
first hand, this extra-Washington perspective. (1978, 252)

Put another way, the central expectation in Fenno's work is that politics cannot
be viewed through the lens of secondary sources. Direct observation of facts on
the ground will almost always give us better insights into politics, regardless of
whether the focus is on Washington work or home styles. Fenno's strategy of
"soaking and poking" is rightly celebrated because he showed that observation
and deep study were compatible with the goal of working toward general
explanations of the legislative process.

Have researchers heeded Fenno's admonitions? For the most part, yes.
The gold standard in legislative studies remains primary source data, gathered
through interviews or observation. As a contributor to this volume once put it,
"There is no substitute for some first-hand contact with members of Congress
and some close-up observation of the legislative process for congressional
scholars" (Sinclair 1992b, 5).

A better measure of the perceived value of participant observation can be
seen in the vitae of the contributors to this volume. More than two-thirds have
served as American Political Science Association Congressional Fellows.
Most of the others have some direct contact with politicians, usually in the
form of unstructured interviews. These experiences, I submit, are not all that
exceptional. They reflect the example of Dick Fenno's career-long demonstration of the value of seeing politics firsthand.

The value of participant observation can be observed in several contributions to this volume. DeGregorio, for example, focuses on the House under
Republican rule and on why the Republicans make different institutional and
policy choices than their Democratic predecessors. Her explanation stresses
that the new Republican majority was driven by a new culture of governing,
one that emphasized inclusion over coercion, corporate-style management
practices, and principles over pragmatism. It is hard to imagine how this
insight could be developed, except by (paraphrasing Fenno) watching, seeing,
and talking with the people you are studying.

Forgette's contribution also uses participant observation to similar advantage. In part, his essay focuses on the failure of the Republican majority leadership to work effectively as a team. As he asks,

> How did those in Gingrich's inner circle, including Armey, DeLay, and Boehner, lose their ability to effectively coordinate work, openly communicate, and anticipate the reactions of the rank and file and opposition? This breakdown appears even stranger considering that these leaders had functioned well as a minority team, were ideologically unified, and had always voiced a commitment to party building.

The answer, he argues, lies in the difficulties inherent in the transition to majority status. In part, Republicans faced the problem of having to learn how to run the House—something that no member of the new Republican majority had ever experienced. The move to majority status also exacerbated policy differences, both within the Republican rank and file and among the leadership. Because of their longtime status as a minority party, Republicans lacked the mechanisms for and the experience with devising intraparty compromise. In this light, the Republicans' inability to exploit their majority status to the degree they expected is no surprise.

Soaking and Poking around Districts

Most interesting about the use of participant-observation methods in legislative studies is that which is absent: research that focuses on behavior in the district. With the notable exceptions of work by Larson (1990) and Swain (1990), I am not aware of any research that is based on direct observation of what members of Congress say and do in their districts.

In part this asymmetry is no surprise. The Congressional Fellowship program provides a ready-made mechanism for legislative scholars to spend a year observing how Congress operates. Many schools allow faculty to spend time in Washington to supervise their internship programs. Organizations such as the Brookings Institution provide a base of operations for visiting faculty.

In contrast, district-level fieldwork is both an organizational and financial nightmare. There are no obvious sources of funding such as the Congressional Fellowship. Moreover, would-be soakers and pokers must handle all of the logistic details themselves, from charting their target's itinerary to making travel arrangements. Scholars in Washington know where politicians live and work. Out in the field, much energy must be expended to find and get to politicians. And for all of these reasons, district-level research is also expensive.

Nevertheless, the continuing and profound impact of *Home Style* on how scholars think about Congress suggests that a shift in funding priorities might be in order. Many important questions concerning how legislators win and hold their districts and the policy implications of these behaviors remain unanswered. No one doubts the importance of getting up close and personal to politicians in Washington. What is needed are the means to send legislative scholars out into the country to examine the external forces that shape behavior and outcomes in Washington.

Conclusion

In this essay I have identified some essential pieces of the conventional wisdom on contemporary Congress that in one way or another can be traced to Dick Fenno's research program. Others no doubt exist. And given Fenno's continued travels with members of Congress, it is clear that any summary of his impact on the field is premature, a snapshot of a moving target.

One thing is certain. Dick Fenno's research, both the findings and how they are developed, has changed how scholars think about the Congress and about legislatures. And it will continue to do so. In that sense, his wisdom is in no way conventional. It serves as a compelling example to those who study legislatures with the benefit of his insights.

NOTE

1. The time period for the search ended in 1997 for the *American Journal of Political Science* and 1995 for the *American Political Science Review* and the *Journal of Politics*, because these were JSTOR's limits as of January 1999. *Legislative Studies Quarterly* was omitted because this journal has not been incorporated into JSTOR.

REFERENCES

Abramowitz, Alan I. 1991. "Incumbency, Campaign Spending, and the Decline of Competition in U.S. House Elections." *Journal of Politics* 53 (1): 34–56.
Alder, E. Scott, and John S. Lapinski. 1997. "Demand-Side Theory and Congressional Committee Composition: A Constituency Characteristics Approach." *American Journal of Political Science* 41 (3): 895–918.
Alford, John, Holly Teeters, Daniel S. Ward, and Rick K. Wilson. 1994. "Overdraft: The Political Cost of Congressional Malfeasance." *Journal of Politics* 56 (3): 788–801.
Austen-Smith, David. 1992. "Explaining the Vote: Constituency Constraints on Sophisticated Voting." *American Journal of Political Science* 36 (1): 68–95.
Austen-Smith, David, and John R. Wright. 1994. "Counteractive Lobbying." *American Journal of Political Science* 38 (1): 25–44.

Bianco, William T. 1994. *Trust: Representatives and Constituents.* Ann Arbor: University of Michigan Press.

Bianco, William T., David B. Spence, and John D. Wilkerson. 1996. "The Electoral Connection in the Early Congress: The Case of the Compensation Act of 1816." *American Journal of Political Science* 40 (1): 145–71.

Born, Richard. 1991. "Assessing the Impact of Institutional and Election Forces on Evaluations of Congressional Incumbents." *Journal of Politics* 53 (3): 764–99.

Brown, Robert D, and James A. Woods. 1991. "Toward a Model of Congressional Elections." *Journal of Politics* 53 (2): 454–73.

Browne, William P. 1992. "Review of 'Gaining Access: Congress and the Farm Lobby, 1919–1981.'" *Journal of Politics* 54 (4): 1188–90.

Calvert, Randall L., Mathew D. McCubbins, and Barry R. Weingast. 1989. "A Theory of Political Control and Agency Discretion." *American Journal of Political Science* 33 (3): 588–611.

Cameron, Charles M., Albert D. Cover, and Jeffrey A. Segal. 1990. "Senate Voting on Supreme Court Nominees: A Neoinstitutional Model." *American Political Science Review* 84 (2): 525–34.

Cohen, Cathy J., and Michael C. Dawson. 1993. "Neighborhood Poverty and African American Politics." *American Political Science Review* 87 (2): 286–302.

Cook, Timothy E. 1988. "Press Secretaries and Media Strategies in the House of Representatives: Deciding Whom to Pursue." *American Journal of Political Science* 32 (4): 1047–69.

Cox, Gary W., and Jonathan N. Katz. 1996. "Why Did the Incumbency Advantage in U.S. House Elections Grow?" *American Journal of Political Science* 40 (2): 478–97.

Dion, Douglas. 1992. "The Robustness of the Structure-Induced Equilibrium." *American Journal of Political Science* 36 (2): 462–82.

Dion, Douglas, and John D. Huber. 1996. "Procedural Choice and the House Committee on Rules." *Journal of Politics* 58 (1): 25–53.

Dion, Douglas, and John D. Huber. 1997. "Sense and Sensibility: The Role of Rules." *American Journal of Political Science* 41 (3): 845–57.

Durr, Robert H., John B. Gilmour, and Christina Wolbrecht. 1997. "Explaining Congressional Approval." *American Journal of Political Science* 41 (1): 175–207.

Evans, Diana. 1994. "Policy and Pork: The Use of Pork Barrel Projects to Build Policy Coalitions in the House of Representatives." *American Journal of Political Science* 38 (4): 894–917.

Fenno, Richard F., Jr. 1973. *Congressmen in Committees.* Boston: Little, Brown.

Fenno, Richard F., Jr. 1978. *Home Style: House Members in Their Districts.* Boston: Little, Brown.

Fleisher, Richard. 1993. "Explaining the Change in Roll-Call Voting Behavior of Southern Democrats." *Journal of Politics* 55 (2): 327–41.

Franklin, Charles H. 1991. "Eschewing Obfuscation? Campaigns and the Perception of U.S. Senate Incumbents." *American Political Science Review* 85 (4): 1193–1214.

Gerber, Elizabeth R. 1996. "Legislative Response to the Threat of Popular Initiatives." *American Journal of Political Science* 40 (1): 99–128.

Gilligan, Thomas W., and Keith Krehbiel. 1989. "Asymmetric Information and Leg-
    islative Rules with a Heterogeneous Committee." *American Journal of Political
    Science* 33 (2): 459–90.
Gilligan, Thomas W., and Keith Krehbiel. 1990. "Organization of Informative Com-
    mittees by a Rational Legislature." *American Journal of Political Science* 34 (2):
    531–64.
Green, Donald Phillip, and Jonathan S. Krasno. 1988. "Preempting Quality Challengers
    in House Elections." *Journal of Politics* 50 (4): 920–36.
Grenzke, Janet M. 1989. "PACs and the Congressional Supermarket: The Currency Is
    Complex." *American Journal of Political Science* 33 (1): 1–24.
Grier, Kevin B., and Michael C. Munger. 1993. "Comparing Interest Group PAC Con-
    tributions to House and Senate Incumbents, 1980–1986." *Journal of Politics* 55
    (3): 615–43.
Groseclose, Timothy, and Keith Krehbiel. 1994. "Golden Parachutes, Rubber Checks,
    and Strategic Retirements from the 102d House." *American Journal of Political
    Science* 38 (1): 75–99.
Gurian, Paul-Henri. 1993. "Candidate Behavior in Presidential Nomination Cam-
    paigns: A Dynamic Model." *Journal of Politics* 55 (1): 115–39.
Hall, Richard L., and C. Lawrence Evans. 1990. "The Power of Subcommittees." *Jour-
    nal of Politics* 52 (2): 335–55.
Hall, Richard L., and Bernard Grofman. 1990. "The Committee Assignment Process
    and the Conditional Nature of Committee Bias." *American Political Science
    Review* 84 (4): 1149–66.
Hall, Richard L., and Frank W. Wayman. 1990. "Buying Time: Moneyed Interests and
    the Mobilization of Bias in Congressional Committees." *American Political Sci-
    ence Review* 84 (3): 797–820.
Herrick, Rebekah, Michael K. Moore, and John R. Hibbing. 1994. "Unfastening the
    Electoral Connection: The Behavior of U.S. Representatives When Reelection Is
    No Longer a Factor." *Journal of Politics* 56 (1): 214–27.
Jackson, John E., and John W. Kingdon. 1992. "Ideology, Interest Group Scores, and
    Legislative Votes." *American Journal of Political Science* 36 (3): 805–23.
Jacobson, Gary C., and Michael Dimock. 1994. "Checking Out: The Effects of Bank
    Overdrafts on the 1992 House Elections." *American Journal of Political Science*
    38 (3): 601–24.
Kerr, Brinck, and Will Miller. 1997. "Latino Representation: It's Direct and Indirect."
    American Journal of Political Science 41 (3): 1066–71.
Kiewiet, D. Roderick, and Mathew D. McCubbins. 1988. "Presidential Influence on
    Congressional Appropriations Decisions." *American Journal of Political Science*
    32 (3): 713–36.
Kolman, Ken. 1997. "Inviting Friends to Lobby: Interest Groups, Ideological Bias, and
    Congressional Committees." *American Journal of Political Science* 41 (2): 519–44.
Krehbiel, Keith. 1997. "Restrictive Rules Reconsidered." *American Journal of Political
    Science* 41 (3): 919–44.
Krehbiel, Keith, and Douglas Rivers. 1988. "The Analysis of Committee Power: An
    Application to Senate Voting on the Minimum Wage (in Workshop)." *American
    Journal of Political Science* 32 (4): 1151–74.

Larson, Stephanie Greco. 1990. "Information and Learning in a Congressional District: A Social Experiment." *American Journal of Political Science* 34 (4): 1102–18.

Lau, Richard R., Richard A. Smith, and Susan T. Fiske. 1991. "Political Beliefs, Policy Interpretations, and Political Persuasion." *Journal of Politics* 53 (3): 644–75.

Lindsay, James M. 1990. "Parochialism, Policy, and Constituency Constraints: Congressional Voting on Strategic Weapons Systems." *American Journal of Political Science* 34 (4): 936–60.

Lindsay, James M. 1991. "Testing the Parochial Hypothesis: Congress and the Strategic Defense Initiative." *Journal of Politics* 53 (3): 860–76.

Maisel, L. Sandy. 1984. "Teaching the Congressional (Legislative) Process." *News for Teachers of Political Science,* 78 (3): 1

Maltzman, Forrest. 1995. "Meeting Competing Demands: Committee Performance in the Postreform House." *American Journal of Political Science* 39 (3): 653–82.

McAdams, John C., and John R. Johannes. 1988. "Congressmen, Perquisites, and Elections." *Journal of Politics* 50 (2): 412–39.

McCurley, Carl, and Jeffery J. Mondak. 1995. "Inspected by $#1184063113$: The Influence of Incumbents' Competence and Integrity in U.S. House Elections." *American Journal of Political Science* 39 (4): 864–85.

McDonagh, Eileen L. 1989. "Issues and Constituencies in the Progressive Era: House Roll Call Voting on the Nineteenth Amendment, 1913–1919." *Journal of Politics* 51 (1): 119–36.

McGraw, Kathleen M. 1991. "Managing Blame: An Experimental Test of the Effects of Political Accounts." *American Political Science Review* 85 (4): 1133–57.

McGraw, Kathleen M., Samuel Best, and Richard Timpone. 1995. " 'What They Say or What They Do?' The Impact of Elite Explanation and Policy Outcomes on Public Opinion." *American Journal of Political Science* 39 (1): 53–74.

Mouw, Calvin J., and Michael B. Mackuen. 1992. "The Strategic Agenda in Legislative Politics." *American Political Science Review* 86 (1): 87–105.

Munger, Michael C. 1988. "Allocation of Desirable Committee Assignments: Extended Queues versus Committee Expansion." *American Journal of Political Science* 32 (2): 317–44.

Overby, L. Marvin, Beth M. Henschen, Michael H. Walsh, and Julie Strauss. 1992. "Courting Constituents? An Analysis of the Senate Confirmation Vote on Justice Clarence Thomas." *American Political Science Review* 86 (4): 997–1003.

Parker, Suzzane L., and Glenn R. Parker. 1993. "Why Do We Trust Our Congressman?" *Journal of Politics* 55 (2): 442–53.

Pelissero, John P., and Timothy B. Kreps. 1997. "City Council Legislative Committees and Policy-Making in Large United States Cities." *American Journal of Political Science* 41 (2): 499–518.

Powell, G. Bingham, and Guy D. Whitten. 1993. "A Cross-National Analysis of Economic Voting: Taking Account of the Political Context." *American Journal of Political Science* 37 (2): 391–414.

Radcliff, Benjamin. 1988. "Solving a Puzzle: Aggregate Analysis and Economic Voting." *Journal of Politics* 50 (2): 440–55.

Roberts, Brian M. 1990. "A Dead Senator Tells No Lies: Seniority and the Distribution of Federal Benefits." *American Journal of Political Science* 34 (1): 31–58.

Schickler, Eric, and Andrew Rich. 1997. "Controlling the Floor: Parties as Procedural Coalitions in the House." *American Journal of Political Science* 41 (4): 1340–75.

Schiller, Wendy J. 1995. "Senators as Political Entrepreneurs: Using Bill Sponsorship to Shape Legislative Agendas." *American Journal of Political Science* 39 (1): 186–203.

Searing, Donald D. 1991. "Roles, Rules, and Rationality in the New Institutionalism." *American Political Science Review* 85 (4): 1239–60.

Segal, Jeffrey A., Charles M. Cameron, and Albert D. Cover. 1992. "A Spatial Model of Roll Call Voting: Senators, Constituents, Presidents, and Interest Groups in Supreme Court Confirmations." *American Journal of Political Science* 36 (1): 96–121.

Sellers, Patrick J. 1997. "Fiscal Consistency and Federal District Spending in Congressional Elections." *American Journal of Political Science* 41 (3): 1024–41.

Shamir, Michal. 1991. "Political Intolerance among Masses and Elites in Israel: A Reevaluation of the Elitist Theory of Democracy." *Journal of Politics* 53 (4): 1018–43.

Shipan, Charles R. 1992. "Individual Incentives and Institutional Imperatives: Committee Jurisdiction and Long-Term Health Care." *American Journal of Political Science* 36 (4): 877–95.

Sinclair, Barbara. 1988. "The Distribution of Committee Positions in the U.S. Senate: Explaining Institutional Change." *American Journal of Political Science* 32 (2): 276–301.

Sinclair, Barbara. 1992a. "The Emergence of Strong Leadership in the 1980s House of Representatives." *Journal of Politics* 54 (3): 657–84.

Sinclair, Barbara. 1992b. "Framing, Interpreting, and Explaining Senate Behavior: The Importance of Looking Up-Close-and-Personal." *Extension of Remarks,* November, 4–5.

Squire, Peverill. 1988. "Member Career Opportunities and the Internal Organization of Legislatures." *Journal of Politics* 50 (3): 726–44.

Stewart, Charles, III. 1992. "Committee Hierarchies in the Modernizing House, 1875–1947." *American Journal of Political Science* 36 (4): 835–56.

Stewart, Charles, III. 1998. "Congressional Politics' Greatest Hits: The 1990's." Massachusetts Institute of Technology.

Sullivan, Terry. 1988. "Headcounts, Expectations, and Presidential Coalitions in Congress." *American Journal of Political Science* 32 (3): 567–89.

Sullivan, Terry. 1990. "Explaining Why Presidents Count: Signaling and Information." *Journal of Politics* 52 (3): 939–62.

Swain, Carol. 1990. "Bargaining with the President: A Simple Game and New Evidence." *American Political Science Review* 84 (4): 1167–95.

Swain, Carol. 1994. *Black Faces, Black Interests.* Cambridge: Harvard University Press.

Talbert, Jeffery C., Bryan D. Jones, and Frank R. Baumgartner. 1995. "Nonlegislative Hearings and Policy Change in Congress." *American Journal of Political Science* 39 (2): 383–405.

Taylor, Michelle M. 1992. "Formal versus Informal Incentive Structures and Legislator Behavior: Evidence from Costa Rica." *Journal of Politics* 54 (4): 1055–73.

Verba, Sidney, Kay Lehman Schlozman, Henry Brady, and Norman H. Nie. 1993. "Citizen Activity: Who Participates? What Do They Say?" *American Political Science Review* 87 (2): 303–18.

West, Darrell M. 1988. "Activists and Economic Policymaking in Congress." *American Journal of Political Science* 32 (3): 662–80.

Whitby, Kenny J., and Franklin D. Gilliam Jr. 1991. "A Longitudinal Analysis of Competing Explanations for the Transformation of Southern Congressional Politics (in Research Notes)." *Journal of Politics* 53 (2): 504–18.

Wooley, John T. 1993. "Conflict among Regulators and the Hypothesis of Congressional Dominance." *Journal of Politics* 55 (1): 92–114.

Wright, John R. 1990. "Contributions, Lobbying, and Committee Voting in the U.S. House of Representatives." *American Political Science Review* 84 (2): 417–38.

Explaining Institutional Change:
Soaking, Poking, and Modeling in the U.S. Congress

John H. Aldrich and Kenneth A. Shepsle

Introduction

Students of the U.S. Congress (like students of other institutions) are often fascinated by the details of institutional change. Inasmuch as the institutional ways and means of conducting an organization's political business often have significant if not decisive effects on what actually happens there, it is not surprising that scholars and journalists alike freight occasions of institutional change with great significance. Institutional arrangements are akin to the rules of the game, and it is supposed—sometimes formally, other times implicitly—that these arrangements surely stack the deck for some outcomes and against others, in favor of some programs and against alternatives. They may even create, change, or destroy equilibrium ways of doing things. Consider some well-known examples from congressional history.

Clay and the Growth of Standing Committees in the House

In 1811, the year Henry Clay of Lexington, Kentucky, first entered the House of Representatives and was elected its Speaker, there were 10 standing committees (most established in the first few years of the new Constitution) to which was referred somewhat less than half of the business of the House. In 1825, his last year in both roles, there were 26 standing committees to which were referred nearly 90 percent of all bills. Moreover, during that period a powerful Speaker's office ensured a durable, (more-or-less) self-selection mechanism for committee assignments and a (relatively) regular procedure for bill referral. In short, the Jeffersonian preference for a House with weak institutional leadership and genuinely collective deliberation and decision had been radically transformed into one with a strong Speaker and a division-of-labor committee system possessing powerful agenda control. By 1825, the Committee of the Whole, once the place where members participated without interference and where significant policy principles were established for a bill before sending it to a select committee for tidying up, had become a venue controlled procedurally by the Speaker and controlled substantively, jurisdiction by jurisdiction, by standing committees. A House that had become disastrously chaotic and inefficient (especially after the war against Britain was concluded in 1815) had, in a few short years, become a much more streamlined organization.

Reed Rules

In 1889, Speaker Thomas Brackett Reed ordered the sergeant of arms of the House of Representatives to bolt the door of the House chamber and then instructed the House clerk to count as "present and contributing to a quorum" all those in the chamber who had refused to answer to their names in a call of the roll. With these instructions he ended, first by fiat and then later in formal rules, the practice known as the *disappearing quorum,* a tactic used by the minority party to grind the chamber's business to a halt and thereby to extort concessions from the majority. When Representative James McCreary protested, "I deny the right of the Speaker to count me as present," Reed imperiously challenged the temerity of this claim: "The chair is making a statement of the fact that the gentleman from Kentucky is present. Does he deny it?" At the same time, Reed enunciated the Speaker's *right of nonrecognition* in which he took to himself the privilege of asking someone seeking the floor, "For what purpose does the gentleman rise?" If the Speaker judged the purpose dilatory, he denied recognition. The House was in an uproar for several days, but when the dust had settled, Speaker Reed and his closest advisers had drafted a new body of rules for the House, rules that facilitated its operation by removing minority veto points and other dilatory opportunities, thereby permitting the majority party to work its will.

Enlarging the Rules Committee

In organizing the 87th Congress in 1961 to prosecute the agenda of the newly elected president of his party and of a newly unified government, Speaker Rayburn anticipated that the plans of this liberal chief executive would be severely compromised, if not defeated altogether, by a conservative coalition of 4 Republicans and 2 southern Democrats on the 12-person Rules Committee. The latter was a decisive procedural veto point in the legislative process of the House. In an era in which committee chairs were lords of their respective jurisdictions, the fact that one of these two Democrats, Howard Smith of Virginia, was chair of the committee boded especially ill for pent-up liberal legislative aspirations (aspirations intensified by the liberal landslide an election earlier and the frustrations in that Congress of many who were then reelected to the next Congress). In a watershed political event charged with considerable drama, Rayburn and Smith led their respective forces in a showdown over the issue of expanding the Rules Committee to 15. Because Rayburn and his minions had sufficient control over committee assignments to Rules, his success would enable them to craft an 8–7 Rules Committee majority. By a 217–212 vote, Rayburn won on the issue. (That Smith remained as chair, that chairs continued to exercise considerable agenda power, and that one of the newly appointed Rules Committee members, James Delaney of New York, was not always a reliable ally of the liberals ultimately took some of the glow off this victory.) Again, a partisan majoritarian effort succeeded (at least nominally) in diminishing veto power.

Filibuster Reform

By the early 1960s civil rights activism and southern opposition had reached colossal levels. The Kennedy and Johnson administrations were eager to pass an historic piece of civil rights legislation. The existence of parliamentary devices and political conditions in the House (enlarged Rules Committee, a Judiciary Committee more or less purged of southerners, discharge petition, 21-day rule) meant that minorities in that chamber would have difficulty stifling these efforts. But a malapportioned Senate that gave extraordinary weight to southern preferences, combined with institutional procedures that gave extraordinary clout to *any* minority, meant that the battle had to be won in the Senate. The device by which Senate minorities in the past either defeated civil rights bills outright, induced them to be watered down beyond recognition, or deterred them from being introduced in the first place was the *filibuster,* the parliamentary right of a senator to hold the floor once recognized for as long as he or she wished. Debate could not be ended by ordinary means (short of adjourning). The extraordinary means, called *cloture,* required that two-thirds of those present and voting had to vote positively to end debate. In highly salient cases in which participation rates were very high, this requirement essentially meant that civil rights proponents needed to secure 67 votes. With 22 southerners almost certain to oppose, and mischievous Republicans willing to help out, civil rights bills were often doomed at the outset. In a major institutional move, the Senate majority (with help, ultimately, from Senate Minority Leader Everett Dirksen of Illinois) revised Senate rules without destroying the filibuster altogether. The criterion for cloture was changed from the relative standard of two-thirds of those present and voting to the absolute standard of 60 votes.

Each of these famous cases, and the legislative historian could easily produce a dozen more, describes how political agents redefined institutional practices in the House and Senate. Each is an instance of a concerted effort to cleanse (sometimes partisan) minority veto points to expedite matters of interest to its proponents. Another category of reform, only slightly different from the examples of eliminating minority vetoes, is often observed when a new partisan majority sweeps into Congress eager to grease the skids for its "mandate." Perhaps the most dramatic example is that of the House Republican majority in 1995, the first in 40 years, that sought to implement its Contract with America through major changes in House structure and practice (Aldrich and Rohde 1997–1998). Other examples include the creation of an explicit Senate leadership structure for the majority Republicans in the 1890s and for the majority Democrats in 1913 (Gamm and Smith 1997).

Admittedly we have conflated a variety of different types of reform: formal with informal, intrachamber with intraparty. A more systematic inquiry into endogenous institutional change would want to make these and other distinctions. In the present essay, however, we are less concerned with explaining institutional change (in which these distinctions would prove important). Rather, we want to explain (or, better, explore) how scholars explain institutional change.

The chambers of the U.S. Congress are charged by the Constitution with the responsibility of organizing themselves. These legislative bodies are self-governing groups. But they do not govern themselves in a vacuum. Long histories serve both as constraints and as bases for expectations and forecasts. When institutional changes arise—and they occur all the time, of course—then scholars want to know why. What conditions are necessary and sufficient for institutional change? What motivates individual agents to seek or block change? What conditions are propitious for the watershed changes such as those recounted earlier? In this essay we examine a small cafeteria of explanatory approaches. We conclude that the principal approach—a theory of rational agents pursuing private objectives through tinkering with the institutional "production function"—is attractive, impressive, and yet incomplete in important ways. We further claim that soaking and poking is a methodological companion to rational choice explanations and that context and sequence are theoretical supplements needed to complete this approach. After reviewing some standard explanatory approaches, we lay out our argument.

Modes of Explanation

Thick Description as Explanation

Watershed events such as those mentioned earlier have been the subject of intensive examination by political scientists, historians, and journalists. Many of the most informative are unprepossessing case study exercises in description. The absence of good institutional histories aside—a gripe about which we feel deeply but won't trouble the reader with here—analyses of the official record and secondary sources for momentous institutional changes give the interested student a glimpse of how these events played out. The best of these—the thickly descriptive ones—often entertain an implicit theory of how things played out so that they are careful to provide the reader with details that would be relevant to this implicit theory. If entertaining an implicit theory of strategic interaction among purposeful agents, for example, they might take the time to describe carefully the sequence in which specific circumstances unfolded, because a sequence of actions provides insights about the strategies that had been implemented. Were there motions to overrule Speaker Reed's ruling on counting people present in the chamber as contributing to a quorum? If so, was it the Speaker's "policy coalition" that supported him on these votes, or were there various stripes of "proceduralists" who went along with the Speaker on counting quorums even though they opposed him substantively? How did Speaker Rayburn sequence the events that were consummated in the 217–212 vote? Why wasn't a deal cut with Smith in advance? Was it incomplete information (neither side knowing quite who had the votes, but each believing ex ante that his chances were good), or the absence of commitment mechanisms (Smith could not credibly promise to be supportive of the Kennedy administration agenda), or something else? Why didn't the Senate leadership cut a deal with southerners short of weakening the filibuster by making it easier to reach cloture? Was it complete information (they knew they had the votes), the inability of southerners to credibly promise not to make mischief when civil rights legislation came to the floor, or something else? In each of these instances, a writer with a prototheory in his or her head would feel compelled to present relevant fine-grained detail.

If, however, one developed a rigorous logic to the theory implicit in a thick description, it would almost certainly be discovered that key elements of the necessary and/or sufficient conditions were not covered in the description. Indeed, one of the virtues of formalizing a verbal argument into propositional form is to discover just what must be assumed to be able to make the argument logically consistent. As a result, the description, no matter how thick, would almost certainly overlook essential empirical pieces of the story—it would be hit or miss. Even if by some chance (or genius) the thick description were to be logically consistent, readers (and perhaps the author) would not know that the prototheory was logically consistent and complete, given only the description itself to read.

Moreover, if a sophisticated describer of the sort just depicted happened to entertain a theory different from the one in which you, the reader, were interested, then the details he or she reports may be of only passing concern to you.[1] Thus, thick description may be hit or miss in this second sense. The early writers about the evolution of legislative practices in Congress—DeAlva Stanwood Alexander, Mary Parker Follett, Lauros McConachie, Woodrow Wilson, Chang-Wei Chiu, Robert Luce, Ada McCown—are sources of admiration and frustration in both of these respects.

The shortcomings, then, of descriptive modes flow from the unpleasant proposition that there are "too many" facts and they do not speak for themselves. Consequently, facts reported are facts *selected*. And they may not be the right ones for one's own purposes, either because the selection principle is inappropriate to these purposes or because there is no apparent selection principle at all.[2] Missing are a clear definition of just what the scholar seeks to explain (i.e., a well-defined dependent variable) and a coherent, logical answer to the central question of science, why? (i.e., a well-specified "equation" for "estimation" of the dependent variable).

It should come as no surprise that description, thick or otherwise, is insufficient to the task of explanation. Once political scientists came to recognize explanation as their business, methods that moved beyond description began to evolve. That is not to say that description disappeared from our agenda. Indeed, on one view (not meant to be uncharitable) the methodological revolution beginning just after World War II, and including survey research and statistical methods, consisted of sophisticated forms of description. These approaches permitted us to appreciate the connection of the data we had to the universe from which they were drawn, to measure with quantitative precision, to infer regularities from these data, and to assess the confidence with which we could draw descriptive conclusions. No mean feat, that! It is our contention that these methods principally enabled us to identify regularities that required explanation; they did not provide a technology of explanation, a method for addressing systematically *why* there are those regularities. Still, it must be emphasized that uncovering regularities is a critical step, without which there would be nothing to understand or explain scientifically.

The "Old" Institutionalism

The early history of the discipline includes a sufficiently large number of descriptions of institutional arrangements that that era is sometimes referred to as that of ("old") institutionalism. It is untrue, as some nonetheless aver, that the "old institutionalism" was simply descriptive of the rules and details of various governmental bodies. The best were theoretical, quite in the sense cited previously, of asking—and seeking to answer—*why* questions. Sometimes the theory was strictly normative (whether revealing Westminster parliamentary envy à la Wilson or a Tory-Labour party system envy à la Schattschneider). Sometimes it was more nearly positive. In those cases, the driving forces of institutional form and change were generally broad, impersonal dynamics. One of the best in this tradition (albeit later in time than the old institutionalism) is Joseph Cooper's explanation for the emergence of standing committees in the House, an explanation based on repetitive and growing workload, increased complexity, and other organization-theoretic factors (*Origins of the Standing Committees* 1970). (It is worth noting that organization theory was developed in the era of the old institutionalism at least partly to provide some explanatory punch to overly descriptive scholarship.) Indeed, Cooper was quite accurate in noting that committees emerged amidst increasing volumes of legislation and recurring problems and topics. That this division of labor and the development of expertise that accompanied it would make matters more efficient is likely. These arguments are, we believe, an advance over ad hoc explanations, as well as those arguing against purpose and intention, of which Sait's famous coral reefs metaphor (concerning the absence of conscious design in institutions) is the exemplar.[3]

Institutional reaction to external forces is highly impersonal in old institutionalist stories and, we believe, essentially apolitical. No doubt, an organization-theoretic explanation such as Cooper's is often a critical part of an explanation of institutional change. In providing background circumstances it may come close to characterizing necessary conditions. But whether necessary or not, such considerations are surely insufficient. For example, the emergence of standing committees in the House and Senate revealed different patterns, yet evidently both were affected at the same moments by essentially the same volume of workload, repetition, and complexity. Why did those of the House emerge sooner but more slowly, the Senate's all at once? The answer we propose—the missing ingredient that renders Cooper's possibly necessary conditions something closer to sufficient—is the motivation of key political figures (Gamm and Shepsle 1989).

Rational Choice (and Maybe Other Purposive) Models

Motivations

The deductive approach most closely connected to legislative studies focuses on the purposes of legislative agents and the context in which they take actions, in effect adding people to the largely impersonal forces of the old institutionalism. The focus on purpose enables the inquiry to create an abstracted version of individual legislators—flesh and blood human beings are replaced by a small set of purposes that are plausible descriptions of what animates the behavior of legislators. In effect, we substitute an objective function for a proper name: a function that generalizes the proper name to some (potentially) well-defined class of actors.

The most common approach of this sort takes legislators as single-minded seekers of reelection, the famous Mayhewian conception. Accordingly, legislators who seek to secure reelection act as agents for their constituents, the latter varyingly operationalized (as per Fenno) as the residents of the geographic district, their reelection constituency (those who voted for the legislator last time), or a primary constituency (those who supported the legislator in intraparty contests in the past) (Fenno 1978). Variations on this theme would include constituents with valuable electoral resources (money, organizational assets, and transferable followers) or even constituents whom the legislator aspires to represent (e.g., a statewide constituency for a House member who seeks a seat in the Senate). However operationalized, reelection-oriented legislators are assumed to be rational agents in the sense that they utilize the opportunities and endowments provided them by their current political office—staff, committee posts, and access to contributors and media—to further their political objectives.

There is nothing inherent in the rational choice approach, however, that demands a singular definition of the contents of the objective function. Thus, Fenno's famous tripartite objective function—that members seek reelection, good public policy, and/or power in the House—provides the major alternative to the single-minded seeking of reelection approach (Fenno 1973). The first of these is the Mayhewian view we have just discussed. The second—the pursuit of "good" public policy—is taken by many implicitly to be Mayhewian as well; that is, the policy preferences attributed to legislators are assumed to be indirect, with legislative agents adopting the perspective of their reelection-relevant, policy-motivated principals.

Fenno, on the other hand, provides for the possibility of legislative preferences that are entirely exogenous (i.e., legislators who really care about policy issues quite apart from their value for reelection) (Canon 1990). Legislators may deviate from reelection seeking in this view because the electoral filter is not relentlessly Darwinian, so that there is often considerable slack (due, for example, to a long-term partisan reputation that permits relatively unobserved shirking from it by policy-motivated members). This slack enables even reelection-seeking legislators to entertain private conceptions of "good public policy" and to act on them. Nevertheless, pure Mayhewians believe that legislators "run scared," leaving no stone unturned and no margin unattended in their reelection quest.[4]

Although a geographic constituency is assigned a legislator as a matter of constitutional practice, a legislator's "constituency" is chosen. We touched on this issue earlier when we noted that progressively ambitious legislators—contemporary House members who wish to win a place in the Senate or nineteenth-century representatives who wanted to go back home to enter state or local politics—might act with an eye to a constituency they hoped to represent at some future time. What we are claiming here is that a legislator's objective function, to incorporate a conception of responsiveness to constituency, is endogenous. Hence there are many different senses to the concept of constituency. Some legislators, for example, depart dramatically from the Mayhewian notion, or even variations that allow for future ambition, by thinking of their constituency as consisting of their fellow institutional partisans. Especially when given the luxury of a nonbinding connection to the folks back home—nonbinding because of entry barriers or local political practices such as machine politics that render congressional elections otherwise noncompetitive—these legislators seek power in the institution by taking other legislators as their "constituents." This, then, is the third of Fenno's conceptions about the motivations of legislators. (Robert Byrd of West Virginia is rightfully famous for simultaneously taking care of both geographic and institutional constituents—for overloading West Virginia with federal largesse on the one hand and paying excruciating attention to the needs of his fellow Democrats in the Senate on the other. He was, in other words, the nearly pure instantiation of a Cox-McCubbins party leader who internalized externalities and provided collective goods for the legislative party [Cox and McCubbins 1993].)

In short, a rational model of legislative practice defines members by their objective function. Legislative objectives, in the most commonly used form, revolve around responsiveness to the somewhat slippery conception of constituency. This approach, as we have suggested, is permissive given that the idea of constituency is a flexible notion, that it is not carved in granite, and that legislators choose it. All manner of observed legislative behavior is compatible with it:

- Legislators who never met a voter they didn't like and are intent on taking care of just about all of them
- Legislators who develop and burnish a reputation for policy expertise and leadership
- Legislators who like to spend time along the rail of the House floor or in the Senate cloakroom ministering to the needs of their colleagues

Legislators, that is, are guided by one or more of Fenno's three political purposes—reelection, good public policy, and power in the chamber. Although the electoral connection is, as noted, not relentlessly Darwinian, its pressures aren't chopped liver, either. Thus different legislative types will be differentially "sorted" by the electoral connection. In equilibrium, we believe a legislative chamber will be populated by all types, given variance in constituencies and electoral conditions.

Context as Strategic Interaction
The rational choice approach is not just about objectives; it is also about opportunities, constraints, and information. All of the objectives noted address the idea of purpose, but the choices that are made in their service (strategies in the argot of game theory) depend on context. The institutional context in which choices are made include the official rules and unofficial norms that regulate legislative life, the clashing and complementary purposes of others, the extralegislative circumstances that prevail at any particular time, and the private beliefs legislators entertain. In short, institutional context is a shorthand term for

a complicated production function that transforms the actions of purposeful legislative agents into (expected) outcomes. In other words, it is a game.

This, too, is a slippery term. Although there may well be some real way the legislative world works, no legislator knows it for certain and all entertain beliefs about it held with more or less confidence. So the game-tree analogy for opportunities, constraints, and information in the legislative setting is suggestive at best, because in the subjective view of legislators it is often not a uniquely and commonly known concrete construct that theorists (like us!) typically assume. Like the blind-man-and-the-elephant allegory, legislators possess only partially overlapping visions of how the legislative game is played—and thus of what the impacts will be of any particular "reform."

We have claimed that the idea of purposive actors—the link missing in macrohistorical and organization theoretic accounts and provided by rationality-based approaches—is nevertheless slippery. This uncertainty arises because legislators are not stamped on their foreheads with any one purpose in particular, because there are many from which to "choose," and because the electoral mechanism is not so insistently selective as to weed out all but one. A legislative body, therefore, is composed of *many* purpose types, and it is an empirical matter to determine the mix of types in a particular legislative body at a particular time.

Likewise we have just claimed, ever so briefly, that the context or game in which purposeful actors pursue their objectives is also slippery, because it consists of so many pieces and because so many of these pieces are understood by the actors in an inherently subjective way. Even legislators with common purposes may proceed on the basis of entirely different understandings about how the legislative world works. They have different hunches, intuitions, beliefs about the mix of purpose types, knowledge of the rules, and understandings about historical precedents and legacies. Some, like Byrd in the Senate and Rayburn in the House, have stellar reputations for their cunning and expertise on all of these things. Others, especially rookie legislators, have only the crudest comprehension and are fortunate if they can rely on a sympathetic cue giver or Washington-wise staffer for guidance. And although getting these things right will surely enhance a legislator's effectiveness in achieving his or her purposes, neither the electoral filter nor the intralegislative selection mechanisms are so unerring or deterministic as to eliminate variance in this respect altogether. A legislative body, therefore, consists of many belief types, and it is an empirical matter to determine the mix of types in a particular legislative body at a particular time.

We will return to "empirical matters"—regarding the mix of both purpose types and belief types—when we shortly give prominence to the methodology of soaking and poking that Richard Fenno has made famous. Before that, however, we briefly digress to a different methodology, indeed an art—that of heresthetic made famous by Fenno's former colleague, William Riker (1986).

Heresthetic, History, and Context

Even though we feature rational choice, we acknowledge, along with cutting-edge rational choice theorists at the present time, that rationality is imperfect. Information is incomplete, calculation capacity is limited and computation costly, and not even the most sophisticated strategist can look very far down immensely complicated game trees, much less engage in the exercises of backward induction and probabilistic updating required in a "full" rationality approach. (Indeed, even if he or she could, it is not altogether clear, as game theorists such as Binmore have emphasized, what conjectures should be entertained about how others have played.)[5] However, even if we do not despair of these limitations in our models, we have also conceded in our earlier discussion of modes of explanation how slippery the very heart of rational choice is when it comes down to hard cases. The purposes of legislators are many-splendored; their beliefs about how the legislative world works are as variable as human perception, cognition, and understanding are in other contexts. But we need to acknowledge another layer of complexity.

In the simplest of consumer behavior models in economics, the representative consumer is assumed to maximize utility, subject to a constraint on endowments in a context of market prices. The consumer knows his or her preferences, knows the resources with which he or she is endowed, and is a price taker. The first of these items is not decidedly more problematic in the legislative context (though we note again that, in a manner not nearly the same as is conceded in a market setting, there will be a mix of purposive types).[6] The second item is somewhat more problematic, inasmuch as a legislator may be more or less knowledgeable about how he or she may transform resources—votes, staff, office budgets, committee posts, access to expertise, and so on—into legislative results; that is, there is a mix of belief types.[7] The last of the items mentioned is entirely problematic, at least at first glance, in the political sphere. The reason is that economic actors, in their roles as consumers, take the context in which they behave as fixed and unaffected by their individual actions. To effect changes in the economic context, consumers must abandon their more narrowly based economic roles and engage in politics—indirectly through their agents in institutions of the political world or directly through collective action. In short, in most circumstances economic actors may reasonably regard the economic setting as unaffected by (at least their own) economic behavior; these contextual parameters are set elsewhere. Voters may be akin to price takers. Legislators, on the other hand, are members of self-governing groups. Context-effecting activity is politics at its purest and must be treated as entirely within the domain of self-governing political activity.

So, in politics much more than in economics, we must take account of the endogeneity of context.[8] Not everything is up for grabs in anything short of revolutionary circumstances. But so many of the practices of a legislature—from establishing an institutional division and specialization of labor, to deciding how to count quorums, to determining the size and composition of an agenda committee, to prescribing the terms of legislative debate—as our introductory examples suggest, are up for grabs. The very act of conceiving how else legislators might practice institutional politics is an instance of a political art that William Riker termed *heresthetic*. In an additional layer of complexity, then, we must add to the variation and fluidity of political purposes and the variation and amenability to revision of political beliefs the imaginative capacities that enable one to conceive of alternative institutional arrangements and to modify them accordingly. Reed, Rayburn, Mansfield, and (allegedly) Clay saw that the objectives they sought were unattainable in the business-as-usual, status quo political context. So they reinvented government.

Summary Thoughts on Modes of Explanation

We have come to praise rational choice theory, not to bury it. In doing so, however, we wish to underscore some of the practical difficulties the researcher in the field encounters when trying to apply it. In most rational choice theories there are many degrees of freedom, much variance, and much fluidity—that is, many matters that cannot conveniently be left as primitive, unexplained, or exogenous. Consequently, the theory of rational choice needs to be wedded to a methodology of rational choice.[9] That this is a real problem may be seen by briefly revisiting one of our historical examples. That there is a way forward is the subject of our final section.

The Emergence of Congressional Committees Redux

In the modern historical literature on Henry Clay,[10] scholars emphasize time and again the man's burning ambition: to escape the meager opportunities of rural western Virginia as a youth; to make his mark as a young lawyer in the prosperous and bustling legal and business community of Lexington, Kentucky; to dominate the faction-ridden Kentucky legislature; to elevate his game, first briefly as a senator, then as a member of Congress, and then again as a senator in the national legislature; and, finally, to dictate the course of national politics, something he managed to do from the very beginning of his Washington career in 1809 to its very end in 1852. The historians portray Clay as an issue entrepreneur who cast about for issues that would serve to advance his ambitions. First, it was war with Britain (propelling him to the speakership); then conquest of Canada and the Floridas; then tariffs, a national bank, and internal improvements via his famous American Plan; then recognition of and encouragement to the newly democratizing former Spanish colonies in

Latin America; and, of course, slavery. Historians concede that Clay had a warm spot in his heart (or a soft spot in his head!) for some of these issues. He regarded the recognition of democracies throughout the world, for example, as a uniquely American responsibility. (It was, perhaps, only coincidental that this issue allowed him to differentiate himself completely from the Monroe administration . . . and from three of Monroe's cabinet secretaries who were his political rivals—see later section for more details.) Implicitly at least, it is suggested that Clay sought out issues because he saw them as ways to hold together a coalition that kept him in the speakership—a position he was never to lose while sitting in the House. The coalition that launched him to the Speaker's chair the very first day he set foot in the House—war hawks mostly from the west and south, but a few in the north as well—had lost its raison d'être after the end of the war with Britain and the Treaty of Ghent. Moreover, the Federalists had been discredited and were on their way to oblivion, leaving the Jeffersonians nearly a coalition of the whole. In this factionalized environment with no large issue or credible opposition to keep the Jeffersonians cohesive, Clay needed a new base to maintain his hold on the speakership.

We address two methodological issues here. First, most rational choice theories of politics hold ambition in high regard, for ambition is but another way to label maximizing behavior. These theories, however, are less satisfactory when addressing the singularly important behavior of someone other than a "representative" politician. Clay cannot be understood merely as a reelection maximizer, or as someone interested in good public policy, or even as one who sought power in the House (at least not for its own sake). His ambition was more than any of these. Indeed, in his unbridled ambition, which many of his contemporaries believed was taken to such lengths as ultimately to be self-destructive, Clay was seen as without peer. How do we come to terms with someone who is sui generis? It is difficult, as just noted, to classify Clay within conventional categories, and this is a difficulty not only for rational choice approaches but for other theoretical frameworks as well. To come to terms with Clay lies outside theoretical discourse; it is an empirical challenge. Yet come to terms with Clay we must if we are to account for the politics of a period in which he occupied center stage.

More generally, no single individual may be representative of (or represented by) *any* objective function. To focus on any single individual is to focus both on what he or she shares in common with others and on what makes him or her unique as an individual. This distinction is akin to that which is represented in the estimable parameters in some statistical equation, aggregated over numerous individual politicians, and that which constitutes the unique properties of each observation, captured in the residual term.

A second issue remains, even if we are not troubled by Clay's sui generis quality. Clay was at the center of politics in the House in a period of momentous institutional change. If Rip van Winkle had fallen asleep in 1815 (the end of the war with Britain) and awoken in 1825, he would have found a remarkably different House of Representatives. If, on the other hand, he had fallen asleep in 1825 and awoken more than a century later, he would, roughly speaking, have found a broadly similar House. To oversimplify, in the decade ending in 1825 many institutional features were set in the House that would prevail for almost 150 years—specifically, a proactive political and substantive policy role for the Speaker of the House (in contrast to the Speaker of the British House of Commons and Speakers of the U.S. House before Clay), limitations on debate, and a refined division- and specialization-of-labor committee system that gives subunits considerable jurisdictional agenda power. It is hard to imagine that Clay was a passive bystander in these developments. Indeed, it has been suggested that Clay was behind them, experimenting with institutional instruments along with floating substantive policy ideas in his quest to shore up a coalition that would maintain him in the speakership and continue to fuel his presidential aspirations.[11]

The institutional reforms of this period, if Clay was indeed behind them, constitute clear cases of heresthetical maneuver. Standing committees with defined jurisdictions and "property rights" to membership extending beyond a single bill or single session of Congress were not unknown institutional forms in the first decades of the nineteenth century; they were invented by the English in the fifteenth century and traveled across the Atlantic to the colonial legislatures in the seventeenth and eighteenth centuries. But they were exceptional institutional devices in most legislatures of the early nineteenth century, reflecting a Jeffersonian suspicion of small, potentially unrepresentative groups; committees, when they were used at all (in contrast to conducting business entirely in the Committee of the Whole), were primarily *select,* temporary creations to consider a single bill or, perhaps, a series of closely related issues within a single legislative session. Clay's vision (if indeed it was his) was to commit credibly to potential allies to a durable deal in which they would have quasi-permanent influence on those issues that most concerned them. After failing to find an enduring issue around which to construct a durable coalition, he engaged in institutional engineering, giving long-term agenda power in jurisdiction after jurisdiction to members in exchange for their fealty. Thus, the account is of the general properties of institutions under various rules and the interaction of that general account with the specific acts of a specific—and at least partially unique—individual.

This is but a story. The makings of a more rigorous argument about credible commitment and durable coalitions lurk behind it. What is problematic is how to explain Clay's imaginative ploy. In effect, he convinced decisive collections of legislators to play a different game. In the new game, the privileges of subsets of House members were enhanced in their respective jurisdictions, on the one hand, and the boundaries defining these jurisdictions were made secure by the routinization of bill assignments, on the other. This arrangement permitted a considerable portion of the House to have extraordinary influence in policy areas to which they attached high priority, which, in turn, secured for Clay support both procedural and substantive from his followers. In short, it was a deal made in heaven. But how did he imagine this scheme? How best might we model, and hence explain, this sort of political ingenuity, this inventive artistry?

An alternative that bears a familial resemblance more to evolutionary biology than to a purposive approach is (paraphrasing Alchian's seminal ideas) to assume that imaginative schemes are hatched by political herestheticians all the time (Alchian 1950). Later observers are victimized by selection bias in the sense that the successful schemes are recorded by historians whereas the failures are relegated to the dustbin of history. Clay, after all, tried lots of things, and turned, we conjecture, to institutional tinkering only after the more conventional maneuvers of an issue entrepreneur failed.

In our view a rational explanation is complemented by a highly nuanced appreciation of the formation of ideas. By embracing a model of cognition, learning, perhaps even imagination, it may come to terms with heresthetical moves that more generic hypotheses cannot accommodate and more generic theories find anomalous. At the very least a theory of idea formation may provide empirical guidance on these matters. Unless we are particularly unlucky, for example, and Clay hatched the idea of a "modern" committee system in the splendid isolation of his boardinghouse rooms, there should be empirical residues of the evolution of his thinking on these subjects. If only we knew where or for what to look! Soaking and poking, as we discuss shortly, is something that ought not to be restricted to the here and now. Historical examination of Clay's interactions with his allies—or Reed's, Rayburn's, and Mansfield's with theirs, for that matter—means soaking and poking in diaries, correspondence, and other archival materials with a theoretical searchlight.

Soaking and Poking as a Methodological Companion for Rational Choice

Deductive approaches, by their very nature, must assume something like the proposition that factors left outside the theory effectively "cancel out." A clear understanding of why something occurs, according to this view, may adequately be accounted for with a small set of included variables and causal mechanisms. And yet, in his or her heart of hearts, even the most extreme rationalist harbors the intuition that shocks, perturbations, and disturbances, while canceling out most of the time, are not always compensating and sometimes are huge in their impact. Only the most stubborn of determinists, economic or otherwise, holds to the view that nothing idiosyncratic can make a real or lasting difference. Nevertheless, in the intellectual division of labor we tend to sort ourselves into those who think contingency is irrelevant and those who think it is everything. As expressed by Hill (1997, 191),

> Within the disciplines that take human beings as their object of study, there are, very broadly speaking, two schools of thought. One school focuses on the universal attributes of human kind, finds a common substratum beneath cultural differences, and looks for convergence among the many separate histories of the species. The other school seizes upon the particular, is preoccupied with the accidents of history, and regards contingency, rather than necessity, as the essence of the human condition.

Hill goes on to note that rational choice theory is one of the favorites of members of the first school, and obviously we would place ourselves in this academy. And yet (isn't there always an "and yet"?) the history of congressional politics is dotted with transforming events and occasions—"contingency rather than necessity"—in which a bold, unexpected, or imaginative interpretation or action moves events off in an entirely unpredicted direction.

Mayhew (1974) was properly impressed by the extent to which a simple rational model—with reelection-seeking agents at its center—could account for so much of everyday political life in the U.S. Congress. And Fenno (1973), by adding other motivations to the mix, permitted the development of a more nuanced picture of congressional life, not to mention qualifying the more cynical view of congressional politics if reelection were all there were. These men have provided us with the conventional categories in which nearly every congressional scholar now organizes his or her thoughts about legislative politics.

Fenno, however, in his presidential address to the American Political Science Association, sought to remind us that politicians not only are "goal-seeking [but also] . . . situation-interpreting individuals" (1986, 4). It is this latter capacity, we suspect, that permits flights of imagination, many of which crash and burn but some of which become the modern committee system, the Reed rules, the expanded Rules Committee, or the end of the strong-form filibuster.

Surely the behavior of even the most imaginative politician is accounted for initially by a more conventional set of categories.[12] Clay never had to worry much about reelection. His Lexington constituency apparently never tired of him even, for example, after he supported the infamous legislative pay raise that, in 1816, cost nearly three-fourths of all incumbents their seats (Bianco, Spence, and Wilkerson 1996). But his close call in that election reiterated what his political antennae already had received—namely, that other legislators (especially the huge class of freshmen in 1817) needed to keep the folks back home happy. Clay needed to run a House that could deliver for its members. The "old" ways would not work in 1817, he surmised, in a context of factionalism and regionalism on the one hand and an influx of amateur politicians on the other.

Clay, as noted, had strong policy preferences, though we are uncertain whether they held an independent, exogenous fascination for him or whether he was entirely instrumental in their advocacy. For the most part we interpret this advocacy mainly in light of Clay's aspiration to be the spokesman for the new states beyond the Appalachians—"Harry of the West," as he was known. Only somewhat later, we surmise, did he appreciate the suitability of this role to the wide-open, one-party politics of faction and region that prevailed from the waning days of the Virginia Dynasty through the election of Andrew Jackson. In short, he was a policy entrepreneur because it seemed to make for good electoral and institutional politics (at least some of the time) and also because it seemed to be normatively attractive (again, at least some of the time). There is nothing particularly novel or unconventional about this reasoning. It surely encouraged Clay to enhance the role of the Speaker as a proactive policy advocate, a legacy that survives to this day.

If Clay's orientation toward reelection and good public policy does not strain the bounds of conventionality of these explanatory categories for legislative behavior, his aspiration to power in the House is slightly more complicated. He sought the speakership in the House initially for much the same reasons he sought (and attained) the same office in Kentucky's lower house—his vanity and ambition pushed him to distinguish himself from, indeed elevate himself over, his peers. He came to Washington already used to the idea that he was the center of attention, always where the action was. (A more contemporary exemplar of this phenomenon is Lyndon Johnson as majority leader of the U.S. Senate.) Released from constraining reelection worries and apparently comfortable as an issue advocate so long as it didn't complicate his other needs, he was free to pursue the trappings of institutional power initially as an ego trip and later as an instrument, a stepping-stone, for higher aspirations. (In this latter respect, again, Lyndon Johnson comes to mind.)

We are suggesting, then, that the standard purposive categories of modern legislative research seem to capture at least a part of Clay's motives and actions. But we would say of these what we said earlier of rational choice theory more generally: they are attractive, impressive, and incomplete in important ways. The matter that continues to puzzle us is how Clay managed to piece together a path toward his ambitious objectives involving the changes in the institutional ways of doing business that he ultimately induced. How does a scholar come to terms with a strategic shift of gears, a new way of seeing one's way through from status quo to desired result, a gambit of such proportions that it endured even if the objective for which it was created was never achieved? If the question is bold and challenging, the answer is as modest as its main practitioner: soaking and poking. This methodology will not solve all problems, but it will, we believe, provide some scientific discouragement to, and systematic constraints on, the temptation to treat the imaginative maneuvers of extraordinary politicians in entirely unique ways utterly uninterpretable in terms of more general theories.

Sequence as Well as Context

Even if soaking and poking is an appropriate addition to the methodological repertoire of institutionalists of the rational choice persuasion, the task of explanation will still not be completed. The conjunction of a general theory of the effect of rules with a specific account of Clay nonetheless leaves us with an institution that was dramatically, even radically, transformed, never to look the same again. That the heresthetician, Clay, appeared in the House in 1811 can never be explained in the scientific sense (or, even granting Alchian's terms their due, it still cannot be explained why this particular heresthetical act succeeded in the second decade of the nineteenth century). This subject is not general-theorem science that focuses on a big bang equilibrium that can ignore the starting point and path to that equilibrium. Rather, this is an historical science (with emphasis on it nonetheless being a science), in which path dependency, sequence, and starting points, and in which the historical appearance of particular individuals and other truly exogenous shocks, matter. The Hempelian notion of a scientific explanation of some phenomena is the conjunction of general principles with particular empirics. The rational choice apparatus provides the general principles, and they are necessary both to the specific explanation and to science in general. But in an historical science, in a path-dependent process, so too are the unique properties, the sui generis individuals, the unanticipated events necessary.[13]

The addition of soaking and poking is a question of methodology, more or less in the narrow sense. The addition of time dependency changes the nature of the scientific explanation and thus is more than mere methodology. No longer can one make general statements meant to transcend time and place. The filibuster was and is important in the Senate but not in the House because their paths of development were different and that which was different did not rest on systematic differences in the motivations of House versus Senate members (Binder 1997). One can make scientific statements, but their application requires as well the specifics of time and place and person. Not just any specifics, of course, but specifics that must be compatible with the general theoretical statements (and vice versa). Together, however, the methodology of soaking and poking and the science of context and sequence are additions to the rational choice enterprise that effectively make it attractive, impressive, and (nearly? actually?) complete.

Tentative Conclusions

Rational choice models now enjoy a great deal of respect and popularity in political science. They may be appreciated for their own sake—for their elegance, power, and parsimony—and many practitioners of the modeler's craft hold precisely this view. But with their growing attractiveness rational choice models require something more than aesthetics; they require a user-friendliness, an adaptability to real problems, perhaps even an owner's manual.

We do not envision returning to earlier modes of explanation, but we believe that rational choice models in practice will acquire some of the earlier features of social scientific explanation. Particularly when utilized to come to terms with historical phenomena, we think rational choice models need to be enriched both theoretically and methodologically.

Regarding the former, we have suggested that context and sequence ought not to be abstracted away. Institutions are embedded in a web of relationships that are historically influenced if not determined. This web, and the time dependency that derives from the importance of sequence, means that general statements will always need to be qualified by the specifics of time and place. But unlike earlier descriptive approaches, rationality, context, and sequence lend themselves to a more analytical rendering. Even though garden-variety, universalistic rationality must be harnessed by the specifics of context and sequence, the explanations produced will possess an analytic sharpness not usually enjoyed by the more descriptive approaches.

We have raised the sui generis issue that must be tackled in any effort to account for the watershed events in the life of an institution. The historically significant events that constitute major instances of institutional change are often heresthetical transformations that entail considerable imagination and creativity by the principal individuals involved. Clay's role in invigorating the speakership and utilizing the standing committees and Reed's in articulating rules to grease the skids for the majority party are instances of instrumental behavior, but the imaginativeness of the ploys remains a puzzle.

Finally, and perhaps most tentatively, we propose that the history of institutions can be a science. An historical science, however, differs from the model of science that has structured the thinking of most rational choice modelers so far. If our hunch is correct, an historical science of institutions retains derived propositions, to which is added context, sequence, and the exogenous interventions of imaginative individuals. But such blendings of formal results with empirical specifics are the ingredients of scientific explanations in all cases. The derived propositions will be conditional, as all rational choice propositions are conditional, but the conditions will, we must expect, be unique to the context, sequence, and appearance of exogenous forces in the life of the particular institution whose history is being explained.

1. Consider the following example. Roger Brown (1971), in his excellent history of the decisions leading up to the War of 1812, informally but explicitly presents an argument that runs counter to the prevailing historical wisdom. His argument is that President James Madison was not a dove that had to be egged on by war hawks to submit a declaration of war. Rather, in the period between the convening of the 10th Congress in November 1811 and the declaration of war in June 1812, Madison worked hand in glove with war hawks (especially Henry Clay, Speaker of the House; Peter Porter, chair of the Foreign Affairs Committee; and John C. Calhoun, chair of the Military Affairs Committee) to build up the nation's military preparedness with two objectives in mind. By increasing the size of the army and navy and expanding the network of military roads, he hoped first to signal the British of American intent in the hopes of getting the British to retract their Orders in Council, which were the stimulus to war in the first place. This is the "to-ensure-peace-you-must-prepare-for-war" principle. Failing this goal, his second objective was to be certain that the nation could prosecute a war if, in fact, it entered one. Brown documents his argument in great detail. But there is virtually nothing in his fine book about how, exactly, Clay employed select committees— stacking their composition and sequencing their activities—to yield the conditions propitious for war in June of 1812. If a student of congressional organization were interested in the latter, there would be slim pickings in the Brown volume. Those facts never made Brown's radar screen.

2. Readers of the various books and *New Yorker* articles of Elizabeth Drew will appreciate that there is another type of thick describer—the one who reports everything, refusing to discriminate the profound from the trivial and thus making it impossible for the reader to do so as well.

Our colleague Morris Fiorina has complained in private conversation of historians whose selection "principle" is, in effect, "whatever happens to be available." Consequently, the web they weave is one that depends entirely on whose diary they read, which desk drawer they opened, or which archive they happened to explore. The representativeness of the evidence is unknown, as are the various selection biases that may have been at work.

3. Some argue the metaphor is so well-known precisely because it was and is so extreme and mystical.

4. Exemplars of this view include Thomas Mann, *Unsafe at Any Margin: Interpreting Congressional Elections* (Washington, D.C.: American Enterprise Institute, 1977); and Anthony King, *Running Scared: Why America's Politicians Campaign Too Much and Govern Too Little* (New York: Free Press, Martin Kessler Books, 1997). Note that the position that even reelection seekers can entertain and act on policy preferences demands that legislators actually have multiple objectives, à la Fenno and in apparent contradiction of Mayhew. It is just that the continual demands of reelection yield a trade-off between or among multiple objectives that continually favors reelection-maximizing strategies.

5. Off-the-equilibrium-path behavior, for which strategic provision must be made by a player in the full rationality approach, implies that something other than a

rational best response must have been made at a prior move by one of his or her opponents. But if this is the case, then what kind of player could have made such a choice— a mistake-prone player? one with a "trembling hand"? or a systematic form of irrationality? Even full rationality approaches are laden with still-unresolved theoretical complexities (see Binmore 1987).

6. Of course, there is preference diversity in markets. If consumer tastes were identical, the circumstances would hardly be propitious for the kind of exchange at the very foundation of markets. But it is assumed that all consumers are engaged in satisfying their consumption desires. This perspective is a far cry from the variance in purpose types we described earlier for legislatures.

7. This step is normally not entertained in models of consumer choice, in which any consumer knows simply that money is transformed, at fixed exchange rates, for utiles.

8. To be fair, parts of modern political economy are all about how economic agents, possessing a political as well as an economic repertoire, may divert resources from nominally economic activities—investment, production, and consumption—to explicitly political activities if the latter improves their welfare. The literature on rent seeking and corruption, for example, describes how economic agents alter (i.e., endogenize) the framework in which economic activity is conducted by intervening in the political sphere.

9. Of course, it is always possible to revise and improve the theory, and this is happening all the time. The toy models of extensive-form game theory (which were a considerable, even revolutionary advance over the toy matrices of the normal form game)—the very stock in trade of the modern legislative theorist—remind us of the revolutions that happen in the world of theory. The present interest in incomplete information, bounded rationality, and evolutionary ideas stands as evidence that rational choice theorists are hardly complacent types.

10. The best known of the secondary and biographical literature on Clay includes that by Mayo (1937), Peterson (1987), Remini (1991), and Van Deusen (1937).

11. This case has been made—purely as an argument lacking smoking-gun empirical evidence—in Gamm and Shepsle (1989). In a recent paper, while expressing sympathy and empirical support for an elaborated version of this position, Jenkins speculates that Clay began plotting his presidential bid 7 years in advance of the 1824 election. In an instance of remarkable foresight, Clay, it is alleged, anticipated that Monroe would be unopposed for a second term in 1820 but that the 1824 election would be a wide-open competition among Monroe's major cabinet secretaries (Adams, Calhoun, and Crawford), potentially ending up in the House of Representatives (in light of the growing regionalism in electoral politics). If that did transpire, and Clay managed to finish at least third in the electoral vote tally, his presidential prospects would depend on his control of that body. He thus engaged in institutional tinkering that would assure him the necessary influence in that event (see Jenkins 1996).

12. We depend heavily here on the fine interpretation of events offered by Jenkins (1996).

13. More accurately, it is unanticipatable events, not unlike the alleged meteor impact as explanation for the demise of the dinosaurs and rise of mammals. These kinds of explanation require good science *and* good history (see Alvarez 1997).

REFERENCES

Alchian, Armen A. 1950. "Uncertainty, Evolution, and Economic Theory." *Journal of Political Economy* 58: 211–21.

Aldrich, John H., and David W. Rohde. 1997–98. "The Transition to Republican Rule in the House: Implications for Theories of Congressional Politics." *Political Studies Quarterly* 112 (winter): 541–67.

Alvarez, Walter. 1997. *T. rex and the Crater of Doom.* Princeton: Princeton University Press.

Bianco, William, David B. Spence, and John D. Wilkerson. 1996. "The Electoral Connection in the Early Congresses: The Case of the Compensation Act of 1816." *American Journal of Political Science* 40: 145–71.

Binder, Sarah A. 1997. *Minority Rights, Majority Rule: Partisanship and the Development of Congress.* New York: Cambridge University Press.

Binmore, Kenneth. 1987. "Modeling Rational Players, I." *Economics and Philosophy* 3: 179–214.

Brown, Roger. 1971. *The Republic in Peril: 1812.* New York: Norton.

Canon, David. 1990. *Actors, Athletes, and Astronauts: Political Amateurs in the United States Congress.* Chicago: University of Chicago Press.

Cooper, Joseph. *The Origins of the Standing Committees and the Development of the Modern House.* 1970. Houston: Rice University Studies.

Cox, Gary, and Mathew McCubbins. 1993. *Legislative Leviathan.* Berkeley and Los Angeles: University of California Press.

Fenno, Richard F., Jr. 1973. *Congressmen in Committees.* Boston: Little, Brown.

Fenno, Richard F., Jr. 1978. *Home Style: House Members in Their Districts.* Boston: Little, Brown.

Fenno, Richard F., Jr. 1986. "Observation, Context, and Sequence in the Study of Politics." *American Political Science Review* 80: 3–15.

Gamm, Gerald, and Kenneth Shepsle. 1989. "Emergence of Legislative Institutions: Standing Committees in the House and Senate, 1810–1825." *Legislative Studies Quarterly* 14: 39–66.

Gamm, Gerald, and Steven S. Smith. 1997. "Emergence of Senate Leadership, 1833–1946." Paper read at the annual meeting of the American Political Science Association, Washington, D.C.

Hill, Greg. 1997. "History, Necessity, and Rational Choice Theory." *Rationality and Society* 9: 189–213

Jenkins, Jeffery A. 1996. "Property Rights and Institutional Selection: The Emergence of Standing Committee Dominance in the 19th Century House of Representatives." Paper read at the annual meeting of the Southern Political Science Association, Atlanta.

Mayhew, David. 1974. *Congress: The Electoral Connection.* New Haven: Yale University Press.

Mayo, Bernard. 1937. *Henry Clay: Spokesman of the New West.* Boston: Houghton Mifflin.

Peterson, Merrill D. 1987. *The Great Triumvirate: Webster, Clay, and Calhoun.* New York: Oxford University Press.

Remini, Robert V. 1991. *Henry Clay: Statesman for the Union.* New York: Norton.

Riker, William H. 1986. *The Art of Political Manipulation.* New Haven: Yale University Press.

Van Deusen, Glyndon. 1937. *The Life of Henry Clay.* Boston: Little, Brown.

Building Reputations and Shaping Careers: The Strategies of Individual Agendas in the U.S. Senate

Wendy J. Schiller

Introduction

The structure of a Senate delegation offers a unique opportunity to study the effects of dual representation—two legislators sharing the same exact geographic constituency—on legislative agenda setting. To date, most work on Senate delegations focuses on the partisan composition of the delegation as a function of electoral and state characteristics (Alesina, Fiorina, and Rosenthal 1990; Herrick and Thomas 1993; Powell 1990; Segura and Nicholson 1995). A smaller set of work in this area (Jung et al. 1994; Uslaner 1998) focuses on senators' institutional behavior—namely, the roll call voting patterns of Senate delegations—and suggests that senators use roll call votes to attract the support of particular constituencies in their states. In contrast to Jung et al., Bernstein (1992) found that partisan and ideological differences between senators from the same state do not translate into differences in approval ratings among constituents. The same group of constituents displayed similar levels of support for senators from different parties.

My work explores the effects of sharing the same geographic constituency on other legislative activities—notably, how senators select the issues and interests that comprise the core of their agendas. Existing work tells us that senators perceive the need to establish reputations as effective legislators among their constituents (Fenno 1991; Schiller 1995). Because of the power afforded to each senator, individual choices as to which issues and interests they champion in the Senate will influence, and in some cases determine, the aggregate legislative output of the Senate. To construct a more complete explanation of the individual choices that comprise Senate behavior, it is important to examine the effects of the two-person structure of Senate delegations.

From a representational standpoint, we should expect to see senators from the same state representing similar issue areas and economic interests in their legislative portfolios. From an electoral standpoint, we might also expect to see senators addressing similar issues—if they are perceived to be popular among voters—because they each seek a majority voting coalition in the state. For example, senators from Nebraska, a heavily agricultural state, should both be expected to address farm interests. Senators from the same state should also be expected to respond equally to an overriding policy concern in that state; that is, senators from Florida should both make immigration a primary focus of their legislative agendas.

However, what we actually observe is that senators from the same state do not build legislative agendas based on similar issues and interests; on the contrary, they build very distinct and separate legislative agendas on which they base much of their reputation as senators, regardless of same- or split-party affiliation. We are therefore faced with the following puzzle: *Why do senators who represent the same state, but who never compete for the same senate seat, use different issues as the core of their legislative agendas?*

In this essay, I argue that legislative differentiation within Senate delegations emerges as a result of each senator's individual response to the staggered nature of Senate elections and the institutional structures that determine his or her legislative opportunities.

Agenda Setting

Initial Decisions to Differentiate

In their early years, freshman senators generally adjust to the Senate as an institution; they choose which issues will be the foundation of their first term and decide which legislative tools they will use to formulate their agendas.[1] They seek out open territory—issue areas in which they can build a name for themselves, inside and outside the Senate. In doing so, senators rely most heavily on their prior experience, personal interests, campaign promises, and state concerns as the bases for legislative initiatives (Fenno 1991, 1996). They use these factors as guidelines for seeking particular committee assignments, introducing bills, and offering amendments (Schiller 1995).

In making these early choices about the content of their first-term agendas, senators pay close heed to which committee assignments and issue areas are already the property of the other senator from their state. Several variables explain why freshman senators choose alternative committees and issue areas from their state colleagues. One variable is the structure of Senate elections; because Senate elections are staggered by 2, 4, or 6 years, one senator almost always enters the Senate facing a senior colleague who has already begun to build a reputation as a senator from that state. If the junior senator decides to specialize in areas similar to those of his or her more senior colleague, he or she faces higher costs of reputation building because of the senior colleague's established visibility in those areas.

The importance of staggered elections may depend heavily on the number of years that divide the two senators. If the two senators from the same state are only 2 or 4 years apart, then the incentives to differentiate may not be as great.

At those early stages of a Senate career, reputations are not yet firmly established and the junior senator in that case may be willing to incur the costs of encroaching on the senior senator's chosen issue areas. The longer the senior senator from the state has been in office, the more likely he or she is to have successfully built a reputation in issue areas, thereby increasing the costs of encroachment by the junior senator. The effects of seniority within a Senate delegation are most obvious in cases in which the senior senator has secured a committee chair or ranking position on a committee. Faced with that kind of constraint, pursuing similar issue areas is clearly an inefficient strategy.

Senate party caucus rules governing committee assignment also exert an independent effect on legislative agenda formation within Senate delegations. In both the Democratic and Republican party caucuses, rules prohibit two senators from the same party and the same state from sitting on the same committee together. Automatically, then, a junior senator must adjust his or her preferences for committee assignments to those not already taken by the senior senator.

If two senators are from the same state but opposite parties, then they are not constrained to seek different committee assignments. In most cases of split-party delegations, a newly elected senator is technically free to pursue the same committee assignment(s) as his or her state colleague. Senators from the same state (but different parties) might feel less pressure to adopt distinct legislative agendas, relying instead on partisan differences to establish reputations, and pursue the same issue areas. However, I argue that the same incentives hold for differentiation among split-party delegations as same-party delegations. Even if the junior senator is set apart by a different partisan affiliation, the senior senator still has the advantage of institutional seniority and established reputation in specific issue areas; it remains an inefficient strategy to encroach on those issue areas.[2]

Staggered elections, which result in senior and junior senators, and caucus rules may explain initial decisions to differentiate among same-state senators, but they do not fully explain the persistence of differentiation. Given turnover in the Senate, each senator will have opportunities to switch committee assignments and we might expect them to expand their legislative agendas to address the issues most attractive to their state constituents. Surprisingly, there is not a great deal of movement toward the same issue areas among senators from the same state over time. The puzzle then becomes *what sustains differences in legislative specialization among Senate delegations over time?*

Sustained Differentiation over Time

The explanation for sustained differentiation within Senate delegations over time rests on the requirements for successful reputation building—namely, media attention and constituent recognition—and the benefits of institutional seniority. Media coverage is often the primary way that senators establish reputations as legislators, nationally and in their home states. Cook (1989) details the efforts legislators expend to attract media attention: press releases, editorial boards, town meetings, and so forth. Hess (1981, 1986) found that reporters seek out senators who are considered experts on an issue via their committee jurisdiction because those senators are viewed as the key policymakers in that issue area. Consequently, senators' efforts to gain publicity, nationally and in their state, often depend on their institutional positions.

Once the media establishes contact with particular senators in issue areas, the tendency is to return to the same senators over and over again. This media bias toward "the usual suspects" makes it difficult for a senator to establish himself or herself in issue areas normally associated with a state colleague, even if the opportunity arises within the Senate to do so.

Moreover, because two senators occupy the same media market, it is inherently difficult for both of them to obtain solo press coverage; for example, any article on Senate votes will mention both senators. Therefore, a senator has strong incentive to distinguish his or her legislative accomplishments in the Senate from those of his or her colleague to attract individual publicity in the state.

In turn, constituents' evaluations of their senators are often based on what they read in the newspaper or see on television. Sinclair (1990) found that national media coverage increases senators' exposure to their constituents and usually results in more favorable evaluations. Franklin (1993) and Sinclair (1990) both demonstrate that the higher constituents' education level and attention to media, the more likely they are to be able to name specific reasons for liking or disliking their senators. Once both senators have used their legislative agendas to become associated with success in distinct issue areas among the media and constituents, it makes little sense for them to branch out into each other's territory.

There are also costs to switching committee assignments midway through a term or Senate career in terms of seniority and legislative power. A senator invests a certain amount of time and energy in specializing, forging working relationships with other senators, and ultimately proving himself or herself to be an effective legislator in particular issue areas. As a senator becomes more senior on a committee, the costs of establishing a reputation in new issue areas, within the institution itself, increase. Consider the previous example of senators from Nebraska; in this case, Senator A has established himself as an expert in defense and rural transportation issues based on his seats on the Armed Services and Commerce Committees and Senator B has specialized in Agriculture issues. Senator B leaves the Senate and thus provides the opportunity for Senator A to move to the Agriculture Committee and begin to forge a new reputation as an agriculture specialist. However, Senator A calculates that the costs of starting over, and the loss in seniority, outweigh any possible benefits from switching committee assignments, despite the fact that agriculture is a major interest in his state. Subsequently, Senator C, who replaced Senator B, takes the seat on the Agriculture Committee and thereby maintains the differentiation within the delegation.

Simply stated, then, senators from the same state continuously take into account the behavior of their state colleagues when constructing their legislative agendas. Where we might expect senators from the same state to address the same set of important issues and interests, we find that the incentive structure that they face pushes them in opposite directions. From their first choices of committee assignments and issue areas, to their attempts to get media attention and constituent recognition at home, to their eventual rise up the institutional ladder of seniority, senators from the same state behave as if they are in competition with each other.

Research Design

One single illustration of the differentiation among senators from the same state posited in this essay is highlighted by Fenno (1996, 46), who quotes former Senator Paul Tsongas comparing himself with his Massachusetts colleague, Senator Ted Kennedy:

> Yes, the issues that I'm into reflect another generation. He tends to be into human resources issues, Great Society issues. Mine are more technological, more future-oriented-energy, environment, Africa, the restoration of cities. Those are different kinds of issues than health care, the criminal justice system, or welfare would be.

To demonstrate more systematically that same-state senators purposely seek to differentiate themselves, and that the media, interest groups, and constituents recognize these differences, I examine the legislative behavior of senators that served in office during the years 1987–92. During this period, 28 state delegations (56 senators) were represented by the same pair of senators over the entire 6 years and 22 state delegations (44) changed composition.

My sources of data include interviews with Senate staff members in 42 Senate offices, conducted in 1991 and 1992 as part of a larger project that examined how senators formulated their legislative agendas. The interview data used in this essay come from questions addressed to senators' staffs about what factors influenced their choice of committee assignments and the issue areas on their agendas. I also collected data on individual senators, including seniority, party, state size, size of economy, number of bills introduced, ideology, committee assignment, committee position, proximity of a reelection campaign, and whether the senator ran for president.

Unfortunately, the number of states for which media coverage is available electronically for these years is limited to 10: Georgia, Illinois, Texas, New York, Massachusetts, Florida, Nebraska, Minnesota, Kentucky, and California.[3] Using the data from these states, I have analyzed patterns of relevant trends in local coverage of senators from the same state.[4] I also use qualitative data from a questionnaire sent to editors and reporters at the newspaper with the largest circulation in each of the 50 states; 28 surveys were returned, for a response rate of 56 percent.

To test whether constituents recognize differentiation by their Senate delegation, I use the 1988–92 pooled Senate Election Study's like and dislike questions about senators. Issue mentions are delineated by the National Election Survey (NES) codebook, which distinguishes between domestic and foreign policy; I include both in my analysis. In general, committee jurisdictions are broader than the NES categories, and I matched like and dislike issue mentions with committee jurisdictions based on the descriptions set forth in the Senate Rules as well as Smith and Deering (1990).[5]

Differentiation over Time: Qualitative Evidence

We know that senators enter the Senate with policy interests and prior experience that can often dictate their committee preferences (Fenno 1973). Senators often come to the Senate with a preexisting reputation in an issue area by virtue of holding a prior elected office in the state such as representative, attorney general, or governor. The logical choice for these senators is to try to translate their existing reputation in certain issue areas into a broader reputation as a senator. However, these senators often discover that the other sitting senator has already cornered the market on "their" issues.

Such was exactly the case for Senator Jim Jeffords (R-VT), who was elected in 1988. Senator Jeffords had specialized in dairy issues, a crucial interest for his state, during his career as a member of the House of Representatives. In the House, he could distinguish his role in dairy issues because he was the only congressman from his state involved in his issues and faced no direct competition from other home state representatives. In the Senate, all that changed. When he arrived in the Senate, he found that the issue had been "taken" by Senator Leahy (D-VT), who was 14 years his senior. As Senator Jefford's legislative director put it:

> Senator Leahy is considered something of an expert in the dairy industry. He was the ranking member on the House Subcommittee on Livestock,

Dairy and Poultry. He probably knew more about the dairy industry than anyone in the House. Also [state] is dairy and dairy is about it in the state. It has a big impact on other industries in the state like tourism. . . . The thing about dairy is that with Senator Leahy being Chairman of Agriculture, there is not too much mileage to be gained in spending time on that issue.

Because of his fellow state senator's prominence on dairy issues, Senator Jeffords, the former congressman, had to focus on other issues to forge a reputation for himself *as a senator.* He chose to take the seat on the Environment and Public Works Committee, where he has actively sponsored several bills that deal with pollution and hazardous materials. Notably, in this case the two senators had different party affiliations and still Senator Jeffords perceived the need to contrast himself legislatively with Senator Leahy.

Because senators from the same state share office for longer periods of time, one might expect the competition between them for publicity and recognition to subside. Interestingly enough, the competitive nature of the relationship does not greatly diminish. If one senator has a lot of seniority over the other one, as in the case mentioned earlier, then the junior senator may view himself or herself in competition with the senior senator indefinitely. A case in point is that of Alaska, where Senator Ted Stevens (R-AK) is senior to Senator Frank Murkowski (R-AK) by 12 years. Although Senator Murkowski has been in office for 17 years, he still remains overshadowed by Senator Stevens. One Alaska reporter described their relationship this way:

For Stevens and Murkowski, the problems between them arise not just because of party, but because of the varying lengths of tenure. Stevens has been around since 1968, Murkowski since 1980. But the Republican turnover has meant that Murkowski has progressed steadily up the seniority chart, culminating in the chairmanship of the Energy and Natural Resources Committee—arguably the most influential panel in the Senate on a federal land state. Still, Alaskans are used . . . to Stevens getting things done for them. . . . Stevens thinks he has the better ideas and the better strategy for accomplish(ing) the state's goals. Murkowski, always looking for ways to climb out from behind Stevens' shadow, tries to strike out on his own only to find that there are subtle roadblocks and sniping coming from his colleague.

In Oregon, Senators Mark Hatfield (R-OR) and Bob Packwood (R-OR) were elected only 2 years apart and served together for more than 25 years. As an editor and a reporter from an Oregon newspaper described it, each chose to pursue distinct legislative issue areas:

> Packwood and Hatfield, over time, carved out niches that rarely met and almost never overlapped. Hatfield was the details guy on Oregon issues; Packwood was more national, focusing on broader issues like taxation matters that almost never had any direct connection to a specific Oregon constituency. (Reporter)

> Locally, he [Hatfield] has brought a number of projects to the state and was the most influential player on natural resources issues and on the fate of the Bonneville Power Administration. Packwood has played a big role in the 1986 tax reform bill and was influential as one of the first pro-choice members of the U.S. Senate. He also was a big champion of deregulation on the Commerce Committee. . . . Overall, I would say Packwood had fewer accomplishments for Oregon and was more of a lone wolf. (Editor)

In each of these cases, senators from the same state, regardless of same- or split-party affiliation, diversified their portfolios to establish individual legislative reputations and to sustain their differences throughout their Senate careers.

Although most senators from the same state choose different committee assignments, there are some exceptions. In the 6-year period studied here, four pairs of senators shared a committee assignment for all 6 years, five pairs of senators shared a committee assignment for only 4 years, and nine pairs of senators shared a committee assignment for only 2 years. Importantly, even among state delegations with shared committee assignments, few freshman senators chose to sit on the same committees as their more senior colleagues—only 6 out of 29 senators who were freshmen during this time sought out a seat on the same committee as their more senior colleagues. If senators share the same committee assignment, it is usually because a junior senator has joined the committee of his or her more senior colleague, for the most part after the junior senator has been in the Senate long enough to establish the basis for an independent reputation.[6] Overall, the extent to which senators from the same state share committee assignments is very minimal.

Trends in Recognition of Same-State Senators

Thus far I have argued that senators set out from the very beginning of their tenure to distinguish themselves from their state colleagues and therefore join different committees and sponsor legislation in different issue areas. But are these distinctions recognized outside the Senate? To see whether constituents show any signs of recognizing specific issues associated with the two senators from their state, and whether these issues differ, I performed several tests. The first test uses the full sample of all senators who held office at some point during the 6-year period between 1987 and 1992. Using these data, I explain the

variation in the number of specific issue likes or dislikes associated with senators as a function of seniority, state size, reelection, committee assignment,
partisan composition of the delegation, and number of issue likes or dislikes
associated with the other senator from the state.[7]

Table 1 presents the findings of Model 1 for six major issue areas organized as committee jurisdictions: Judiciary, Labor and Human Resources,
Energy and Environment, Finance, Agriculture, and Defense and Foreign Relations. The number of issues mentioned as likes or dislikes about a senator in an
issue area is strongly positively correlated with a committee assignment in that
issue area, thereby confirming the importance of committee assignment in determining a senator's visibility in specific issue areas.

The table also reveals that the number of issue mentions in an issue area
for one senator exerts little statistical or substantive impact on the number of
issue mentions in that issue area for the other sitting senator from the same
state. The only area for which there appears to be a substantively significant
correlation between senators from the same state is agriculture. Although there
is not a strong negative correlation, at the very least it suggests that the constituents can tell the difference between their senators by assigning them credit
for differing issue areas. One explanation for the weak coefficient is that the
decision to differentiate, and the legislative reputation that comes with such
differentiation, is measured primarily in committee selection. In sum, the
results of Model 1 support several conclusions about the relationship between
senators' legislative activity and constituent impressions of them. First, holding a particular committee assignment translates into recognition by constituents of accomplishment in that committee's issue areas. Second, constituents identify their two home state senators with distinct issue areas.

Clearly, media coverage of senators is an important intervening variable
in the relationship between senators and their constituents. Variations in the
amount and content of media coverage may explain variation in constituent
evaluations across senators from the same state. We know that national media
coverage exerts an effect on constituent approval ratings (Sinclair 1990), but
the effects of state-based newspaper coverage on constituent recognition are
still relatively unexplored. Senators perceive each other as much stronger competition for publicity at home than on the national level, where they compete
against all other senators, not just their state colleague. This type of competition for visibility is well described in the following *Chicago Tribune* article
about Senators Alan Dixon and Paul Simon:

> Having spent the third year of his first Senate term on the presidential
> campaign trail, Simon acknowledged that he needs to devote his full
> attention to the Senate and getting re-elected. . . . If there was a weekend
> radio or television public affairs show he did not tape, it wasn't for lack of

demand or effort by his staff. *In fact, his chief rival for media attention seemed to be his colleague and Downstate neighbor, Democratic Sen. Alan Dixon, who doesn't face re-election until 1992* [emphasis added]. . . . [M]embers of Simon's Washington staff have taken to bombarding the press room [at the *Tribune*] with phone calls and press releases about Simon's activities, including "fact sheets" about "Simon related provisions" in various bills moving through Congress. (May 15, 1988)

To test for the effects of two senators competing for media coverage in the same media market in their state, I constructed Model 2 to predict and explain the amount of local newspaper coverage that senators receive in the six issue areas as a function of state size, seniority, committee assignment, committee

TABLE 1.   Model 1: Determinants of Constituent Like and Dislike Issue Mentions about Senators, 1987–92

	Judiciary	Labor	Energy/Epw
Intercept	1.69**	1.21**	.12
	(.56)	(.46)	(.43)
Seniority	.06	−.06	−.02
	(.10)	(.08)	(.07)
Reelection	.97**	.81**	.67**
	(.26)	(.21)	(.19)
State size	.04**	.01	−.02
	(.02)	(.02)	(.02)
Numcom	−.27**	−.09	.07
	(.13)	(.10)	(.10)
Judiciary	1.49**		
	(.36)		
State colleague issue mentions	.12**	.10*	.05
	(.06)	(.06)	(.06)
Labor		1.31**	
		(.27)	
Energy			.65**
			(.24)
Epw			1.10**
			(.26)
Same party	−.24	−.11	.12
	(.24)	(.20)	(.19)
Adjusted R^2	.12	.12	.11
N	259	259	259

position, prior experience as a member of Congress or governor, running for president, and amount of coverage allotted to the other sitting senator.[8] As noted earlier, the availability of data to explore local media coverage is limited for 1987–92, but some patterns of coverage emerge for the 10 states examined.

As table 2 reveals, sitting on the Judiciary, Labor, Finance, or Armed Services Committee significantly increases the number of local newspaper articles about a senator in those issue areas. Interestingly, sitting on the Foreign Relations Committee has no effect on state media coverage. The local nature of the defense industry may enable senators to make much better use of a seat on Armed Services than on Foreign Relations for the purposes of attracting state media coverage. Sitting on the Agriculture Committee also increases media coverage, but the impact of the coefficient is very minimal.

TABLE 1 — *Continued*

	Finance/Economy	Agriculture	Defense/Foreign
Intercept	.80	.08	−.19
	(.44)	(.24)	(.42)
Seniority	−.02	−.009	.11
	(.08)	(.039)	(.07)
Reelection	1.22**	.10	.14
	(.20)	(.10)	(.18)
State size	.004	−.02*	−.02
	(.017)	(.01)	(.02)
Numcom	−.06	−.05	.18**
	(.10)	(.05)	(.09)
Finance	.62**		
	(.22)		
State colleague issue mentions	.16**	.43**	.05
	(.06)	(.05)	(.06)
Agriculture		.79**	
		(.12)	
Foreign relations			.65**
			(.23)
Armed services			.63**
			(.23)
Same party	−.005	−.22**	.09
	(.187)	(.10)	(.18)
Adjusted R^2	.15	.39	.05
N	258	259	259

Source: Pooled Senate Election Study, 1988–92.
Note: Standard errors in parentheses.
*$p < .10$ **$p < .05$

The effects of holding prior office on media coverage are mixed. Being a former member of Congress decreases coverage in the areas of judiciary and foreign relations but increases it in economic issue areas. Being a former governor increases coverage in judiciary, labor, and the environment. It may be the case that governors can carry over their preexisting reputations statewide in traditionally domestic issue areas more easily than former members of Congress.

The relationship between media coverage for one senator and media coverage for the other senator from the state are also mixed. The parameter estimates for this variable are only significant in the areas of labor and agriculture issues, where the coverage for one senator suppresses coverage for the other. In two other areas, defense/foreign relations and judiciary, the effect is also negative but the parameter estimates are insignificant. Again, the small sample size reduces our ability to generalize, but these results give some, albeit minimal, support for the assertion that senators compete for media attention and that it is difficult for both senators from the same state to get media attention in the same issue areas.

TABLE 2.   Model 2: Determinants of State Media Coverage of Senators in Specific Issue Areas, 1987–92

	Judiciary	Labor	Energy/Epw
Intercept	40.9**	25.0**	17.5
	(10.4)	(12.7)	(11.8)
Seniority	−5.8**	5.4*	−1.9
	(2.9)	(3.2)	(2.8)
Reelection	1.8	5.7	18.1**
	(6.6)	(7.5)	(6.6)
Congress	−17.3**	−6.1	−2.05
	(8.2)	(9.0)	(8.3)
Governor	10.1	23.0**	51.3**
	(9.1)	(10.3)	(9.6)
Judiciary	72.3**		
	(11.5)		
State colleague media	−.02	−.20*	.10
	(.11)	(.12)	(.12)
Labor		24.7**	
		(11.3)	
Energy/Epw			−6.0
			(8.3)
Adjusted R^2	.38	.30	.41
N	58	58	58

(continued)

The last step in the process of explaining differentiation among senators from the same state is to connect institutional behavior, local media coverage, and constituent recognition. Model 1 demonstrated that constituents recognize senators' legislative activity, and Model 2 illustrated the direct connections between a senator's committee jurisdictions and the issues for which he or she receives local press attention.

Model 3 builds on the results of the other models by using media coverage to test for patterns of recognition of senators among their constituents. In this model, committee assignment is excluded because of its high multi-collinearity with media coverage and because Model 2 confirms that media coverage is in part based on a senator's committee assignment, controlling for other variables.[9] The results of Model 3 indicate that constituents respond to local media attention in specific issue areas when naming like and dislike issue

TABLE 2 — *Continued*

	Finance/Economy	Agriculture	Defense/Foreign
Intercept	−1.2	.29	53.2*
	(8.7)	(.14)	(29.4)
Seniority	4.6**	−.07*	8.0
	(2.3)	(.04)	(7.3)
Reelection	6.6	.01	−3.7
	(5.7)	(.09)	(17.0)
Congress	24.4**	−.10	−44.6**
	(8.3)	(.10)	(21.2)
Governor	24.1**	−.19	−27.0
	(7.9)	(.13)	(24.6)
Finance	27.2**		
	(7.7)		
State colleague media	.07	−.005*	−.02
	(.12)	(.002)	(.12)
Agriculture		.014**	
		(.002)	
Foreign relations			−3.9
			(19.8)
Armed services			64.5**
			(21.7)
Adjusted R^2	.34	.47	.35
N	58	58	58

Source: Dow Jones News Retrieval Service 1987–92.
Note: Standard errors in parentheses.
*$p < .10$ **$p < .05$

mentions associated with the senators from their state (table 3). In five out of six issue areas—judiciary, labor, finance, agriculture, and defense/foreign affairs—media coverage increased constituent like or dislike responses about the senator.

The effects of the issue mentions for one senator on the issue mentions for the other senator vary across issue areas. In three out of six issue areas—finance, agriculture, and the environment—there is a statistically significant correlation between issue mentions for one senator and issue mentions for the

TABLE 3.   Model 3: Effects of State Media Coverage on Constituent Recognition of Senators in Issue Areas

	Judiciary	Labor	Energy/Epw
Intercept	.39	−.28	−.31
	(.81)	(.63)	(.41)
Seniority	−.34*	−.09	−.08
	(.19)	(.16)	(.10)
Reelection	.87	.24	.85**
	(.49)	(.40)	(.28)
Presidential candidate	−1.5*	−.77	−.43
	(.84)	(.68)	(.43)
Congress	.23	−.07	−.16
	(.54)	(.44)	(.28)
Governor	.90	.33	.94**
	(.63)	(.53)	(.44)
Judiciary media	.03**		
	(.01)		
State colleague judiciary issues	.10		
	(.14)		
Labor media		.02**	
		(.01)	
State colleague labor issues		−.001	
		(.149)	
Energy/Epw media			−.002
			(.005)
State colleague energy/Epw issues			.36**
			(.13)
Same party	−.48	.99**	.43
	(.65)	(.48)	(.29)
Adjusted R^2	.31	.25	.29
N	52	52	52

(*continued*)

other senator from the state; for judiciary, labor, and defense/foreign affairs, no such correlation exists. It may be the case that senators from the same state have a more difficult time distinguishing themselves in areas that are of great concern to the state, especially in the case of agriculture. Even if one senator from the state does not actively address the issue, constituents may simply assume the senator is attentive because the interest is so important to the state. For more ideological areas, such as judiciary and labor, it may be easier for senators to stake out a clear position on issues or adopt distinctly different portfolios because the areas are less intrinsically connected to state interests.

TABLE 3 — *Continued*

	Finance/Economy	Agriculture	Defense/Foreign
Intercept	1.14**	−.19	.002
	(.68)	(.40)	(.806)
Seniority	−.14	.15	−.03
	(.16)	(.09)	(.21)
Reelection	1.03**	.43**	.69
	(.40)	(.22)	(.48)
Congress	−.19	.10	.90
	(.51)	(.24)	(.60)
Governor	−.83	−.01	−.41
	(.56)	(.30)	(.66)
Finance/economy media	.003		
	(.009)		
State colleague finance/economy issues	.40**		
	(.14)		
Agriculture media		.011**	
		(.005)	
State colleague agriculture issues		.33**	
		(.14)	
Defense/foreign media			.012**
			(.004)
State colleague defense/foreign issues			−.08
			(.14)
Same party	.06	−.09	.17
	(.46)	(.24)	(.58)
Adjusted R^2	.19	.23	.16
N	52	52	52

Source: Dow Jones News Retrieval Service 1987–92; pooled 1987–92 Senate Election Study issue mentions

Note: Standard errors in parentheses.

$*p < .10$ $**p < .05$

It is important not to overestimate the import of the findings of these three models. I am not suggesting that all constituents are fully aware of the distinctions between their two senators, on any dimension. This work is a more modest endeavor to illustrate the influence of having a two-member delegation on strategic agenda setting and the extent to which agenda setting pays off in terms of building reputations. To this end, these quantitative results provide support for the anecdotal evidence discussed earlier; same-state senators' choices to differentiate their legislative agendas are recognized by the national and local media, whose coverage of senators in turn directly influences constituents' evaluations of their senators.

Conclusion

In this essay, I have argued that the dynamics of a two-person Senate delegation strongly influences the choices that individual senators make about their legislative agendas. Establishing a successful Senate career depends on building a reputation inside and outside the Senate as an effective legislator. Senators choose particular committee assignments and use legislative tools to accomplish that goal. At every stage of the process, senators from the same state confront each other as an obstacle. Within the Senate, staggered elections automatically provide seniority to one senator over the other, and Senate party caucus rules often preclude joining committees alongside a state colleague. At home, local media tend to identify senators with specific issues early on in their tenures, based on committee assignments, and thus make it difficult for one senator to encroach on the other senator's territory. Constituents subsequently form impressions of each senator from their state based in part on media coverage of the senator's legislative portfolio. Like media attention, once constituents have formed an impression of a senator, there are high costs to changing that reputation. All these factors result in a counterintuitive finding: legislators who share the same geographic constituency address distinctly different interests and issue areas.

Despite their efforts to differentiate, some evidence suggests that constituents sometimes identify both senators from the state with the same issue. Although these correlations between like and dislike mentions for both senators are very weak, they exemplify the challenge that senators, especially those who share the same party, face in differentiating themselves. The evidence that senators perceive the need to do so is more than compelling; it is less clear the extent to which they actually succeed.

One important variable that I do not include in the model is interest group support for senators from the same state. Using economic interest groups as a proxy for state interests, we would expect patterns of support for senators from the same state to reflect differences in legislative specialization. Do state-based interest groups tend to throw their support behind both senators from the same state, or do they tend to align more closely with one senator over the other? One way of measuring interest group support is to examine campaign contributions from affiliated political action committees (PACs) in the state. Schiller (2000) indicates that, in fact, economic interest groups do not invest equally in both senators from the same state but rather invest more in the senator who demonstrates a stronger willingness to address their particular concerns. More work needs to be done, however, to capture the full effects that incentives for interest group support may exert on the legislative activity of senators from the same state.

Some might argue that a viable alternative explanation for differentiation within Senate delegations rests on a model of tacit cooperation among senators to divide up the responsibilities of representing their state. If one senator addresses an important state interest, the other senator can divert his or her attention to other areas; the division of labor allows each senator to narrow his or her legislative focus, use resources efficiently, and thereby appear more effective. As long as all the important issues are covered, constituents will form positive evaluations of both senators from the state.

If we were to accept a division-of-labor theory, then two assumptions would have to hold. First, one or both senators from the same state would have to be willing to give up the issue areas that are most attractive to their constituents as part of the division of labor. In this essay, I have tried to demonstrate that senators expend time and energy building a reputation they believe will be most appealing to their constituents. It makes little sense, then, that senators would voluntarily pass up the opportunity to address issues they knew to be important to their constituents. Second, the division-of-labor explanation assumes that constituents know little about their senators and are incapable of distinguishing between them, to the point that constituents mistakenly associate the work of one senator with that of his or her state colleague. The results of this study, though by no means definitive, demonstrate that constituents can and do associate distinctly different legislative issue areas with each of their home state senators.

Ultimately, this study has implications for how we perceive senators' efforts to represent their states. When we study representation in American politics, we normally posit a relationship between a single legislator and his or her constituency, in both the House and the Senate. But in the Senate, there is really a relationship between a single constituency and two legislators. Though they do not face each other in competitive elections, senators from the same state compete to establish themselves with their home state constituents. The result of that competition is representation on a wider range of issues and interests than we might expect from a single legislator, even if both senators share the same party affiliation.

APPENDIX: MEASUREMENT OF VARIABLES

Seniority	Number of terms served in the Senate
Reelection	Dummy variable coded 1 if the senator was up for reelection and 0 if not
State size	State population in millions
Numcom	Number of standing committee assignments
Presidential candidate	Dummy variable coded 1 if the senator ran for or was considered as a potential presidential candidate and 0 if not
Congress	Dummy variable coded 1 if the senator had served in Congress before entering the Senate and 0 if not
Governor	Dummy variable coded 1 if the senator had served as governor before entering the Senate and 0 if not
State colleague issue mentions	Number of constituents' like or dislike mentions about the other sitting senator from the state
State colleague media	Number of newspaper articles that mention the other sitting senator from the state
Judiciary	Dummy variable coded 1 if the senator was a member of the Senate Judiciary Committee and 0 if not
Labor	Dummy variable coded 1 if the senator was a member of the Senate Labor and Human Resources Committee and 0 if not
Energy	Dummy variable coded 1 if the senator was a member of the Senate Energy Committee and 0 if not
Epw	Dummy variable coded 1 if the senator was a member of the Senate Environment and Public Works Committee and 0 if not
Finance	Dummy variable coded 1 if the senator was a member of the Senate Finance Committee and 0 if not
Agriculture	Dummy variable coded 1 if the senator was a member of the Senate Agriculture Committee and 0 if not
Armed services	Dummy variable coded 1 if the senator was a member of the Senate Armed Services Committee and 0 if not
Foreign relations	Dummy variable coded 1 if the senator was a member of the Senate Foreign Relations Committee and 0 if not
Same party	Dummy variable coded 1 if the senator shared the same party affiliation as his or her state colleague and 0 if not

NOTES

I would like to thank Sarah Binder, Frances Lee, Fiona McGillivray, Kent Weaver, and Darrell West for their thoughtful comments on this project.

1. For a general examination of the behavior of freshman senators, see Levy (1996).

2. As Sinclair (1989) has demonstrated, committee assignments are central to legislative agenda building but they are not the sole determinants. The access to the floor that all senators possess enables them to at least try to influence policy areas outside their committees through amendments and speech making. But as both Sinclair (1989) and Smith (1989) point out, success rates for floor activity are limited and the floor is not the most efficient source of reputation building in an issue area.

3. Data for Kentucky were available only for the years 1989–92.

4. Over the 6 years, 24 senators held office in these states. The newspapers used in the study of state media coverage were, respectively, the *Atlanta Constitution*, the *Chicago Tribune*, the *Houston Chronicle*, *Newsday*, the *Boston Globe*, the *St. Petersburg Times*, the *Omaha World-Herald*, the *Minneapolis Star-Tribune*, the *Louisville Courier-Journal*, and the *Los Angeles Times*. The state media data were organized and coded in the following way: I searched each newspaper for articles that mentioned the names of the senators from the state and downloaded the list of all articles by their headlines for each year from 1987 to 1992. I divided the search into three categories: articles that included the senior but not the junior senator, articles that included the junior but not the senior senator, and articles that mentioned both senators. Using a combination of headlines and the full text of articles, I coded the content of the articles according to 14 categories: foreign policy/defense, judiciary, education, environment/energy, infrastructure, health, welfare/labor, agriculture, budget/tax/trade, banking/housing, state politics/issues, pork, presidential politics, and other.

5. For example, when a respondent mentioned Social Security, labor, and nuclear energy, I coded the responses as Finance Committee, Labor and Human Resources Committee, and Energy/Environment and Public Works Committees, respectively.

6. The Senate Appropriations Committee also presents a test of the differentiation hypothesis. Senators from the same state may not choose the same committee assignments, but there may be a correspondence between Appropriations Committee work in an issue area and the jurisdiction of another committee. The most extreme example might be one senator from a "farm" state joining the Agriculture Committee while his or her state colleague joins the Appropriations Subcommittee on Agriculture. The two senators technically sit on different committees, but they can both use their committee assignments to address the same relevant state issue. Because only 29 senators can sit on the Appropriations Committee, seeking to encroach via this committee is not an available strategy for 70 senators. Moreover, a preliminary study of the state delegations with senators who held office for 6 years and one senator sat on the Appropriations Committee indicates that there is some overlap but not a significant amount.

7. I treat each senator as an independent observation. The inclusion of the issue likes and dislikes for the other senator from the state might be considered a problem because of the potential correlation between the disturbance terms. However, a comparison of the residuals from regressions using the issue mentions for one senator as an independent variable to predict the issue mentions for the other yields no significant correlation for any of the six issue areas. The same is true for the models that use media coverage of one senator as an independent variable to predict media coverage of the other senator.

8. As in the case of the larger sample, I treat each senator as an independent observation.

9. The correlations between committee assignment and state media coverage in committee jurisdiction areas are as follows: Foreign Relations = −.14, Armed Services = .48**, Finance = .43**, Labor and Human Resources = .36**, Judiciary = .58**, Energy/EPW = .02, Agriculture = .62**.

REFERENCES

Alesina, Alberto, Morris Fiorina, and Howard Rosenthal. 1990. "Why Are There So Many Split Senate Delegations? A Model of Opposite Party Advantage." Harvard University.

Bernstein, Robert A. 1992. "Determinants of Differences in Feelings toward Senators Representing the Same State." *Western Political Quarterly* 45: 703–23.

Cook, Timothy E. 1989. *Making Laws and Making News.* Washington, D.C.: Brookings Institution Press.

Fenno, Richard F., Jr. 1973. *Congressmen in Committees.* Boston: Little, Brown.

Fenno, Richard F., Jr. 1991. *Learning to Legislate: The Senate Education of Arlen Specter.* Washington, D.C.: Congressional Quarterly Press.

Fenno, Richard F., Jr. 1996. *Senators on the Campaign Trail.* Norman: University of Oklahoma Press.

Franklin, Charles H. 1993. "Senate Incumbent Visibility over the Election Cycle." *Legislative Studies Quarterly* 2: 271–90.

Herrick, Rebekah, and Sue Thomas. 1993. "Split Delegations in the United States Senate: 1920–1988." *Social Science Journal* 30: 69–81.

Hess, Stephen. 1981. *The Washington Reporters.* Washington, D.C.: Brookings Institution Press.

Hess, Stephen. 1986. *The Ultimate Insiders: U.S. Senators in the National Media.* Washington, D.C.: Brookings Institution Press.

Jung, Gi-Ryong, Lawrence W. Kenny, and John R. Lott Jr. 1994. "An Explanation for Why Senators from the Same State Vote Differently So Frequently." *Journal of Public Economies* 54: 65–96.

Levy, Dena. 1996. "Mapping the Effects of Previous Experience: The Transition and Legislative Activities of First-Term Senators." Ph.D. diss., University of Iowa.

Powell, Lynda W. 1990. "Explaining Senate Elections: The Basis of Split Delegations and Party Polarizations." University of Rochester.

Schiller, Wendy J. 1995. "Senators as Political Entrepreneurs: Using Bill Sponsorship to Shape Legislative Agendas." *American Journal of Political Science* 1: 186–203.

Schiller, Wendy J. 2000. *Partners and Rivals: Representation in U.S. Senate Delegations.* Princeton: Princeton University Press.

Segura, Gary M., and Stephen P. Nicholson. 1995. "Sequential Choices and Partisan Transitions in U.S. Senate Delegations: 1972–1988." *Journal of Politics* 57: 86–100.

Sinclair, Barbara. 1989. *Transformations of the U.S. Senate.* Baltimore: Johns Hopkins University Press.

Sinclair, Barbara. 1990. "Washington Behavior and Home-State Reputation: The Impact of National Prominence on Senators' Images." *Legislative Studies Quarterly* 15: 475–93.

Smith, Steven. 1989. *Call to Order.* Washington, D.C.: Brookings Institution Press.

Smith, Steven, and Christopher Deering. 1990. *Committees in Congress.* 2d ed. Washington, D.C.: Congressional Quarterly Press.

Uslaner, Eric M. 1998. *The Movers and the Shirkers.* Ann Arbor: University of Michigan Press.

Majority Party Leadership, Strategic Choice, and Committee Power: Appropriations in the House, 1995–98

Bryan W. Marshall, Brandon C. Prins, and David W. Rohde

Introduction

This essay is part of a continuing effort to elaborate and apply a theory of legislative organization in Congress that has been labeled "conditional party government." Developed by David Rohde (1991) and John Aldrich (1995) and extended further in joint work (Aldrich and Rohde 1996a, 1996b, 1997, 1997–98, 1998), the theory deals with the role of parties in Congress and the willingness of members to empower their parties and their leaders to influence the legislative process. In this analysis our specific purpose is to follow up on an earlier study of the appropriations process in the House (Aldrich and Rohde 1996b). The earlier research focused mainly on the process in 1995 as compared with previous Congresses: the theoretical expectations about appropriations politics under the new Republican regime and how the events of 1995 measured up to those expectations. Here we want to extend that analysis through 1998 by exploring the ways that changing contexts and changing choices by relevant actors affected appropriations politics. In so doing, we also hope to shed light on questions raised by Dodd and Oppenheimer (1997) about the degree to which conditional party government would continue to apply to the House after the revolutionary 104th Congress.

We begin by elaborating the theoretical expectations that follow from conditional party government regarding this situation. Then we consider quantitative evidence regarding three stages of the decision-making process related to appropriations: voting within committee, decisions on special rules, and floor voting for the period 1995–98, with some comparisons to earlier years. Next, we focus on specific decisions by the majority leadership on structuring the agenda for appropriations bills in 1997–98. Finally, we return to the theoretical issues that motivated this study and draw conclusions.

Theoretical Issues

Conditional Party Government: A Brief Outline

The theory of conditional party government is discussed extensively in the work cited earlier, so we will confine ourselves to a very brief consideration here. The modifier *conditional* is used to indicate the theoretical contention that the strength of party organizations within the legislative setting (both the powers granted to parties by members and the willingness of those members to tolerate or support the exercise of such powers) depends on certain things that are mainly determined by the exogenous patterns of electoral politics. Specifically, the condition involves the degree of preference agreement within legislative parties and the degree of preference conflict between them. In general, the theory contends that as intraparty homogeneity and interparty conflict increase, members will be more inclined to support the grant of strong powers to party leaders and to support the use of those powers. As intraparty homogeneity increases, members see that the use of leader powers is less likely to result in policy outcomes that are significantly different from their preferences; as interparty conflict grows, the consequences to members of one party of legislative victory by the other party become increasingly adverse. In addition to expectations about the grant and exercise of leadership power, the theory predicts that rank-and-file members will also seek to develop mechanisms to ensure that those colleagues to whom the party grants power (e.g., committee chairs) will not use that power to frustrate the party's legislative goals.

As noted, the impetus for the theory depends on the results of exogenous electoral forces—the pattern of preferences among members who get elected. In addition, the theory's expectations are conditional in another way, also related to electoral forces. We do not expect the party organization to be active or efficacious on all issues. The theory explicitly assumes that legislators have a variety of motives—election, policy, and power—that affect their behavior (Fenno 1973). Only some issues—those that are linked to partisan divisions in the electorate, either among voters or among activists—invoke partisanship. These issues make up the party's issue agenda, which varies over time (Cox and McCubbins 1993). Thus the theory's expectations relate only to a subset of issues, and we would anticipate that the dynamics of legislating on other types of issues would be very different (Rohde 1994). The issues that constitute the party's agenda are relevant to the operation of conditional party government.

Because the basic framework of our theory was articulated before the election of 1994, the new Republican majority offered an excellent opportunity to empirically evaluate a variety of its implications. In particular, because both general perceptions and specific measurements (Aldrich and Rohde 1998) support the conclusion that the House after 1994 saw the greatest degree of intraparty homogeneity and interparty conflict in many decades, the theory offers the clear expectation that the leadership of the parties (especially that of the majority) would seek the grant of significant new powers and that members would possess strong incentives to support new powers and their exercise. The evidence presented in the collaborative research between Aldrich and Rohde cited earlier provides strong support for the theory's predictions. Speaker Newt

Gingrich received new powers, especially relating to the operation of committees, that made him the strongest Speaker since Joe Cannon. The members of the House GOP Conference supported the exercise of these powers to pursue the party's legislative agenda—indeed, they often insisted on it. Of course the Republican membership did not agree with every application of leadership power. When there was disagreement, Republican members often resisted and succeeded in blocking the leaders' actions.

Although most analysts have agreed that the theory of conditional party government was applicable to the 104th Congress and that the evidence from that Congress supported its predictions, some have questioned whether the theory would continue to apply in the 105th Congress and beyond. Specifically, Dodd and Oppenheimer (1997) have argued that even though the parties in the House continued to be internally homogeneous and divided from each other, constraints would limit the applicability of the theory. These constraints include (1) the close seat distribution between the parties, (2) the existence of a significant number of competitive districts, (3) the emergence of issues that split the majority party, and (4) member willingness to trust party leaders. As the authors note, Aldrich and Rohde recognized that because of the multiple goals of members, other factors would influence the degree to which partisan considerations dominated in the legislative process, so we see no necessary conflict between the basic theory and these arguments. In the succeeding pages, we intend to examine the continued applicability of conditional party government to the appropriations process in 1997–98 and to shed some light on the relevance of the constraints that Dodd and Oppenheimer have noted.

Previous Work on House Appropriations Politics

Before proceeding to a discussion of the most recent Congress, it is necessary to convey the highlights of earlier work dealing with House Appropriations, both before the 104th Congress and during those "revolutionary" years.[1] It is sufficient to our purposes to note the main findings from the work of Fenno (1966, 1973), Smith and Deering (1984), and White (1989). Fenno's research (1973) showed that House Appropriations was the least partisan of the six committees studied in his comparative analysis. Subcommittees were largely autonomous, and "[c]ommittee unity on the floor is the ultimate and critical product of the norm system" within the committee (1973, 123, 127). In his earlier study of Appropriations, Fenno found that the norms included "bargaining and compromise as methods of decision making," and every subcommittee was expected to observe the norm of "minimal partisanship" (1966, 25, 164). Following up on Fenno's work as part of a general study of House and Senate committees, Smith and Deering (1984) found that Democratic party reforms decentralized the committee's operations even further but also made the committee more responsible to the Democratic Caucus. Furthermore, the committee's control over expenditures continued to decline, undermining its prestige and influence even more, and an increasing proportion of members sought assignment for policy reasons rather than the institutional power motives that Fenno found to predominate. The system of subcommittee specialization and relative autonomy persisted but in noticeably weakened form.

The most recent full-scale study of the committee is by White (1989). The time period captured in his analysis overlaps with the increase in party government in the House during the 1980s. White found that both parties sought to put loyalist members on the committee but that both also sought "responsible" members of the type Fenno's research had described more than 20 years earlier. His interviews indicated that "philosophical zealots" did not make it on the committee and that it operated "with a premium on being non- or bi-partisan, and on consensus operation" (1989, 142). White argued that the picture of the committee retained strong similarities with the portrait Fenno had offered. "The committee remained one of the most nonpartisan on the Hill. Chairmen still dominated subcommittees, through the command of staff more than the norms of deference" (White 1989, 15).

Having provided this summary picture of the working of House Appropriations before the GOP takeover, we now outline the results of the previous research on the politics of appropriations in the 104th Congress. The evidence is strong that, as expected by the theory of conditional party government, the impact of the change in membership and party control was profound. First, as we noted previously, at the opening of the new Congress, Gingrich and the party leadership were granted significant new powers. Of particular import here were the Speaker's assertion of the right to name new major committee chairs (including for Appropriations) in violation of seniority,[2] greatly enhanced leadership influence over committee assignments (which was used to place seven freshmen and four sophomores on the committee), a 6-year term limit for chairs, a one-third reduction overall in committee staff, and a shift from the committee's leaders to the majority leader in control over appropriations bills on the floor. In addition, after enhancing leadership control over committee chairs, the GOP undermined subcommittee independence by giving the full committee chairs the power to appoint subcommittee members and their chairs. (Previously members had been self-selected, and subcommittee chairs secured their positions by seniority.)

Although these changes in formal powers were important, it is clear that the significant changes in the politics of appropriations that occurred in the 104th Congress were mainly the result of deliberate strategic choices by the GOP leadership. The enhanced powers were instruments in the pursuit of the leadership strategy. Specifically, before 1995 the Appropriations Committee had a great deal of independence within its sphere. The committee focused principally on constraining overall spending, providing specific dollar amounts for individual programs, and ensuring the passage of their funding bills. This focus tended to mitigate the propensity for partisan conflict (White 1989). Disagreements, then, were relatively rare on the floor and even less frequent within the committee.

In 1995, however, the majority leadership decided to pursue a very different course. The Republicans were committed to a policy agenda that would substantially change existing government policy (Aldrich and Rohde 1996a; Bader 1996; Gimpel 1996). The segment of the GOP Conference most committed to change (particularly freshmen and sophomores) was very concerned that senior Republicans on many committees would be too committed to the status quo to support new policies. This concern reflected a long-standing division within the GOP Conference (Connelly and Pitney 1994). Also, stand-alone bills with large changes in policy would be inviting targets for Senate Democratic resistance and presidential vetoes. To avoid these problems, the Republican leadership decided to use the Appropriations Committee as a major vehicle for legislative policy change.

The evidence in Aldrich and Rohde (1996b) clearly shows that doing so was a leadership-originated strategy and that it was imposed on the Appropriations Committee over the determined objections of the senior committee leadership. The leadership also played a substantial role in pressuring and monitoring the committee's actions on individual bills. The GOP efforts to impose policy changes through appropriations bills transformed the committee's decision-making patterns. There was a nearly 10-fold increase in partisan votes on amendments, and the source of most of the increase was the legislative items (called riders) imposed from outside the committee. For example, the Veterans Administration–Housing and Urban Development bill contained 30 pages of legislative language dealing with the Environmental Protection Agency and other agencies.

Another aspect of leadership activity in pursuing its strategy was the molding of the floor environment through the Speaker's control of the Rules Committee. The inclusion of legislative language in appropriations bills is a violation of the rules of the House. It was possible, however, to protect riders (either in the original bill or in amendments that will be offered) from points of order on the floor by barring such actions in the special rules that set the terms of floor debate. Legislative language had long been included in committee bills by bipartisan agreement in situations in which the authorizing committee had not completed its work and the protection of those provisions had generally been noncontroversial. The use of riders for partisan purposes had been comparatively rare before 1995, but in that year it was pervasive, and partisanship in the debates over rules for the bills also soared. The rules were often drafted to advantage GOP proposals or to frustrate Democratic efforts to revise or defeat those proposals. Senior or moderate Republicans were often pressured to support these special rules, even though the rules would produce policy outcomes the members did not favor.

Similarly, when the bills came to the floor, the majority leaders used their powers to try to keep GOP members in line, and they used their control over floor activity to influence outcomes (e.g., by choosing when to take votes or by pulling bills from the floor when the strategic situation turned against them). The contrast in preferences between the more senior members of Appropriations and the hard conservatives in the conference was further illustrated in floor action in 1995 by conservative-sponsored amendments that tried to push policy even further to the right; many of these amendments passed over the objections of committee Republicans.

The eventual result of these policy conflicts is well-known.[3] The Senate resisted many of the House GOP's policy initiatives, which (along with delays in the budget process) considerably slowed the passage of appropriations bills. As anticipated, President Clinton found many of the initiatives that survived the interchamber negotiations to be unpalatable. He vetoed a number of appropriations bills and threatened to veto others. As a result, the new budget year arrived without the passage of appropriations for all agencies. To prevent those agencies from shutting down, Congress proposed a continuing appropriations resolution, along with the budget reconciliation bill to complete that process and a bill to increase the debt ceiling. All of these measures, however, contained major policy changes that Clinton opposed. Contrary to the expectations of many House Republicans, including many leaders, the president stood his ground and vetoed the bills. In the ensuing weeks, two partial government shutdowns occurred. Also contrary to GOP expectations, the public's reaction was mainly to blame the Republicans in Congress for these events; citizens sided with the president on most of the specific policy conflicts (Rohde 1996).

These events dragged on into 1996, and the House Republican leadership eventually became seriously concerned about the potential for this conflict to undermine its chances of maintaining majority control. Republican leaders decided to shift strategy and were able to persuade a sufficient number of their members to go along. They struck a compromise with Clinton that favored the president on most issues, and the process was finally completed in April 1996, with the fiscal year half over. With the 1996 elections looming, the GOP leaders decided not to repeat the process in the fiscal 1997 appropriations. Although efforts to make policy changes through appropriations and the use of riders did not stop completely, they were reduced substantially. As we show in a later section, conflict dropped markedly within the committee, in the debates over special rules, and on the House floor. The majority leaders decided to focus on producing some legislative results for which their members could claim credit with the voters, and the 1996 appropriations process was brought to an expeditious conclusion.

Leadership Strategy and Partisan Conflict

The previous work on conditional party government, both the general analysis and the specific research on Appropriations, contains the basic ideas of the view we want to elaborate here. As we have said, the theory contends that the propensity of members to empower party leaders and to support their exercise of powers depends directly on the degree of intraparty homogeneity on policy and of interparty divergence. It also contends that legislators have a variety of motives that vary in import from one to another. The key point of relevance here is that these motives tend to vary systematically among party leaders, committee members, and rank-and-file members. This variance in motives can lead to different perspectives on what strategies should be followed and what policies should be proposed.

Consider the three major goals assumed in the theory. First, the desire to be elected and reelected has two relevant aspects: the reelection of a particular member and the retention (or for those in the minority, the achievement) of majority control. The second and third goals are the adoption of good public policy and the achievement of institutional power. Most party leaders—despite former Speaker Tom Foley's unfortunate experience—do not have to worry about their personal reelection, but majority status is of great import and concern to them. Relatedly, just by seeking leadership posts they have demonstrated that institutional power is of significant consequence to them. The importance of policy goals varies from individual to individual, as is true of committee and rank-and-file members.

Appropriations members can serve all three goals through committee service, but previous research indicates that the desire for institutional power has been a dominant motive for seeking assignment, with policy a stronger second from the 1980s on than before. Consequently, the committee's members (especially the more senior ones) have jealously sought to protect the panel's power and influence. These interests were clearly behind the efforts by the committee chair, Livingston, and many subcommittee chairs (the group collectively known as the cardinals) to resist the extensive use of riders in 1995 and more recently. They frequently asserted that this approach undermined what they saw as their principal task: the timely passage of 13 appropriations bills that adequately funded the government programs Congress had authorized. For this group as well, the maintenance of majority status was of special import, although most of the senior members were personally safe from serious electoral challenge.

Rank-and-file members' perspectives varied substantially with regard to these goals. One systematic element was that policy motives were generally more important (at least relatively) among the more junior members of the GOP Conference, among whom those elected in 1992 and 1994 constituted a majority. We would usually expect policy to be relatively more important than power goals among junior as opposed to senior members; they have achieved less within the body and thus would have less to lose if majority status shifted. Among junior GOP members in the 104th and 105th Congresses, however, policy goals appear to have been more prominent than usual relative even to electoral interests. Of course, policy goals are a matter of individual preference, but in this case systematic forces appear to have been at work. Many of these junior members were motivated to seek office in the first place by the desire to change the direction of policy in Washington. This motivation was reinforced in many instances by the personal commitment of members to serve only a short time; some had pledged to quit after only three terms. Although not legal pledges, most were sincere (and others, perhaps, constrained). For such members, traditional institutional power positions were out of reach, and even majority status would be of relatively little import.

This variable mix of goals interacts with the grant of power within the majority party in the House. The party leaders play a predominant (albeit certainly not exclusive) role in setting the policy agenda for the body.[4] To be sure, they are not free agents. Indeed, it is a central expectation of the conditional party government theory that rank-and-file members will monitor leadership efforts in this regard and will move to pressure or sanction leaders if they move too far from expectations. Yet the decisions about what bills to bring up, when, and under what procedures basically rest with the leaders. They also must decide whether to take a prominent role in shaping the development of a given bill in committee or leave the committee to its own devices. Furthermore, the Rules Committee can be used not only to shape the floor procedures for consideration of a bill but also to alter the bill's content after the committee with legislative jurisdiction has completed its work but before the bill hits the floor. The Speaker must decide whether to use this option.

All of these choices will be shaped by the strategies the leadership has decided to follow, and the choice of strategies is made in light of the leaders' goals. Committee members and rank-and-file members react to the leaders' choices in terms of *their* goals. The events of 1995–96 are clearly comprehensible in these terms. Most of those at the Republican Conference in 1995, including a significant portion of the leadership, were strongly committed to major policy changes. Moreover, in the heady days after November 1994, few GOP members saw any conflict between this and electoral goals, collective or individual. The Democrats were down, and it looked like they would go further down. Most Republicans saw Clinton as seriously vulnerable for 1996 and expected that it would be easy to add to the party's ranks in the House and Senate. As the political context changed and the possibility of the majority's vulnerability became increasingly apparent, however, some actors altered their calculations. The theory would expect that the impetus for a change in strategy would come disproportionately from members of the leadership (who would be relatively more concerned about collective electoral success), from party moderates (who would have less investment in radical policy change), and from members who felt individually vulnerable to defeat. This trend would be reinforced by Appropriations Committee members, who had independent reasons for forgoing reliance on the committee for radical change. The analysis of 1995–96 is largely consistent with these expectations.

This elaboration on the implications of the motivational assumptions of the theory sets the stage for the analysis of the politics of appropriations in 1997–98. The scope and character of partisan conflict in the House and the degree of impact parties have on policy outcomes depend on the interaction of the mix of goals among the leadership, committee members, and rank-and-file members and on the strategic choices made based on those goals. If, as in 1995, the majority leadership decides to press for significant policy changes on issues that divide the parties' electoral bases (either because they actually anticipate enacting them or to satisfy activist elements of their electorate), partisan conflict will be amplified. If, instead, as in 1996, the leadership chooses to focus on producing legislative achievements in collaboration with the minority, for which electoral credit can be claimed, partisan conflict will be muted. Similarly, leaders will exacerbate the level of partisan conflict within the committee if they decide to try to use the committee as a vehicle for partisan policy purposes. If instead the committee is left to its own devices, the level of partisanship will depend on the interaction of choices made based on the goals of the committee's members. As the theory of conditional party government has contended since its origins, the patterns of partisanship and the impact of party organizations on policy and behavior depend not only on the amount of power granted to the party by the members but also on the strategic choices that are made on how to use those powers.

Finally, although we will elaborate further as we proceed, this discussion permits some preliminary comments on the points Dodd and Oppenheimer raised. The strategic choices of leaders (and the members' reactions to them) clearly are shaped by the numerical balance in the chamber, as well as by the degree of homogeneity on issues within the party. Saying that homogeneity in the House GOP in 1995 was higher than that in any majority party in decades is not to say that the homogeneity is perfect or the same on all issues. Where there is numerically significant resistance within the majority party to what the leadership wants to do, and where that resistance is sufficiently intense to outweigh the incentives the leaders can bring to bear, they may have to compromise their plans or accept defeat. The results are the same whether the resistance is due to actual policy disagreement or to contrasting electoral calculations. Also, as the original exposition of the theory made clear, the willingness of rank-and-file members to support the exercise of power by leaders depends in part on the degree to which those members believe that those leaders largely share their interests and goals.

Empirical Analysis: Change and Continuity in the Appropriations Process

In 1995, the House Appropriations Committee was at the center of the Republican effort to enact broad policy change. As Aldrich and Rohde (1996b) observed, Gingrich and the GOP leadership helped structure the committee to better facilitate the use of these funding measures to substantively alter federal social policy, as well as cut spending for programs the Republicans did not endorse. After the 1996 elections, however, there was little change in the composition of the Appropriations Committee. It continued to advantage the GOP majority as much as, if not more so than, during the 104th Congress. As table 1 illustrates, the number of seats assigned to GOP members in the 105th Congress remains considerably larger than the Republican majority in the chamber would warrant (56.7 percent in committee to 51.7 percent in the chamber). Moreover, the mean number of majority subcommittee assignments in 1997

TABLE 1. Partisan Division on the Appropriations Committee

	1994	1995	1996	1997	1998
Committee division	37D–23R	32R–24D	33R–25D	34R–26D	34R–26D
Majority percentage in the House	59.3%D	52.9%R	54.3%R	52.1%R	51.7%R
Majority percentage on the committee	61.7%D	57.1%R	56.9%R	56.7%R	56.7%R
Committee percentage minus House percentage	+2.4%D	+4.2%R	+2.6%R	+4.6%R	+5.0%R
Division of subcommittee seats	89D–46R	90R–49D	91R–49D	94R–57D	94R–57D
Majority percentage on subcommittees	65.9%D	64.7%R	65.0%R	62.3%R	62.3%R
Subcommittee percentage minus House percentage	+6.6%D	+11.8%R	+10.7%R	+10.2%R	+10.6%R
Mean majority subcommittee assignments	2.41	2.81	2.76	2.76	2.76
Mean minority subcommittee assignments	2.00	2.04	1.96	2.19	2.19

continues to be nearly as high as in 1995. Consequently, the Republican majority leaders in the House have maintained the potential to affect legislative change through the appropriations process, if they so choose.

Voting within the Appropriations Committee

The strategic choices of the House Republican leadership clearly influenced the debate surrounding the 13 regular appropriations bills.[5] In 1995 alone, 80 recorded votes were taken in the House Appropriations Committee, of which 73 were partisan amendments. More than 97 percent of all votes involved the majorities of the two parties voting in opposite directions, and, quite remarkably, all five of the votes taken to report funding measures out of committee were partisan. Given the importance of this committee's jurisdiction, such conflict may not seem surprising. Yet, as Fenno (1966, 1973) and White (1989) observed, Appropriations has long been a committee that attempts to mitigate such intense conflict by accommodating the interests of the minority. In contrast to 1995, the incidence of partisanship on the committee from the 96th to the 102nd Congresses was considerably less, with only about six partisan amendments being offered, on average, each Congress (see table 2).

As striking as the pivotal role the committee played in the Republican revolution in 1995 was the leadership's calculated move away from using the

TABLE 2. Partisanship on Roll Call Votes in the House Appropriations Committee, 96th–105th Congresses

Congresses	All votes	First-degree amendments	Passage	Number of partisan amendments
96th–102nd	90.0%	93.0%	50.0%	6.1
	($N = 51$)	($N = 46$)	($N = 2$)	(average per Congress)
103rd	100%	100%	—	
	($N = 8$)	($N = 8$)	($N = 0$)	8
1995	97.5%	97.3%	100%	
	($N = 80$)	($N = 75$)	($N = 5$)	73
1996	95.7%	95.7%	100%	
	($N = 47$)	($N = 46$)	($N = 1$)	44
1997	91.3%	94.7%	75.0%	
	($N = 23$)	($N = 19$)	($N = 4$)	18
1998[a]	83.3%	84.2%	75.0%	
	($N = 42$)	($N = 38$)	($N = 4$)	32

Note: Cell entries give the percentage of floor roll calls on which majorities of the two parties voted on opposite sides.

[a]Data are up through July 30, 1998.

committee in 1996 and 1997. As a direct consequence of this change in strategy, we find a conspicuous change in the incidence and level of partisan conflict. Table 2 shows that the number of recorded roll call votes was nearly halved in 1996 and halved again in 1997, and the relative level of partisanship within the committee dropped as well. Yet even 1996 and 1997 demonstrate (when compared with earlier Congresses) that the accommodating consensus-oriented environment discussed extensively by Fenno (1966) and White (1989) has been affected by the diverging interests of the two parties, and decision making within the committee still tends to reflect the pursuit of partisan priorities. Indeed, in earlier Congresses the committee rarely experienced conflict on final passage votes. However, 80 percent of these votes from 1996 and 1997 involved partisan splits.

As might be expected, conflict within the Appropriations Committee varied dramatically across the different funding measures. In 1995, for example, a large portion of the activity occurred on the Health and Human Services spending bill. Indeed, 2 days were devoted to debating over 30 amendments offered within the committee, and multiple legislative riders created intense conflict on the House floor (*CQWR*, August 5, 1995, 2365).[6] While conflict within the Appropriations Committee continued in 1996, by 1997 only two recorded votes were taken on this measure. In contrast, the Agriculture and Military Construction funding bills experienced very few recorded roll call votes in committee in each of the first 3 years of Republican rule.

It appears, then, that the appropriations process generated less conflict within the committee during 1996 and 1997. Yet the conflict manifested invariably broke along partisan lines, and a number of issues continued to provoke intense controversy. In 1997, for instance, conservative appropriators forced a postponement on reporting out the Health and Human Services bill by threatening to offer more than 100 amendments (*CQWR*, December 6, 1997, 2982). And conflict erupted in committee on the Treasury–Postal Service bill because GOP appropriators included a controversial provision to allow certain types of firearms to be imported (*CQWR*, December 6, 1997, 2984). Thus, although there was an overall decline in the incidence and level of partisan conflict within the committee during 1996–97, on those policies that the leadership chose analogous strategies to those used in 1995, we tend to observe analogous levels of partisan conflict.

Emerging GOP Differences in Committee

Despite the Republicans' perceived electoral mandate in 1994, there was still disagreement within the party as to both goals and strategies. Tension existed between ideologues, who desired rapid and dramatic policy change, and more moderate members, who generally saw the legislative process as an incremen-

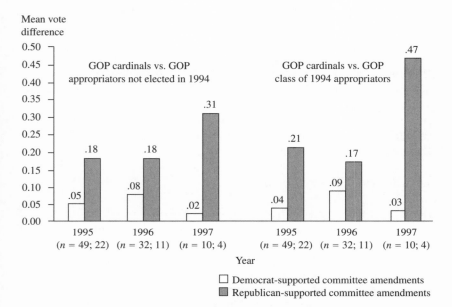

Fig. 1.   **Mean vote difference between GOP cardinals
and GOP appropriators, controlling for party support for amendments
(all first-degree committee amendments)**

tal enterprise (Aldrich and Rohde 1997–98; Fenno 1997; Pomper 1997). Seniority, then, generally tended to distinguish these factions much like it did for the Democrats during the 1960s and 1970s. Many junior members elected in 1992 and 1994 demonstrated an unwillingness to accommodate the interests of Democrats, whereas their more senior colleagues had become accustomed to collaborating with opposition members in the 1980s.[7]

Even in 1995, when Appropriations was at the heart of the Republican revolution, differences emerged within the GOP ranks. Figure 1 shows that the mean vote difference between the Republican cardinals and the rest of the GOP members on the Appropriations Committee was considerable.[8] Yet more interesting is how these differences increased from 1995 to 1997. Indeed, although the number of GOP-supported committee amendments was admittedly quite small in 1997, the difference between the cardinals and the rest of the committee, particularly the members of the class of 1994, was more than two times greater than in 1995.[9] It appears, then, that as the subcommittee chairs were allowed more autonomy in crafting these regular spending bills, disagreements over their content increasingly emerged within the committee between the different GOP factions.

As a result of the Republican leadership's strategic choices, conflict within the Appropriations Committee in 1997 was largely confined to a few issues on only a handful of the funding measures. Furthermore, the intensification of differences among Republican appropriators was largely restricted to GOP proposals. Indeed, from 1995 to 1997, tension was rarely manifest between the cardinals and the other Republican members on Democratic-supported committee amendments. In fact, in 1997 the difference between subcommittee chairs and the GOP class of 1994 appropriators on Republican-supported amendments was over 15 times more than the difference evinced on Democratic-supported amendments.

1998: Renewed Reliance on Appropriations

In contrast to 1996 and 1997, preliminary evidence from 1998 appears to show the GOP leadership once again choosing to use appropriations as a principal vehicle for realizing its goals. Consequently, patterns similar to those observed in 1995 on appropriations decision making have appeared in 1998 because of the strategic choices of the GOP leadership. In table 2, we see that the number of recorded committee roll call votes has nearly doubled from 1997, as has the number of partisan amendments. Although the overall level of partisanship appears to have decreased somewhat from 1997, the Foreign Operations funding measure has yet to be reported to the floor by the committee. Historically, this appropriations bill has generated considerable conflict (*CQWR*, May 31, 1997, 1258). Given the recent debates over International Monetary Fund funding and United Nations dues, any committee activity following the August recess has the potential to produce further partisan strife.

Like 1995, then, appropriators in 1998 have once again been called on to carry a substantial legislative load, and many programs are being targeted for sizable funding cuts (see *Washington Post,* June 28, 1998, A4). Many of the legislative issues raised in 1998 involve attempts by conservative Republicans to legislate social policy. At least as far as the leadership is concerned, however, many of these attempts appear to be intended for immediate electoral purposes rather than a genuine attempt to make substantive changes in public policy. Indeed, according to Pianin (1998, A4), "some riders are intended only to make a political point by drawing a distinction between the parties and have little chance making it into final versions of legislation." Worried about the maintenance of their majority, the Republican leaders sought to emphasize issues that were salient to their base voters. "Republicans are seeking to energize conservative voters—those most likely to turn out on their behalf in November" (Stevenson 1998). The White House, though, appears to have taken these GOP moves seriously. As in 1995, President Clinton has vowed to veto more than half of these funding measures, potentially setting the stage for another government shutdown in the months ahead (*The Hill,* August 12, 1998, 2–3; *National Journal,* August 8, 1998, 1848–53).

Additionally in 1998, differences have resurfaced in committee between the cardinals and the class of 1994. For example, Representative Neumann (R-WI) and other conservative budget hawks demanded a special GOP Conference meeting that determined that a $2.25 billion provision in the Treasury/Postal Service/General Government appropriations bill designated to fund year 2000 (Y2K) computer-related glitches should be stripped out and considered in a separate supplemental bill (see *CQWR,* June 20, 1998, 1700). Neumann and other members of the conference were concerned that committee leaders (Livingston [R-LA] and Kolbe [R-AZ], in particular) attempted to circumvent budgetary spending caps by inappropriately designating certain funds as emergency related.[10] Neumann's attempt to strip the provision was defeated, but the committee vote was 14–32, pairing most of the Democrats and cardinals against nearly all of the members from the class of 1994.[11]

Floor Voting: The Linkage between Goals and Strategies

Special Rules

Similar to the evidence within committee, we find the change in leadership strategies also to affect debate on the floor on the regular appropriations bills. Table 3 reflects changes in the leadership's use of special rules. In particular, the level of partisan conflict on these rules declined between 1995 and 1997. For example, in 1996 and 1997, although 92 percent of the regular appropriations bills received rules, only 15 percent of these measures in 1996 and 23 percent in 1997 found partisan majorities opposed. In 1995, on the other hand, more than two-thirds of them generated as much partisan conflict. These differences reflect a change in what the leadership was attempting to do with these special rules. In 1995, the GOP leadership used the rules to include controversial policy riders. However, in 1996 and 1997 a similar strategy was not pursued to the same extent. Thus, as indicated in table 3, the incidence of partisan conflict observed on these rules was lower in 1997 than it had been in 1995. The decreased incidence of conflict reflects both the change in leadership strategy and the extent that the conference had sought to constrain the actions of the committee in 1995.

Floor Debate

Further consequences of the leadership's change in strategy are evident from floor roll call voting.[12] Indeed, the changes we find in floor decision making on appropriations appear to be less the result of policy moderation and more the

TABLE 3. Characteristics of Special Rules on Regular Appropriations Bills, 96th–105th Congresses

	96th	100th	103rd	1995	1996	1997	1998[a]
Number of bills	25	26	26	13	13	13	11
Percentage of bills with rules	68%	58%	81%	100%	92%	92%	100%
Percentage of bills with nonconsensual rules	8%	35%	39%	77%	15%	31%	63.6%
Percentage of bills with partisan rules	0%	31%	38%	69%	15%	23%	63.6%
Percentage of rules with waivers for rule 21(2)	100%	100%	100%	100%	100%	100%	100%
Mean party difference	11.2	64.8	94.6	78.3	91.0	78.0	82.1
(all rules with votes)	$(N = 6)$	$(N = 10)$	$(N = 10)$	$(N = 11)$	$(N = 2)$	$(N = 4)$	$(N = 8)$
Mean party difference	23.0	69.6	94.6	82.7	91.0	78.0	82.1
(nonconsensual votes)	$(N = 2)$	$(N = 9)$	$(N = 10)$	$(N = 10)$	$(N = 2)$	$(N = 4)$	$(N = 8)$
Mean party difference	—	74.1	94.6	91.9	91.0	95.0	93.7
(partisan votes)	$(N = 0)$	$(N = 8)$	$(N = 10)$	$(N = 9)$	$(N = 2)$	$(N = 3)$	$(N = 7)$

[a]Data are up through July 30, 1998.

result of strategy moderation employed by the GOP leadership. Table 4 indicates the reduction in the frequency of partisan conflict across different types of votes. Looking at the second column in the table, the proportion of party-unity votes drops from 75 percent to 61 percent between 1995 and 1997. In addition, columns 4 and 5 indicate substantial decreases from 1995 to 1997 for final passage votes, 57 percent to 42 percent, and conference reports, 42 percent to 8 percent.[13]

The frequency of votes from 1995 to 1997 tells a similar story. The number of first-degree amendments (column 3 from table 4) and the subset that were partisan in 1997 (column 6 from table 4) were both less than half their numbers in 1995. Based on the dramatic decrease in the frequency of proposed floor changes, as well as the magnitude in which these proposed changes generated partisan divisions, we can infer that the 1997 regular appropriations bills were handled very differently by the Republicans on the House floor. Indeed, the content of the bills in 1997 was very different from that in 1995. Specifically, the lower levels and decreased incidence of partisan conflict during 1997 were due to the leadership's practice of restraint in using the appropriations

TABLE 4. Partisanship on Roll Call Votes on Floor Voting (All Members) on Appropriations Bills, 96th–105th Congresses

Congresses	All votes	First-degree amendments	Passage	Conference reports	Number of partisan amendments
1979	41.1%	57.1%	23.1%	0%	32
	($N = 95$)	($N = 56$)	($N = 13$)	($N = 4$)	
1980	41.9%	60.0%	20.0%	0%	27
	($N = 74$)	($N = 45$)	($N = 10$)	($N = 5$)	
1987	80.7%	84.6%	60.0%	—	33
	($N = 57$)	($N = 39$)	($N = 10$)	($N = 0$)	
1988	45.9%	68.4%	23.1%	16.7%	13
	($N = 61$)	($N = 19$)	($N = 13$)	($N = 12$)	
1995	74.9%	70.5%	57.1%	41.7%	105
	($N = 251$)	($N = 149$)	($N = 14$)	($N = 12$)	
1996	59.8%	66.3%	46.2%	11.1%	61
	($N = 132$)	($N = 92$)	($N = 13$)	($N = 9$)	
1997	61.0%	71.0%	41.7%	8.3%	49
	($N = 141$)	($N = 69$)	($N = 12$)	($N = 12$)	
Total	61.3%	68.2%	38.8%	16.7%	320
	($N = 811$)	($N = 469$)	($N = 85$)	($N = 54$)	

Note: Cell entries give the percentage of floor roll calls on which majorities of the two parties voted on opposite sides.

process as a vehicle to enact the GOP's legislative agenda. This change in leadership strategy resulted in greater exercise of autonomy by the committee, which in turn alleviated some partisan controversy and led to greater moderation in proposed social spending cuts.

The patterns found in table 4 mark significant changes in appropriations decision making between 1995 and 1997. But the departure from the historically normal appropriations process is also apparent when making comparisons with the 96th and 100th Congresses. For example, the last column of table 4 reflects the magnitude of change with respect to the incidence of partisan conflict over time. Specifically, one can see that the number of partisan amendments during 1995 alone was nearly as great as the number from both the 96th Congress (1979–80) and the 100th Congress (1987–88) combined. The stark change in the incidence of partisan conflict in 1995 reflects the extent to which the leadership was attempting to employ the appropriations process as a vehicle to carry out the majority party's policy priorities.

Certainly, Fenno's insights from 25 years ago seem remarkably applicable to these findings (1973, 24). Indeed, the bipartisan process of decision making on appropriations has largely given way to partisan conflict as the debate has become more focused on prosecuting party priorities. Left to its own device, there will be more partisanship on appropriations than seen in past Congresses because of the more homogeneous preferences within the parties and their reflection in the committee membership. However, our evidence also demonstrates that the conflict observed on appropriations decisions depends to a large extent on the strategic choices made by the GOP leadership.

Emerging GOP Differences on the Floor

The changes in the appropriations process become more evident when the analysis is focused on some of the major factions in committee and on the floor. Indeed, the differences in voting behavior we present in the following figures and table not only reflect the change in leadership strategy from 1995 to 1997 but also represent the different mix of goals among the GOP membership. For example, figure 2 shows that on Republican-supported amendments, a majority of the cardinals voted differently than a majority of Republicans on the floor nearly 31 percent of the time in 1995, 59 percent of the time in 1996, and nearly 40 percent of the time in 1997. Yet, once again, the cardinals were very united with the rest of the conference on Democratic-supported amendments between 1995 and 1997. It would appear, then, that many of the cardinals were united and dissatisfied with a large number of the proposed changes to their bills that had the support of the GOP Conference. We conclude that the cardinals were increasingly unwilling to accede to the leadership's attempts at legislating through these funding measures.

Percentage
of divergence

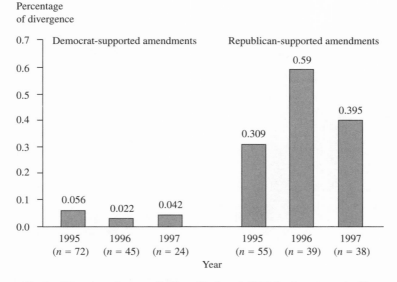

Fig. 2.   **Divergence between GOP cardinals and GOP Conference, controlling for party support for amendments (conflictual first-degree amendments only)**

In addition, figure 3 presents a comparison among appropriators from the GOP class of 1994, nonappropriators from that class, and the rest of the GOP Conference. On those amendments supported by a majority of Democrats, a majority of either appropriators or nonappropriators from the class of 1994 rarely voted differently than a majority of the GOP Conference. In fact, between 1995 and 1997 on Democratic-supported amendments, the two groups from the class of 1994 were indistinguishable. However, on the subset of amendments supported by a majority of Republicans, substantial differences emerged between the two groups in terms of their divergence with the GOP Conference. The biggest differences were seen in 1995 and 1996. For example, on GOP-supported amendments, a majority of appropriators from the class of 1994 voted opposite a majority of the GOP Conference nearly 22 percent of the time in 1995 and nearly 26 percent of the time in 1996, whereas the nonappropriators from that class voted opposite a majority of the GOP Conference only half as often.

The evidence from 1995 and 1996 suggests that class of 1994 appropriators may have been somewhat different from the rest of their classmates. These differences may have played a role in the leadership's selection in 1995 of these particular freshmen to sit on the Appropriations Committee. In 1997 the pattern for appropriators from the class of 1994 is somewhat different from in

Percentage
of divergence

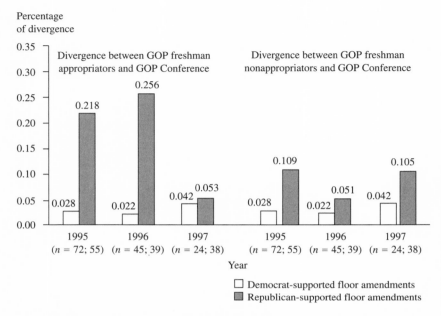

Fig. 3.   Proportion of floor amendments in which a majority of the GOP class
of 1994 voted opposite the GOP Conference, controlling for party support for
amendments (conflictual first-degree amendments only)

1995. A majority of those junior appropriators voted opposite a majority of the
conference on GOP-supported amendments only one-fourth as often as in
1995. If the junior appropriators were more moderate than their GOP classmates, the changes in 1997 may reflect that the recent election heightened their
perception of vulnerability to a greater extent than it did for the more conservative members in their class. In contrast, little change is found from 1995 and
1997 (11 percent in both years) in divergence between the GOP Conference
and class of 1994 nonappropriators on Republican-supported amendments.

Party cohesion on Republican- and Democratic-supported amendments
tends to parallel the divergence findings. On the subset of amendments in
which a majority of members from both parties were opposed, the average proportion of GOP appropriators from the class of 1994 voting aye on Republican-
supported amendments was 69 percent in 1995, 57 percent the following year,
and back up to 76 percent in 1997. These findings suggest that the junior
appropriators were just as, or slightly more, cohesive in support of GOP-
preferred changes to appropriations bills in 1997 as they were in 1995.[14] Alternatively, the cohesion of nonappropriators from that class on GOP-preferred
changes went from 85 percent (the highest of any GOP subgroup) in 1995 to 80

percent by 1997. There was even less change in cohesion among the other GOP subgroups. For members of the GOP Conference, cohesion on Republican-supported amendments was 81 percent in 1995 and 76 percent in 1997. For the cardinals, cohesion on the same amendments was 59 percent in 1995 and 54 percent in 1997. Overall, then, we can conclude that there was relatively little change in behavior among the membership on Republican-supported amendments to appropriations bills.

Although there appears to be relatively little change within groups over this 3-year period, differences among the groups are clearly apparent. The cohesion scores suggest that the GOP cardinals were significantly less supportive of the party position than the class of 1994 appropriators and even less so compared with their nonappropriator classmates on GOP-supported amendments. Interestingly, in 1995–96 the cardinals were notably more cohesive against Democratic-supported amendments than either appropriators or nonappropriators from the class of 1994. This difference disappeared in 1997 when both GOP subgroups voted more cohesively than the cardinals against Democratic-supported amendments.

What we have observed, then, is strong Republican unity against Democrat changes to funding legislation from 1995 to 1997. This finding is not surprising given the clear differences in party preferences. However, within the Republican party differences emerged when GOP-supported proposals were considered. If we consider voting with the GOP Conference as a baseline for conservative policy support, we find very limited evidence of the different subgroups moderating their behavior between 1995 and 1997. In fact, from the evidence presented, the GOP class of 1994 appropriators appear to be both less likely to vote against the conference and more cohesive in their support of Republican-preferred changes to appropriations in 1997 than they were in 1995. However, it also appears that the freshmen appointed to the Appropriations Committee in 1994 may have been less ideologically driven than their fellow classmates. Although the evidence illustrated in figure 3 and table 5 demonstrates that they disagreed with the conference on GOP-supported amendments considerably less often than did the cardinals, they did so more often than the rest of the 1994 class. If policy moderation was occurring on appropriations in 1996–97, our evidence suggests that it is the result not of moderating policy preferences within the GOP Conference but of moderating leadership strategies. When the leadership chooses to regress back to strategies such as those employed in 1995, parallel changes in the incidence and character of conflict are the result.

Some Legislative Specifics from 1997–98

We can amplify the discussion of the shifting strategies of the GOP leadership, and the reactions to those strategies by House Republicans, by briefly considering a few particular bills from 1997 and 1998. Here we outline both matters of policy content and efforts to use control of the floor to shape the agenda to the Republicans' advantage.

Appropriations in 1997

We have seen from the aggregate evidence that overall the regular appropriations bills considered in 1997 did not provoke the level of partisan conflict that characterized 1995. Only 3 of the 13 bills had special rules that triggered party conflict on the floor (although others involved disagreements before they reached their final form). These three cases reflected the use of controversial rules provisions that were included by the Rules Committee at the behest of the GOP leadership rather than because of actions of Appropriations Committee members. As David Obey (D-WI), the ranking Democrat on Appropriations said during debate on a rule, "On the Committee on Appropriations on each of these bills except one, we have worked out a very effective bipartisan working

TABLE 5.   Cohesion on Party-Unity Votes by Year (First-Degree Amendments Only)

		1995	1996	1997
GOP-supported				
amendments		$N = 35$	$N = 19$	$N = 27$
	Republicans	79%	72%	75%
	GOP Conference[a]	81%	75%	76%
	GOP class of 1994			
	(nonappropriators)	85%	82%	80%
	GOP class of 1994[b]			
	(appropriators)	69%	57%	76%
	GOP cardinals	59%	34%	54%
	Democrats	20%	18%	11%
Democrat-supported				
amendments		$N = 57$	$N = 40$	$N = 20$
	Republicans	16%	21%	20%
	GOP Conference[a]	17%	22%	21%
	GOP class of 1994			
	(nonappropriators)	15%	21%	21%
	GOP class of 1994[b]			
	(appropriators)	16%	22%	19%
	GOP cardinals	8%	9%	16%
	Democrats	76%	76%	79%

Note: Cohesion is defined as the percentage of specified members voting aye averaged across votes.

[a]GOP conference excludes Appropriations Committee members.

[b]GOP freshmen were sophomores in 1997.

relationship. . . . The problem is that . . . the Committee on Rules has imposed a partisan straightjacket on the debate for those bills, and it has in the process turned those bipartisan products into partisan war zones" (*Congressional Record*, July 23, 1997, H5653).

The legislative branch appropriations bill and its rule were largely uncontroversial except for the decision by the Rules Committee to bar a single Democratic amendment that sought to block the use of money from a disputed contingency fund for an investigation of labor laws and union activity. Similarly, the dispute about the rule for the Interior appropriations bill revolved only around the usual conflict over funding for the National Endowment for the Arts (NEA). NEA supporters wanted an up-or-down vote on agency funding, but GOP conservatives objected, and the Rules Committee refused to permit a vote on the grounds that it would involve authorizing language in the bill. However, the Rules Committee permitted a leadership-supported alternative amendment (that involved 28 pages of authorizing language). The amendment would have completely restructured federal arts funding, but it had received no committee hearings. The rule squeaked by on a 217–216 vote, after strong efforts by the Republican leadership and last-minute vote switches by members. One NEA supporter, moderate Republican Sherwood Boehlert of New York, said: "I am still against the [proposed restructuring of the NEA]. . . . My vote today was for the party and for the leadership" (*CQWR*, July 12, 1997, 1617).

The final rule controversy occurred on the agriculture bill, because of a dispute over another rule (for the foreign-aid appropriation), in which the Rules Committee had proposed to bar an amendment by Nancy Pelosi of California, a senior Appropriations Democrat. To protest that action, Democrats delayed debate on the agriculture bill with numerous time-wasting procedural motions. In response, the GOP leadership had the Rules Committee propose a rule for that bill that would severely limit amendments and motions for the remainder of its consideration. The difference in perspective between the majority leadership and GOP members of Appropriations was illustrated during the debate on the rule. Sonny Callahan (R-AL), the chair of the Appropriations Subcommittee on Foreign Operations, sympathized with the Democrats: "I happen to agree with the minority. . . . I think they should have had a different rule." Similarly, Appropriations chair Livingston said: "Is there legitimacy to some of their complaints? Of course there is," although he criticized the Democrats for carrying their protest too far (*CQWR*, July 26, 1997, 1756).[15]

Of course, the conflicts over special rules were not the only partisan matters on appropriations bills in 1997; there were also substantive disputes over funding levels and other things. However, as we have seen from the aggregate evidence and the discussion here, both on the rules for the 13 regular appropriations bills and on the legislation, partisan conflict was more limited and less intense than it had been in 1995. Left largely to its own devices, in 1996 and

1997 the Appropriations Committee reverted generally to the bipartisan patterns of decision making of its past. In 1997 this tendency was reinforced and facilitated by the budget agreement that the Clinton administration and congressional Republicans concluded early in 1997; they agreed to set the amounts available for discretionary spending in advance. The partisan conflicts that still occurred revolved largely, as we have seen, around a small number of specific decisions by the majority leaders, who sought to advantage their party's interests.

The Strategy Shift in 1998

The GOP leadership's actions related to special rules on 1998 appropriations bills reveal clearly their decisions to assert stronger influence over the committee's product and across a wider range of issues than in 1996 and 1997. As we saw in the data in table 3, as large a proportion of rules were partisan as in 1995 (7 of the 11 considered so far) and with about the same level of partisan conflict. Some of the bills involved disputes mainly over a single item, similar to the situation we discussed with regard to the 1997 bills. For example, disagreement on the Interior bill again centered solely on funding the NEA. This year the Appropriations Committee decided, contrary to the plans and wishes of the GOP leadership, to include funding for the NEA in the bill (*CQWR,* June 27, 1998, 1771). Because the funds had not been authorized, this rider would have needed protection in the special rule to escape deletion on the floor on a point of order. Under pressure from conservatives who wanted to kill the agency, the majority leadership refused to supply protection.[16] However, in response to demands of GOP moderates, they protected a proposed floor amendment that would restore NEA funding. Moreover, in an effort to extract a bit of electoral advantage from this move, the rule provided that the NEA amendment could only be offered by threatened Representative Nancy Johnson of Connecticut rather than by the agency's longtime champion Sidney Yates (D-IL), who was retiring that year. This action angered many Democrats and chagrined some committee Republicans, but it was not enough to bring down the rule.

On the Defense bill, the only dispute involved a decision by the Rules Committee to remove from the bill the funds appropriated to deal with the Y2K problem in the Defense Department's computers; the funds had been designated emergency funds. The emergency label freed the committee from the necessity, under the budget agreement, of offsetting the money with cuts in other accounts. Republican fiscal conservatives objected and demanded that the leaders block this effort; they complied. David Obey, the full committee's ranking Democrat, attacked the decision on the floor; he contended that it was important to have the funds in the bill to deal with the problem immediately, and Bill Young (R-FL), the chair of the Appropriations Subcommittee on

National Security, stated on the floor that he agreed with Obey (*Congressional Record,* June 24, 1998, H5216, H5219). The legislative branch appropriations bill only involved Democratic complaints that the GOP, as in 1997, refused to protect a proposed amendment that would have restricted the use of money from the committee contingency fund. Democrats stated that it was otherwise "a fair rule" and "otherwise a good bill."

On other rules, the conflicts were more extensive or unusual. The rule for the treasury appropriations bill, like that for defense, stripped emergency funds for the Y2K problem; that provided the principal objection for Democrats. However, the rule protected legislative language that would have required health plans for federal employees to provide coverage for many contraceptives. The rule thus provoked opposition from GOP pro-life members. The rule could not survive the combination, and it was defeated 125–291. After a recess, a new rule was brought to the floor. In it the majority leadership took the unusual step of giving protection to only a single instance of legislative language that would block a pay raise for members of Congress. This limited protection satisfied GOP conservatives because it left vulnerable the provision on contraceptives, but it similarly exposed all other legislative provisions. The protection for the pay raise provision was a device to induce members to vote for the rule by permitting supporters to claim that a vote against the rule was a vote for a congressional pay raise. The chair of the Republican Congressional Campaign Committee issued a news release before the vote stating that Republicans would do just that against any Democrat who voted no on the rule (*CQWR,* July 18, 1998, 1949). It may have worked, because although 23 Republicans voted against it, the rule passed with the support of 20 Democrats. Democrats, however, took their revenge during consideration of the bill. While Republicans struck the Y2K funds and the contraceptive language on points of order, Democrats similarly objected to a host of provisions, many favored by the GOP. About 50 provisions were struck in all.

The District of Columbia bill's rule included protection for four major controversial riders that appealed to social conservatives. These riders included funding for school vouchers, a prohibition of needle exchange programs, and a ban on adoptions by unmarried couples. Finally, the Republicans decided to use the usually uncontroversial Veterans Administration–Housing and Urban Development bill as a vehicle to try to compel passage into law of their proposed revamping of federal housing programs. To this end, they authorized inclusion as a rider the entire housing reform bill that had been passed earlier in the session; statements in floor debate made it clear that this was specifically a leadership decision (*Congressional Record,* July 16, 1998, H5645). Additionally, the rule failed to protect a provision that would raise the limits on mortgages approved by the Federal Housing Administration (FHA), a provision that Democrats and moderate Republicans supported. In the Rules

Committee's hearings on the rule, the chair of the Veterans–Housing and Urban Development Subcommittee objected to the inclusion of the housing bill, and during floor debate one Republican member of the subcommittee spoke against the rule because of its failure to protect the FHA provision. Recognizing that they were in danger of losing the rule, the majority leaders took the unusual step of adopting an amendment to the rule that shielded the FHA language. This tactic reduced Republican defections to one, and the rule passed. However, the retention of the housing provisions led nearly three-fourths of Democrats to oppose the bill's passage.

In addition to provoking greater partisanship over the structure of floor debate, the GOP leadership strategy amplified party conflict over the final form of the appropriations bills in 1998. Historically, appropriations bills had usually been passed by large bipartisan majorities because such bills contained many benefits for the constituents of most members. A member would only oppose passage of an appropriations bill if he or she were extremely dissatisfied with its contents. As we saw in table 4, in 1979–80 partisan opposition to passage of appropriations bills was rare. With the resurgence of partisanship in the 1980s and 1990s, such opposition became more frequent. Partisan conflict on these bills peaked in 1987 and 1995, with party-unity votes on passage of 6 of the 13 bills in the former year and 8 of 14 in the latter. We saw at least equivalent levels of controversy in 1998, with party votes on 6 of 11 bills considered so far.

Thus we see that the Republican leadership's strategy in 1998 was to use appropriations bills much more extensively than in the previous 2 years to advance the GOP's legislative agenda. Although this strategy was used in some instances at the leaders' initiative, in other cases it was a response to pressure from the conservative wing of the party's conference. As the appropriations season began, moreover, moves were begun to empower further the central party organization's ability to reinforce party homogeneity. In late June, Robert Ehrlich (R-MD) began circulating a petition demanding that members of the party "support the Conference on procedural matters and to abstain from divisive action" (*Roll Call,* June 22, 1998, 32). It also called on the Speaker to establish a formal mechanism for removing committee and subcommittee chairs who violated the call. The letter quickly garnered more than 100 signatures, and one of the first to sign was Speaker Gingrich. In addition, according to one member involved in the effort, Majority Whip Tom DeLay of Texas encouraged the group to demand that the leadership punish the "5 percent of Members who make life difficult for 95 percent of us" (*Roll Call,* June 22, 1998, 32). Ehrlich and other supporters made clear that the appropriations process was a particular focus of their efforts. "The appropriations season is when you really need to have your act together as the majority party. . . . It's the true test of whether you can govern" (*USA Today,* July 13, 1998, 7A).

Conclusion

The theory of conditional party government asserts that the realization of conflict, particularly partisan conflict, depends not only on the distinctness of preferences between the two parties and the powers granted to leaders by the rank and file but also on the precise strategic choices members and their leaders make. In 1995, the appropriations process was deliberately used by the new Republican leadership to enact important components of its conservative legislative agenda. Yet the culmination of events from 1995 to 1996 that led to the shutdown of several federal agencies and the nail-biting closeness associated with many GOP (especially freshman) electoral victories had important implications for member goals and strategies. The Speaker's and the Republicans' plummeting support in the polls in late 1995 and early 1996 heightened the concern among the leadership and many members about maintaining their majority in the impending elections.

The appropriations evidence from 1997 and 1998 clearly demonstrates the importance of strategic choices made by party leaders. In 1997, the GOP leaders continued the strategy of 1996 by refraining from frequent use of the appropriations bills as vehicles for advancing the party agenda. As a result, the patterns of party conflict on those bills were similar to those in 1996. Then, in 1998, the majority leadership again decided (partly for electoral reasons) to serve partisan interests by shaping the content of many appropriations bills and the structure of floor consideration. The consequence was patterns of party conflict more like those in 1995 than those in 1996–97.

In addition to the amplified discussion we have offered here of the role of leadership goals in the theory of conditional party government, inferences from the theory depend heavily on the relationship among party leaders, committee members, and the rank and file. The evidence regarding the appropriations process in 1997–98 has provided us with significant new information related to these relationships. First, we saw new evidence of contrasting preferences and goals between the senior membership of the Appropriations Committee and members of the GOP Conference. These contrasts provoked frequent complaints from the appropriators about leadership strategies, and the strategies were in turn usually responses to the demands of rank-and-file members whose preferences differed from those of the appropriators. The committee-conference difference was also one reason for the Ehrlich effort to further enhance leadership power to pressure recalcitrant Republicans.

Regarding conference-leader relationships, we saw that the leaders generally had encountered dissatisfaction from members when they emphasized electoral moderation over partisan policy pursuits. Most of the dissatisfaction came from the conservative wing of the party and not from moderates. Moreover, we did not observe any rank-and-file reluctance to continued empower-ment of the leadership, as the discussion of the Ehrlich effort indicated.

We can now also offer some final comments regarding the issues Dodd and Oppenheimer (1997) raised. Clearly, the narrow GOP majority has constrained the party and its leadership from 1995 to the present. That constraint, moreover, has become a greater problem as further divisions emerge within the GOP Con-ference. Our analysis demonstrates, however, that this constraint has not blocked the operation of the implications of the theory of conditional party gov-ernment in the 105th Congress. Within the appropriations process, partisan leadership action and party conflict over policy did not decrease over time. Rather, they sharply increased in 1998 relative to 1996–97. Similarly, although leader and member concern over electoral interests increased in 1996 and later, this concern did not prevent significant and increased party organization activity within the legislative process. To the contrary, it is important to note that mem-bers usually complained about the actions of the majority leadership when the leaders sought to soft-pedal the pursuit of partisan policy interests, not when they attempted full use of their power on behalf of the party agenda.

So we conclude that the present analysis provides further support for the view that the role of party organizations in the House and the relationships between leaders and members are basically consistent with the predictions of the theory of conditional party government. A relatively homogeneous major-ity party, with sharply different preferences from the minority, provides the logical basis for empowering party leaders and supporting the exercise of those powers in pursuit of the party agenda. Whether and how those leaders use those powers depends on their goals and the possible strategies they perceive to achieve them. How rank-and-file members respond to particular strategy choices of the leadership depends, in turn, on the mix of goals and perceptions among the members.

NOTES

1. For a more extensive discussion, see Aldrich and Rohde (1996b) and Mar-shall, Prins, and Rohde (1997), on which these few paragraphs are based.

2. Shortly after the 1994 election, Gingrich chose fifth-ranking Robert Liv-ingston of Louisiana to be the new chair.

3. For a more extensive discussion of these events and the strategic maneuvering surrounding them, see Maraniss and Weisskopf (1996) and Rohde (1996).

4. Although this agenda-setting role was more predominant in the GOP leader-ship in 1995–98 than before, it had been growing for some time. See Sinclair (1995, 1997), Bader (1996), Aldrich and Rohde (1996a), and Rohde (1991).

5. We focus only on the 13 regular appropriations bills each year to maximize the comparability of the data across Congresses.

6. *Congressional Quarterly Weekly Report* is cited as *CQWR* in this essay, and the individual articles cited do not appear in the list of references.

7. In fact, the GOP newcomers charged that they would change government before it changed them. "We are not going to be housebroken, period" (quote by Representative Souder [R-IN] in *CQWR*, October 28, 1995, 3254).

8. Mean vote differences are computed similarly throughout the analysis for different subgroups. For figure 1, the variable is computed from the absolute value of the proportion of cardinals voting aye minus the proportion of the remaining GOP contingent on appropriations voting aye averaged across votes.

9. We control for party support on amendments throughout our analysis. In figure 1, GOP-supported amendments represent the subset of first-degree amendments in which the number of Republicans in support of the amendment is greater than the number of Democrats. The subset of Democratic-supported amendments is similarly defined.

10. Under the 1997 Budget Agreement, funds designated as emergency related do not require offsetting cuts in other areas.

11. Of the 13 GOP appropriators voting to strip the provision, 10 were from the class of 1992 or later.

12. Because the fiscal year 1999 appropriations process is still in progress, we do not have available for analysis roll call data comparable to that for earlier years. We offer some limited discussion of 1998 roll calls in a later section.

13. In 1995, there are 14 final passage votes rather than 13 because the legislative branch appropriations bill was passed for a second time after being vetoed by President Clinton. In both votes, Republican unity was nearly identical; however, 56 percent of Democrats voted aye on the first vote and only 46 percent on the second vote. We included both votes to prevent biasing our analysis because the first vote was bipartisan whereas the second was a party-unity vote.

14. Cohesion scores in table 5 are based on the subset of first-degree amendments to appropriations bills in which a majority of members from both parties vote in opposition to one another. No substantive differences exist when all amendments are included. Still, selecting on the subset of party-unity votes allows us to refine our comparisons among the different subgroups even more on those amendments in which clear differences exist between the parties.

15. Although it does not involve a regular appropriations bill, it is worth noting the 1997 supplemental appropriation here because it further illustrates the gap between committee Republicans and the leadership. As with the 1995 budget fight, the GOP leadership sought to include a number of desired legislative policy changes in the bill that dealt mainly with disaster aid for flood victims in the Midwest. Livingston objected to the inclusion of the riders, but he was overruled. The leaders made clear that they would not recognize the independent authority the appropriators wanted. As Majority Leader Dick Armey of Texas said on the floor, "The supposition that the supplemental bill . . . or any appropriations bill . . . is the property of that committee and that committee alone is a supposition of course that is errant and could only provoke mischief" (*Roll Call,* June 2, 1997, 14).

16. Rules Committee Chair Gerald Solomon of New York stated that protection was denied because of the GOP's policy of not protecting riders when the committee

with legislative jurisdiction objected, which was the case here (*Congressional Record,* July 21, 1998, 5975).

REFERENCES

Aldrich, John H. 1995. *Why Parties?: The Origin and Transformation of Political Parties in America.* Chicago: University of Chicago Press.

Aldrich, John H., and David W. Rohde. 1996a. "A Tale of Two Speakers: A Comparison of Policy Making in the 100th and 104th Congress." Paper presented at the annual meeting of the American Political Science Association.

Aldrich, John H., and David W. Rohde. 1996b. "The Republican Revolution and the House Appropriations Committee." Paper presented at the annual meeting of the Southern Political Science Association.

Aldrich, John H., and David W. Rohde. 1997. "Balance of Power: Republican Party Leadership and the Committee System in the 104th House." Paper presented at the annual meeting of the Midwest Political Science Association.

Aldrich, John H., and David W. Rohde. 1997–98. "The Transition to Republican Rule in the House." *Political Science Quarterly* 112: 541–67.

Aldrich, John H., and David W. Rohde. 1998. "Measuring Conditional Party Government." Paper presented at the annual meeting of the Midwest Political Science Association.

Bader, John B. 1996. *Taking the Initiative: Leadership Agendas in Congress and the "Contract with America."* Washington, D.C.: Georgetown University Press.

Connelly, William F., Jr., and John J. Pitney Jr. 1994. *Congress' Permanent Minority?* Lanham, Md.: Rowman & Littlefield.

Cox, Gary W., and Mathew D. McCubbins. 1993. *Legislative Leviathan: Party Government in the House.* Berkeley and Los Angeles: University of California Press.

Dodd, Lawrence C., and Bruce I. Oppenheimer. 1997. *Congress Reconsidered.* 6th ed. Washington, D.C.: Congressional Quarterly Press.

Fenno, Richard F., Jr. 1966. *The Power of the Purse: Appropriations Politics in Congress.* Boston: Little, Brown.

Fenno, Richard F., Jr. 1973. *Congressmen in Committees.* Boston: Little, Brown.

Fenno, Richard F., Jr. 1997. *Learning to Govern: An Institutional View of the 104th Congress.* Washington, D.C.: Brookings Institution Press.

Gimpel, James G. 1996. *Fulfilling the Contract: The First 100 Days.* Boston: Allyn & Bacon.

Maraniss, David, and Michael Weisskopf. 1996. *Tell Newt to Shut Up!* New York: Touchstone.

Marshall, Bryan W., Brandon C. Prins, and David W. Rohde. 1997. "Partisanship and the Purse: The Money Committees and Procedures in the Postreform Congress." Paper presented at the annual meeting of the Southern Political Science Association, Norfork, Virginia.

Pianin, Eric. 1998. "GOP to Use Spending Bills as Battleground." *Washington Post,* June 28, A4.

Pomper, Gerald M. 1997. *The Election of 1996: Reports and Interpretations.* N.J.: Chatham House.

Rohde, David W. 1991. *Parties and Leaders in the Postreform House.* Chicago: University of Chicago Press.

Rohde, David W. 1994. "Partisanship, Leadership, and Congressional Assertiveness in Foreign and Defense Policy." In *The New Politics of American Foreign Policy,* ed. David A. Deese, 76–101. New York: St. Martin's Press.

Rohde, David W. 1996. "Parties, Institutional Control, and Political Incentives: A Perspective on Governing in the Clinton Presidency." Paper presented at the Colloquium Mise en perspective des annees Clinton [The Clinton Years in Perspective], October 6–8, Université de Montreal.

Sinclair, Barbara. 1995. *Legislators, Leaders, and Lawmaking: The U.S. House of Representatives in the Postreform Era.* Baltimore: Johns Hopkins University Press.

Sinclair, Barbara. 1997. *Unorthodox Lawmaking: New Legislative Processes in the U.S. Congress.* Washington, D.C.: Congressional Quarterly Press.

Smith, Steven S., and Christopher J. Deering. 1984. *Committees in Congress.* Washington, D.C.: Congressional Quarterly Press.

Stevenson, Richard W. 1998. "Clinton and G.O.P. Brace for Budget Battle." *New York Times* on the Web, July 21.

White, Joseph. 1989. "The Function and Power of the House Appropriations Committee." Ph.D. diss., University of California.

What We Don't Know
about Congressional Party Leadership

Richard Forgette

The success of Richard Fenno's works on Congress is partly due to his ability to always tell a good story while presenting a clear, provocative conceptual framework. In this essay, I critically discuss the framework in Fenno's recent monograph *Learning to Govern,* a book on the House Republican leadership. The remainder of this essay is an elaboration on what, I think, we do not know about congressional leadership. Particularly, I pose some questions that, in true Fenno style, are central to bridging the current gap between theoretical and descriptive accounts of congressional leadership.

The current House Republican leadership has generated a number of intriguing stories. The most personal and widely known of these stories is the rise and fall of Speaker Gingrich's political capital inside and outside of Congress (Gingrich 1998; Maraniss and Weisskopf 1996). Specifically, how did the Speaker manage to go from exalted leader among his copartisans to only narrowly surviving a failed coup attempt in 3 years? With a junior-dominated rank and file, a nonincremental policy agenda, an emotional high coming from an historic election, and a need for immediate administrative restructuring given the party change, House Republicans' substantial grant of authority to Gingrich was an understandable yet unique circumstance. This grant of leadership authority by the Republican rank and file in the first half of the 104th Congress is the exception that demonstrates the rule of congressional leadership. We might have expected that Gingrich's control over the agenda and these copartisans' votes to fray. Nonetheless, the depth of Gingrich's fall—he survived only after substantial conference lobbying from leaders—indicates the volatility of the current leadership arrangement.

From a management perspective, the sometimes fractious relationship among party leaders is another interesting story of the Republican leadership. How did those in Gingrich's inner circle, including Armey, DeLay, and Boehner, lose their ability to effectively coordinate work, openly communicate, and anticipate the reactions of the rank and file and opposition? This breakdown appears even stranger considering that these leaders had functioned well as a minority team, were ideologically unified, and had always voiced a commitment to party building. Since Speaker Wright, House leadership has been more aggressive in courting the media and proactive in coordinating the party's media message and strategies. The success of the Contract with America as a media event further signaled that the Republican leadership would focus on coordinating its media message. Nonetheless, wanting greater control, Speaker Gingrich centralized media responsibilities and shifted responsibilities from the conference to the Speaker's office. This shift contributed to the dissension among Gingrich's inner circle. It also partly explained rank-and-file members' complaint that the leadership fluctuated in reliable strategic information and was unable to control the media's portrayal of the congressional agenda.

Finally, from the rank-and-file perspective, Republican members' internal dissension presents another intriguing story. How has a party that has voted so much in line (historically high rates of party line votes and average party cohesion) generated so much political infighting? House Republicans' high floor unity has belied their factionalism over strategic premises and distrust of their leadership. Trust in Gingrich's tactical judgment was first challenged during the government shutdown. His later ethics problems and handling of the disaster relief supplemental bill in the 105th Congress further eroded support within the conference.

In *Learning to Govern,* Richard Fenno (1997) weaves together these personal, management, and membership stories of the current House Republicans to make a few key points about legislative governance. By *governance,* he means both strategic agenda setting and interbranch and interparty compromise. In Congress, governing expertise means having "a practical grasp of lawmaking as a lengthy, incremental, multilevel, coalition-building process. And it involves a seasoned strategic sense in matters such as establishing priorities, negotiating outcomes across the separated institutions of government, and calculating feasibility, trade-offs, and timing at every decision making juncture" (Fenno 1997, 20).

His first key point is that legislators every 2 years face the task of electoral interpretation. In the House, majority partisans must organize and minority partisans must adapt. That is, the majority has the job ultimately to decide what the voters' message was from the preceding election and how that message is to be fashioned into a legislative agenda. The minority is merely charged with responding to a majority-controlled organization and agenda. For 40 years, Republicans merely adapted, never organized. Additionally, since the emergence of Gingrich as a minority leader, more Republicans had adopted or endorsed Gingrich's confrontationalist minority leadership style that emphasizes clear partisan contrasts and intentionally provocative rhetoric. This lack of majority leadership experience and confrontational style of minority adaptation contributed to Republicans' overreaching, overestimating the message of the 1994 election. Republicans began to believe that an electoral message, the Contract with America, was a mandate and could serve wholly and unequivocally as their legislative agenda.

Fenno's second point about governance and the Republican leadership relates to institutional bargaining. Once majority leaders interpret the election, they must devise an operational plan and then initiate a strategic dialogue among other leaders that is respectful of political context—the Senate, public opinion, media, and, most important, the president. Legislative leaders must craft strategy that anticipates points of interbranch and interparty conflict. Fenno argues that Republican leaders lacked the natural temperament and experience for this institutional bargaining. Rather than establishing a narrower list of priorities and a corresponding schedule anticipating the process of incremental, negotiated agreements, the new Republican leadership applied an all-or-nothing, take-it-or-leave-it attitude toward policy making. They applied their minority confrontationalist strategy to a Republican-controlled House.

Fenno's criticisms have been made by others, though perhaps not as lucidly or with as much substantiation. Although his tone is decidedly critical, in the end, his conclusions are not judgmental. He carefully avoids premature assessments. The Republican leadership may still "learn to govern." But will leaders learn from these mistakes or will they be repeated? I think that Republican leaders are getting a firmer hold of how to use their office. The political context during and since the Republican transition partly explains their mistakes. As for electoral interpretation, Republicans were implementing a huge administrative reshuffling inside the House during the first 6 months of the 104th Congress. Staff and members were learning new jobs in new surroundings. A ready-made agenda, the Contract with America, bought them time to adjust. As for institutional bargaining, even most junior House Republicans now acknowledge that they were too rigid in the 1995 budget confrontation. That was a heady time for House Republicans after wandering in the desert for 40 years, and junior, self-styled citizen legislators strongly believed that *their* supporters wanted budget balance and smaller government. Despite their public relations fiasco, House Republicans by 1997 succeeded in getting a multiyear budget agreement that achieved balance with a tax cut.

Republicans still may be learning to govern, and clearly leadership styles have changed from the 104th to the 105th Congress. Nonetheless, governance is not static either. The context and expectations that shape party leadership activities continue to compel innovation. Today's party leaders frame agendas and find majority coalitions using different tools than those used in the past. They frame votes around topics that accentuate partisan conflict rather than those that promote bipartisan compromise. They overwhelmingly form winning coalitions within their party caucus on topics that appeal to reelection and primary constituencies. The pragmatic need for institutional bargaining is balanced with their interest in igniting popular discourse and appealing to an activist base.

Fenno's work enriches our understanding of Congress because it has always been both empirically grounded and conceptually clear. Fitting these empirical and theoretical literatures of Congress is what I turn to next. I discuss some general questions that frame current work to bridge the empirical and theoretical studies on legislative leadership.

Understanding Congressional Leadership

Fenno, in characterizing the role of party leadership during a prereform period of strong committee chairs, wrote that party leaders "organize decision making across committees and across stages, thereby functioning as a centralizing force in the making of House decisions" (Fenno 1965, 61). This Rayburn-era coalition model, a behind-the-scenes leadership style coordinating the agendas of committee leaders, operated within an insular, seniority-driven institutional culture relative to today's Congress. Much of the literature since then on the postreform Congress has described how contextual forces and growing intraparty ideological homogeneity have encouraged party leaders to adapt or expand organizational and procedural tools to maintain their procedural and substantive majorities (Rohde 1991; Sinclair 1992). Some authors have concluded that today's Congress is increasingly partisan, one in which party organization matters.

In his book *Pivotal Politics* (1998), Keith Krehbiel, though, questions these conclusions by asking whether mere party activity can be equated to party effects on policy outcomes. That is, Krehbiel argues that the partisan activities in the end have little or no substantive result. It is the equilibrium behavior of countervailing political pressures among competing partisans that does little to move votes or change policy outcomes. Krehbiel's work is a challenge to more empirical Congress scholars, particularly those who espouse a structural partisan or conditional party government view, to orient more directly their study of congressional leadership toward advancing our theoretical understanding of parties in the legislature. I note three general research questions that are fundamental to bridging this empirical and theoretical work on legislative party leadership.

Measuring Partisanship

A first question is how to conceptualize and measure legislative partisanship. Is Congress "partisan," and is it more "partisan" than in earlier periods? Krehbiel (1993) makes the distinction between preference-induced and structural partisanship. Preference-induced partisanship is merely the coincidence of copartisans' policy preferences. Copartisans may share the same ideology and relatively similar reelection constituencies and thus coincidentally vote alike. Krehbiel asserts that party leadership activity does not have a significant and large independent effect on enhancing partisan cohesion. Structural partisanship, on the other hand, suggests that organization and procedure can and do matter in increasing partisan voting and outcomes. Congressional leaders strategically use institutional incentives, agenda control, and informational power to achieve higher rates of partisan cohesion than would occur in their absence. The effect, ultimately, is that votes and policy outcomes are pulled toward the preferences of the majority party median.

Traditional cohesion-based measures of legislative partisanship operationally define partisan votes as those in which copartisans vote together at a rate exceeding some proportion. Although these measures have descriptive value, they suffer from a circular logic: a partisan vote is one in which partisans vote alike. They provide no clear leverage for distinguishing between structural and preference-induced partisanship. Rather than declaring a vote to be partisan when some arbitrary percentage threshold of Democrats and Republicans vote in opposing directions, Cox and McCubbins (1993) construct measures based on intraparty and interparty leadership voting. Party leadership votes, in particular, are defined as those in which there is intraparty leadership agreement and interparty leadership polarization on any vote. Without a known list of party-whipped votes, empiricists may use leadership voting to provide a means of designating which votes party leaders believe to be important.

Using party leadership voting as a basis for measurement, a partisan model of legislative organization may include three procedural sources of structural partisanship: proposal (or committee) power, scheduling power, and agenda (or amendment) control power. Each is key to measuring the impact of party organization on rank-and-file behavior and, ultimately, policy outcome. Briefly, party leaders' proposal (or committee) power may include an authority to structure or alter committee policy jurisdictions, affect committee member assignment, manipulate bill assignment or committee scheduling, and, ultimately, affect or alter committee bill reporting. Scheduling power is the authority to determine access, order, packaging, and timing of bills to be considered on the floor. Finally, agenda (or amendment) control power is the authority to affect the access, order, content, or packaging of floor amendments.

A legislative partisan model implies that the majority party caucus does not strong-arm its rank-and-file members to ensure party support but instead insinuates the members' collective policy and electoral goals into the very structure of legislative decision making. Proposed legislation is parsed through a series of checkpoints, each of which the majority party potentially controls. This gauntlet of party-dominated checks through which proposed bills must pass shapes legislative content, floor agendas, and floor outcomes. Presumably, the net result of this majority party–dominated structure is that policy making operates to a great extent as if on autopilot, with little overt intervention by majority party leaders. Hence, the votes that majority party members face on the floor are largely confined to the choices that the party leaders want members to face—majority party agenda votes and consensual "hurrah" votes.

Whether partisanship is both preference and structurally based cannot be addressed with cohesion-based measures. Traditional cohesion measures of partisanship are not centered on any structural power of party leadership and thus do not provide any means of assessing the flow of causality between strictly preference-induced and partisan voting. Refining measures of partisanship that relate to the components and constraints of structural partisanship in a legislative setting provides at least some improvement in bridging empirical and theoretical literatures.

Causes of Legislative Partisanship

Separate from conceptual and operational issues is the question of why Congress has or has not become more partisan. Various authors have noted multiple sources of legislative partisanship.

Rohde's (1991) and Aldrich and Rohde's (1998) work emphasizes that preference homogeneity is the condition in conditional party government. With regard to the contemporary House, changes in the ideological makeup of particularly southern members and their reelection constituencies have resulted in greater intraparty ideological homogeneity and interparty heterogeneity. This preference homogeneity among copartisans and divergence between partisans induces majority members' to delegate institutional powers to party leaders, increasing further partisan division.

A related idea is Cox and McCubbins's (1993) concept of electoral inefficiencies. Electoral inefficiencies refer to the national partisan tides that affect individual partisans' reelection prospects. Cox and McCubbins presume that this shared electoral value of the party label compels copartisans to organize and cede power to a central authority. They further presume that leaders exercise these powers and that their actions result in outcomes that significantly affect rank-and-file members' reelection. Notably, unorganized reelection-seeking copartisans risk overproducing particularistic legislation and underproducing policy outcomes that have collective benefits. The common wisdom of congressional elections is that "all politics is local" and that the limited effects of national forces are manifested largely through legislative recruitment and less so campaigns. Nonetheless, little work has been done to assess the varying size and impact of electoral inefficiencies, particularly at an individual level.

Fenno (1997), in *Learning to Govern,* underscores the role of the minority party in causing legislative partisanship. Koopman (1996) and Connelly and Pitney (1994) make similar arguments. The primary tactical issue among minority partisans is whether to be confrontationalists or institutionalists; for House Republicans in the 1980s, members espoused either the Gingrich purist view or the Michel and Madigan pragmatic view. Minority partisans' mischievous use of floor amendments may compel the majority to further cede scheduling and amendment control authority to its leaders. A singular event such as the nuclear freeze vote in the early 1980s compelled the majority leadership to systematically remove agenda-setting opportunities for the minority.

Finally, information control and party-building strategies may contribute to legislative partisanship. Gingrich has adopted a new speakership role that was intended to make the leader much more a national media figure. The party caucuses have become more assertive in disseminating policy information for both internal and external consumption and are meeting with greater frequency. Furthermore, the parties' congressional campaign committees have greatly expanded efforts in candidate recruitment, fund-raising, and electoral services. Although Cantor and Hernnson (1997) conclude that party campaign committees do not condition fund-raising on members' partisanship, the national parties have become much more proactive in recruiting and funding challengers. Any legislative impact of this party-building strategy has yet to be empirically shown.

Consequences of Legislative Partisanship

A final question inviting further work relates to the expected consequences of a more partisan Congress. For empiricists, this question suggests placing partisanship on the right side of the equation. What consequences might a more procedurally empowered and ideological party leadership have on the operation of the institution and on policy outcomes? Interestingly, members' perception of the concept of legislative partisanship often is not of coalition formation or leadership effects within the chamber. Instead, they are just as likely to interpret the word *partisan* in terms of its tangible consequences, consequences that more often have negative connotations. When asked how partisanship has changed in the House, participants often speak about the changes in public perceptions of Congress, the institutional culture, the work style and pace, or the information flow. They may allude to changes in the legislative process or the intensity of campaign-related activities that, again, are things we might view as consequences of party leadership delegation and preference-induced partisanship. In the following, I discuss a few possible consequences, notably process and behavioral effects.

How might legislative partisanship affect the policy-making process inside the House? Sinclair (1997) describes the increasingly evident practice of using procedures to bypass committees and the minority. Notably, she documents the rise of omnibus legislative vehicles, postcommittee adjustments, and special rules. She makes a convincing case that there has been a procedural arms race in the House and this race has partly been driven by the actions of party leaders. What is less certain, though, is whether these process changes have altered rank-and-file members' voting decisions or, even further, changed policy outcomes.

A less formal process change, the information flow among legislators, may also be linked to greater House party delegation. More time is spent and substantive information exchanged within the respective party conferences than in the past. The minutes of the House Republican Conference document this clear movement toward a more policy-active and self-conscious party coalition. The House Republican Conference now meets about four times as often as it did during the 1950s and 1960s. In fact, the number of conference meetings in each of the 100st through 103rd Congresses was about equal to or greater than all the conference meetings during the entire decade of the 1950s. About a third of conference meetings during the earlier period were routinely used for leadership elections and committee appointments. After these early organizational meetings, though, the conference only met intermittently and often with low attendance.

Since the 100th Congress, however, House Republicans meet at least once or twice a week when in session, typically on Wednesdays. Attendance has increased over time to about two-thirds of the members. Press and member accounts of party meetings emphasize that there is a lot of "venting" in conference by rank-and-file members while leaders try to anticipate where party defection is likely to occur on pending business. In the 105th Congress, Republicans passed a rule prohibiting staff attendance to conferences in hopes of minimizing press leaks. The effect of this partisan information flow is that House copartisans are more likely to identify themselves as parts of a party team or family compared with their Senate counterparts. Party caucus meetings have become places for "keeping peace in the family." The greater frequency and substance of House party caucus meetings indicate the greater effort to form and maintain party-based coalitions today than in past decades.

The distribution of informational products and services by the leadership offices to copartisans has also changed. The House Republican leadership distributes a range of political briefs and bill summaries to members, including so-called Boarding Passes, summaries and talking points for pending business distributed to members as they return to their districts. The idea is to get copartisans talking about the same things and using the same language. Whether and how this information flow actually affects individual members' priorities, preferences, or decision making has never been systematically studied. Nonetheless, it can be documented that party leaders are much more aggressive in making the party caucuses a central clearinghouse for policy and political information than in the past.

Another set of possible consequences relates to the institutional culture within the House. Specifically, what, if any, impact has further party delegation had on the norms and behavioral practices of rank-and-file members? These behavioral effects may shape contemporary Hill styles, the expectations and practices of how members routinely conduct their business in Washington.

One behavioral effect may be the rise of uncivil discourse, including personal attacks of partisan opponents on and off the floor. An analysis by Kathleen Hall-Jamieson (1997) of demands to take words down on the House floor indicate that incivility peaked in 1946 and 1995, periods directly preceding or following majority party turnover. The appearance of C-SPAN and the subsequent rise in the number of 1-minute and special orders speeches probably have led to coarser rhetoric and more sound bytes in floor debate. Societal changes also have contributed. Still, it is likely that the increasing agenda power of the majority leadership has added to this decline of partisan comity. The positions of current House Republican leaders are partly due to their successful portrayal to copartisans inside the chamber and sympathetic C-SPAN viewers outside the chamber that House rules unjustly punished minority partisans. Speaker Rayburn's dichotomy of media show horses versus legislative workhorses has been further blurred by minority party leadership's active orchestration of 1-minute and special orders speeches. Managing the party's media message has become one of the most important and demanding jobs of leaders.

Although partisan discourse is not necessarily uncivil, this speech may contribute to an apparent decline in interparty contact among House members. Members, particularly those of opposing parties, often do not know each other. This decline of contact may be due to a number of changes in contemporary legislative life, including shorter legislative weeks, longer district periods, electronic voting (which requires less time on the floor), rising casework and scheduling demands, evening fund-raisers, and the declining proportion of House members relocating their families to Washington. To this list, though, we might add a rise of party leadership delegation. The behavioral norm that minority partisans adopt a combative rather than constructive legislative role took stronger hold at a time when the majority leadership was enhancing its institutional powers. Leadership-dominated budget summitry, omnibus legislation, and restrictive floor rules may drive minority members to use floor debate to express their frustration with a process that offers them a less formative policy role.

It is important to point out that this decline in interparty contact corresponds with the already noted rise in intraparty contacts within the party caucus. The 1997 Hershey Retreat was intended to resolve this congressional version of the "bowling alone" problem by bringing Republicans and Democrats (and their families) together for some community building. It is not known whether retreats can effectively change behavior. A few months after the retreat, a House Rules Committee hearing on incivility was canceled when members had to cast an unexpected floor vote to reproach members for uncivil floor debate. Nonetheless, the retreat recognized that incivility is merely a behavioral symptom of a more basic decline in interaction and, perhaps, trust between partisans. Without trust the capacity to craft compromises and form bipartisan coalitions likewise declines.

Stronger legislative parties may have another behavioral consequence among members. They may be changing the norms about what rights and obligations rank-and-file copartisans have within their party caucus. These norms structure the relationship between leaders and the membership. Well short of a binding or king caucus, the House Republican Conference has expectations that rank-and-file members are to support the party position on procedural votes and to give advance notification for defections on party votes. Enforcement is implicit with the leaders' conditional help in gaining desired committee assignments, district benefits, and floor access for members' pet floor amendments.

What do rank-and-file members receive in exchange for this procedural loyalty and information? Leaders promise to attend to a common agenda that carefully avoids issues that knowingly force partisans to take hard votes, ones that place their vote in opposition with constituents. In short, majority party leaders suppress factionalism within the caucus by exercising their scheduling and amendment power. The leadership's negative power for keeping items off the agenda helps maintain support from rank-and-file members as much as its positive power. House Republicans have a number of ideological factions that belie their apparent floor unity. These factions—the Tuesday Lunch Bunch and Conservative Action Team (CATs)—work to communicate to the leadership what should and should not be acceptable agenda items for the conference. At the same time, the leadership has frustrated bipartisan coalitions from forming. The reduction of committee staff and the defunding of legislative service organizations at the start of the 104th Congress decreased the voice of competing agenda-setting coalitions.

Conclusion

Fenno's *Learning to Govern* (1997) leads readers to think more about the current House Republican leadership and congressional leadership generally. As always, Fenno's work includes some genuine insights. His diagnosis of what went wrong, the political missteps of the Republican leadership in the 104th Congress, is persuasive. His presumed remedy, as implied by the book's title, is that congressional party leadership should work toward interbranch accommodation and institutional comity to accentuate legislative output, albeit with incremental policy change. This remedy, though, may not be a model shared by the current leadership. Instead, the current Republican leadership continues to search for issues and frame votes around areas of political conflict and ideological division between the parties. The leaders do so as much to ignite popular discourse and perhaps change minds as they do to possibly help themselves electorally. In short, their view of legislative governance may not conform to Fenno's.

The active and more ideological party leadership model that is currently being practiced compels us to think more about how we can bridge theoretical and descriptive accounts of congressional leadership. I have suggested that we need to know more about the measures, causes, and consequences of structural partisanship, and I have offered some leading questions and thoughts in hopes of provoking discussion. Do party leaders exert independent authority over their rank-and-file members in the House? Why would rank-and-file members willingly delegate this authority and then later follow their leaders? And, finally, does it matter? Is there any evidence that a partisan Congress is to be judged differently from one that is not?

REFERENCES

Aldrich, John, and David Rohde. 1998. "The Transition to Republican Rule in the House: Implications for Theories of Congressional Politics." *Political Science Quarterly* 112: 541–69.
Cantor, David, and Paul S. Hernnson. 1997. "Party Campaign Activity and Party Unity in the U.S. House of Representatives." *Legislative Studies Quarterly* 22: 393–415.
Connelly, William F., Jr., and John J. Pitney Jr. 1994. *Congress' Permanent Minority? Republicans in the U.S. House.* Lanham, Md.: Rowman & Littlefield.
Cox, Gary W., and Mathew D. McCubbins. 1993. *Legislative Leviathan: Party Government in the House.* Berkeley and Los Angeles: University of California Press.
Fenno, Richard F., Jr. 1965. "The Internal Distribution of Influence: The House." In *The Congress and America's Future,* ed. David Truman. Englewood Cliffs, N.J.: Prentice Hall.
Fenno, Richard F., Jr. 1997. *Learning to Govern: An Institutional View of the 104th Congress.* Washington, D.C.: Brookings Institution.
Gingrich, Newt. 1998. *Lessons Learned the Hard Way.* New York: HarperCollins.
Hall-Jamieson, Kathleen. 1997. *Civility in the House of Representatives.* New York: Annenberg Public Policy Center.
Koopman, David. 1996. *Hostile Takeover: The House Republican Party, 1980–1995.* Lanham, Md.: Rowman & Littlefield.
Krehbiel, Keith. 1993. "Where's the Party?" *British Journal of Political Science* 23: 235–66.
Krehbiel, Keith. 1998. *Pivotal Politics: A Theory of U.S. Lawmaking.* Chicago: University of Chicago Press.
Maraniss, David, and Michael Weisskopf. 1996. *Tell Newt to Shut Up!* New York: Touchstone.

Rohde, David. 1991. *Parties and Leaders in the Post-Reform House.* Chicago: University of Chicago Press.

Sinclair, Barbara. 1992. "The Emergence of Strong Leadership in the 1980s House of Representatives." *Journal of Politics* 54: 657–84.

Sinclair, Barbara. 1997. *Unorthodox Lawmaking: New Legislative Processes in the U.S. Congress.* Washington, D.C.: Congressional Quarterly Press.

Preferences and Governance in the U.S. House of Representatives: The Great Republican Experiment

Christine DeGregorio

By their nature, on paper, Republicans cannot rule. First of all they are not willing to buy their power with American tax dollars. And they're not willing to be the gatekeeper of all funding and power. Inherently, how do you hold power and consolidate it, if you devolve and distribute it out? The Republicans are entirely anti-machiavellian in approach. . . . We are undertaking a great experiment, and we could lose.

Representative Brian Bilbray, CA: 49

Introduction

Many House Republicans characterize the transfer of power into their hands as a great experiment. Academics grapple with the same issue. In scholarly parlance, we wonder how much Republican House leadership deviates from the familiar Democratic model. It is a valid question, considering that for 40 years (1955–95) the Democrats have been the only ones in charge. We hope our theories are sound and generalizable to both political parties. But without an opportunity to verify the claim, no one can be sure.

This essay celebrates the teaching and research of Richard F. Fenno Jr. In keeping with *Congressmen in Committees* (1973) and the *Emergence of a Senate Leader* (1991), among his other works, we see the power of individual goals. Indeed, several Republican innovations in House governance seem to fit the majority party's preference for individual- and market-oriented solutions to societal problems over governmental ones. With cost cutting foremost on the minds of many Republicans and their conservative voters, the new leaders are more constrained than their more liberal predecessors. They cannot get away with inducing good behavior among the rank and file with the same level of pork barrel projects that the Democrats could.

This "good public policy" goal, however, only explains part of the story when it comes to understanding how Republicans comport themselves in the majority. The fuller picture borrows from a theme that Fenno stressed in his presidential address to the American Political Science Association in 1986. At the time, he was urging scholars to benefit from firsthand observation. In his words, "You watch, you accompany, and you talk with people you are studying. Much of what you see, therefore, is dictated by what they say and do. If something is important to them, it becomes important to you" (1986, 3). The approach offers a window onto important experiences and events that, if missed, may end in distorted interpretations of political realities.

The Republicans' decades-long position as a powerless minority is just such an experience that, as they tell it, shapes their approach toward wielding power today. Although they were not as successful in cutting back on restrictive debating rules as they promised (Towell 1994), amending activity has increased under their watch. And one practice that Democrats used to their advantage and that Republicans grew to hate—the king of the hill voting rule—is now extinct. From the Republicans' point of view, these deviations in governance stem from two sources: a preference for unencumbered debate and an aversion to the old status quo.

In this essay, two substantive sections follow the study design. First, I examine what is old and new about Republican House governance, detailing management practices and coalition-building strategies in particular. Second, I offer two explanations for the changes we see. One entails the lingering effects of minority status and the Republicans' attraction to personal freedom and principles of fairness. The other explanation of events is straightforward and devolves from the Republicans' more conservative vision of good public policy.

Study Design

For the descriptive evidence on how House Republicans perform in positions of power I rely on public sources—the Library of Congress Information Service (LOCIS), government watchdog organizations (American Conservative Union), and the media (LEXIS-NEXIS). For insights on why Republicans behave as they do, I rely on personal interviews and observation.[1]

The interviews progressed in stages. The early participants included 40 or so leadership aides and lobbyists. The aides provided background information on what their bosses were attempting to achieve and how they approached House governance. The lobbyists reported on the leaders' outreach to political allies. Next came 41 interviews with senior aides to a random and representative sample of rank-and-file House Republicans (see appendix). These semistructured interviews provided background on members' perceptions of and attentiveness to two important principal groups in their lives—constituents and elected party leaders. In subsequent follow-up interviews, 27 Republican officeholders explained their reasons for voting contrary to constituent opinion in one instance and party leaders in the other. Last, I approached Republican party leaders for answers about what they do to orchestrate policy wins on the House floor. Three high-ranking Democrats (one senior representative and two aides to Minority Leader Richard Gephardt [D-MO]) provide their impressions of Republican governance thus far.

A New Culture of Governing

In January 1995, the Republicans introduced several reforms—some by federal statute with bicameral and executive support, others through chamber rules with bipartisan majorities, and still others by party fiat. Although these reforms are sometimes characterized as dramatic and often likened in importance to the reforms of the mid-1970s (Aldrich and Rohde 1997; Owens 1997), they largely perpetuate trends toward good governing that were already under way (Cloud 1995).

When the chamber rules are analyzed for their effects on the distribution of power across three levels of influence (individual, committee, and party), most observers concur that the top party leaders benefited most from the rearrangements (Evans and Oleszek 1997; Owens 1997; Sinclair 1997). What scholars neglect to assess, probably because of inherent difficulties with measurement, is the degree to which the new leaders attempt to apply influence earlier in the process than is customary. The analysis entails a chronological view of the application of power instead of the hierarchical ones we are accustomed to. I explore the idea in the following section, starting with three management practices that Republicans consider unique to their rule—a unified team approach to staffing; advanced, strategic planning; and therapeutic approaches to self-improvement. The remainder of the section examines the Republican leaders' use of four coalition-building practices that include the strategy of inclusion, service to members, structuring choice, and outreach to the grass roots (Sinclair 1983, 1995). The evidence is at least suggestive that the new majority prefers normative approaches that are applied early in the policy process to coercive approaches that are applied late, just before a vote.

Team Management and Strategic Planning

Journalists Maraniss and Weisskopf (1996) succinctly captured Newt Gingrich's (GA: 6) extraordinary attachment to a combined military and business approach to management. "He had all these little sayings. He broke any mission down into VSTP: Vision, Strategy, Tactics, and Projects. . . . He sent his staff down to the U.S. Army Training and Doctrine centers in Monroe, Virginia, and Fort Leavenworth, Kansas to study management techniques. They learned how to lay out branches and sequences TRADOC-style" (1996, 9). A visit to any Republican office will confirm the pervasiveness of the lessons. Members and high-ranking staffers are all familiar with the mantras, and several admit to incorporating aspects of the techniques into their own daily practices.

According to leadership aides, unified team management is a Republican innovation. Speaker Gingrich, Majority Leader Dick Armey (TX: 26), Majority Whip Tom DeLay (TX: 22), and Conference Chairman John Boehner (OH:

8) coordinated their work and that of their aides. The aim was to eliminate confusion and inefficiency from within the conference by explicitly detailing the roles and functions of every office.[2]

On major initiatives, such as those in the Contract with America and the anticrime bill, the majority leader's staff worked closely with committee and subcommittee aides to anticipate trouble in advance of a floor vote. Like a soldier in battle reminiscing about his trench mates, one Armey aide explains with affection the mutual dependency and trust that developed between him and key committee aides:

> There were probably four or five major contract committees. I lived with the staff directors of those committees. We needed each other to get through this. I remember the Judiciary committee, those poor guys. They were exhausted. They had responsibility for balanced-budget constitutional amendment, the crime bill, legal reform, and welfare reform. Ways and means the same way. . . . We really bonded.

To avert unwanted surprises on the floor of the House, staffers to Majority Whip Tom DeLay and Rules Committee Chairman Gerald Solomon (NY: 22) also engaged in an unprecedented level of advanced planning and teamwork. DeLay's preference for what he calls "growing the vote" (rather than whipping the vote) stems from his involvement in the early formulation of policy. He and his staff start tracking major initiatives at the subcommittee stage of the process. Whips and staff meet weekly with the key policy people, staff, and members. This frequent meeting gives bill drafters a chance to respond to early warning signs from their colleagues. Whips also hear about the subtleties of the issues, which equips them to allay the concerns of their partisan colleagues when preparing for the floor.

A senior Rules Committee aide offers a similar account of his work with the people most in the know about initiatives—the committee leaders and staff:

> We are an arm of the leadership and work very closely with the committees that bring bills to us, as well as the leadership, to fashion fair rules and try to be as open as possible. We ask the Republican members of the [Rules] committee to let us know in advance where they might want to take a leading role, not just in handling the rule when it gets on our doorstep, but prior to that. . . . We hear from committee leaders and staff; they educate us. That helps us a great deal.

The two management approaches of unified staffing and advanced planning are intended to help leaders guard against unnecessary splits within the conference that result from misinformation and ignorance. The leaders rely on more customary channels of troubleshooting as well. Here they list the conference, whip meetings, strategy sessions between party leaders and committee people, leadership staff outreach to policy staff, and ad hoc meetings to air concerns and settle disputes.

By all accounts, this level of coordination and advanced planning best depicts Republican governance on major party initiatives in the 104th Congress. After their success at the polls in 1996, the Republicans reshuffled responsibilities and granted more power to committee chairs. As several staffers see it, however, committees must prove themselves worthy of increased autonomy. "They will have to take responsibility for the functions they usually get from us—communications, coalitions, and internal whipping of their bills in [the Republican] conference. They're going to have to become self-reliant in marketing their bills. In turn, we will let them alone more."

The current practice, while returning power to committees, remains more centralized than it used to be (Deering and Smith 1997; Owens 1997). As one aide to Minority Leader Richard Gephardt explains, it took a shock to the system on a scale of the partisan transfer of control to loosen the grip of Democratic committee leaders:

> We were in the majority a long time. . . . Our leaders came up in a graduated manner; we never had the coups like Charlie Hallick and Gerald Ford in the Republican party. . . . It was difficult for the system of policy making to change much. And you get people coming in, like Jim Wright (TX: 12) and Tom Foley (WA: 5); Wright had been very, very, very connected, loyal to the Public Works Committee, and Foley had been the chairman of Agriculture. The idea that you would think of changing the system by which the chairmen would set the agenda was basically unheard of.

That Wright, and to a lesser degree Foley, made some gains in tilting power back to the Speaker and away from committee leaders is not in question (Peters 1996; Sinclair 1997). Compared with the power arrangements that now exist between committee and party leaders, however, the old advances seem modest. And most important of all, most Republican leaders demured to Gingrich (Evans and Oleszek 1997), whereas Dan Rostenkowski and leaders of his ilk fought back (Barry 1989).[3]

Therapeutic Management

Through numerous and regularized meetings that couple all combinations of players (leaders among themselves, leaders and committee chairs, leadership staffers with committee staffers, whip aides with legislative directors, and more), the current majority works to imbue in all members the idea that they are a team and not 228 individual members with highly distinct constituencies. This practice is not unique to the Republican party, but the emphasis on over-coming the incapacities of minority status is unusual.[4]

The teaching imposed on rank-and-file Republicans by their leaders is different in kind and intensity from that of the Democrats. According to Peters (1996), Gingrich used therapeutic means to help Republicans transcend the latent and debilitating effects of their experience in the minority.[5] Peters captures the dynamic in explaining congressional comity:

> In the legislative body, the minority party, accepting its status, adapts to its circumstances in a pragmatic effort to survive. . . . When fully assimilated to the existing power structure, the minority gets along with the majority. This is called comity in the House of Representatives, the Stockholm Syndrome when it occurs among captives of terrorists. (25)

Connelly and Pitney (1994) remark on Gingrich's early success with making believers out of his doubting colleagues; 40 years of minority status notwithstanding, he convinced them in 1994 that they too could be a majority. Through retreats, role playing, and other so-called New Age approaches to cope with change, the conference took on the task of learning how to be a majority. What is more, the members report wanting to be a different kind of majority.

John Boehner, chairman of the Republican Conference, explains how he sees the cultural change his party seeks:

> We're trying to get chairmen to understand that their job isn't to put a bill out there that meets the chairman's prerogative alone. I watched Dan Rostenkowski and [Jack] Brooks, and [Henry] Gonzales, a whole slew of them, the old bulls. I mean, they had their proposals and they'd ramrod them through their committees, and then they'd ramrod them through the floor. It was a short-circuiting of American Democracy. What we are trying to do now is get our chairmen to understand that they're there through the courtesy and on behalf of the Republican conference, to do what is in the interest of the conference, not what is in the interest of that particular member. That's it; we're in the midst of a culture change.

The passage expresses a theme that is fairly universal in the conference. And although the lessons come hard to some chairmen, such as Bud Shuster (House Committee on Transportation), Republicans up and down the line boast of the openness and accountability their majority has brought to the chamber.

These management techniques were reportedly put into place to help leaders (1) stay in touch with one another and with the rank and file, (2) hear and fine-tune messages that resonate well with constituents, and (3) guard against unnecessary splits from within the conference. The novelty of team management, advanced planning, and therapeutic management is undisputed. Where Republicans reportedly veer little from their predecessors is in their use of four well-accepted coalition-building strategies. The distinction I hear from Republicans, and one rarely discussed by academics and pundits, is the leaders' preference for early, normative approaches of influence over utilitarian and coercive ones. The evidence for the argument follows.

Barbara Sinclair (1983, 1997) identifies four techniques that leaders use in building support for party-backed initiatives: the strategy of inclusion, service to members, structuring choice, and, most recently, outreach to the media and interest group allies. The strategies resemble the influence approaches Etzioni (1968) discussed three decades ago. In his configuration, there are three types of power: coercive, utilitarian, and normative. Each approach requires different amounts of time to take hold, and each exhibits different staying power. Coercive approaches such as structuring choice have a quick response time but do not last long. Furthermore, they can create resentments, which can hurt leaders in the future. Normative approaches such as the strategy of inclusion change individuals' understanding of events. When leaders get members to vote correctly because they have common understandings, there is little fear of future belligerence. Utilitarian methods involve the use of quid pro quos. Compliance from such targeted service is faster acting and less enduring than normative approaches. What follows is a comparison of the way the parties use each of these strategies, starting with the most coercive first.

Structuring Choice

For some time, the Democrats managed uncertainties on the House floor by keeping a tight rein on two features of the decision process—the number of amendments introduced for debate and the terms of voting. Although they gained initial ground in opening up the amendment process, Republicans did not meet the standard they set for themselves. The percentage of open and modified open rules reportedly rose from 44 in the 103rd Congress to 58 in the 104th Congress. The new figure stands at 54 percent.[6] The pattern in amendment activity corresponds, as well, to the party's fits and halts over debating rules. In the 104th Congress, amendment activity reached a high for the research period; major initiatives averaged 10.9 amendments. In the 103rd Congress, major initiatives attracted 8.25 amendments, on average. In the current Congress, the figure is 9.27. Time will tell the extent to which the new majority maintains and intensifies its commitment to procedural openness.

The new leaders' record of openness on voting procedures is straightforward. The old rule, known as the king of the hill, allowed for a series of votes. However, only the last option to gain a majority would win, and by design that would be the party's preference. Under the new rule, the option with the largest majority wins, regardless of its place in the decision cue. Rules Committee Republicans call their rule "most votes wins." But it is more popularly identified as the queen of the prom or queen of the hill rule.

Although there is no evidence as of yet that the party has lost a major policy fight as a result of this relaxation of agenda control, Republicans forfeit two benefits the Democrats previously enjoyed. Under the old system, Democrats could vote twice—once for constituents and once for the party. On tough votes, the new rule deprives majority members of the same political cover; Republicans must sometimes choose between their constituents and the party. The situation has its costs. Vulnerable members who go unprotected on the floor can lose their reelection bids, and the party narrows its seat advantage. There is an immediate drawback for the leaders as well, who must go head to head for votes with renegade committee leaders.

This explanation is consistent with events in May 1997 when Bud Shuster refused to back off from his bid for more transportation funds. And although party leaders admit the incident caused them serious heartburn, no one talks of returning to the old procedure.

Service to Members

Case studies about power politics on Capitol Hill are replete with stories about wily leaders—party officials as well as committee chairs—who secure votes for controversial initiatives by doling out a project here and a campaign donation there (Birnbaum and Murray 1988; Evans 1994; Straham 1990). Special projects (disparagingly called pork), valued seat assignments, convenient floor scheduling, and information are all staples of party governance.

Boehner sees little evidence of "dishing out perks to members. Maybe once or twice, I've seen a conversation like that. The biggest perk we give someone is a promise to hold a vote." When questioned directly about the value he places on the informational materials his staff produces from the Republican Conference, Boehner continues:

> It's a function of the leadership to make sure the members know what we are doing. It's for the greater good. We get nothing back for that, other than grief when there's a comma out of place. . . . I don't think our members want us to do that [perks]. I don't think the leaders want to do that. This is part of the modern Republican party. They're much more idealistic, much more driven about how to change the system to meet the goals we set for ourselves in terms of more freedom, more accountability on the part of government, and that's what drives us for the last few years.

Republicans downplay the effectiveness of service as a means of building consensus, and when they acknowledge granting favors to interested members, a somewhat different mix of inducements comes through. Armey's chief of staff, Kerry Knott, explains the reordering of priorities he sees:

> We try to help vulnerable members in several ways. We help them get their bills on the suspension calendar; there's a lot of that. We get them some help via appropriations—old style pork. But most people aren't asking for that. They want credit for doing something positive. [Randy] Tate (WA: 9) wanted to get the credit for ending pensions for convicted felons. We tried to give some members prominent assignments on Ways and Means, Appropriations, etc. Every conference [House-Senate] had a freshman or vulnerable member on it. Gingrich and Armey travel actively to support members.

Study participants confirm another benefit that leaders selectively confer on rank-and-file Republicans. Articulate representatives such as J. C. Watts (OK: 4), Sue Myrick (NC: 9) , and J. D. Hayworth (AZ: 6) attribute much of their early media exposure to leaders' willingness to share the limelight. Staffers out of the Speaker's office and the conference would routinely encourage reporters and television hosts to include particular members in their stories and programming. Leaders assisted junior colleagues in this way, but both parties to the trade realized immediate benefits from the arrangement (apart from extracting a correct vote), a symmetry not typical of old-style utilitarian approaches to influence.

Strategy of Inclusion

Many rank-and-file Republicans speak about the importance of their shared philosophy toward government. Whether accurate or not, these members believe that their ideology, and not intimidation and buy-offs from party leaders, is what most accounts for consensus on the House floor. The perspective squares well with a point made by the Speaker in his book *Lessons Learned the Hard Way* (Gingrich 1998, 54):

> Those members of the House who had switched from the Democratic Caucus to the Republican Conference . . . kept remarking how surprising they found the lack of intimidation and groupthink in the Republican Conference. They were not used to it. But the Republican Party does after all tend to recruit individualistic entrepreneur types, and we pride ourselves precisely on being a conference rather than a caucus.

Rank-and-file Republicans use different words to convey the same meaning, but over and over again they speak of themselves as individualists and free thinkers. They take pride in "not wanting to control everything" and leave winning on the floor to "our shared philosophies for a smaller government and a balanced budget." When members disagree with the leadership, as they sometimes do, there is a mutual understanding. "You tell them [the leaders] ahead. And they say, 'take a walk.' "

Accounts of leaders applying heavy pressure are rare. This then-freshman's recollection of the pressure he received before a June 12 vote regarding the government shutdown is typical:

> Newt was really good at laying down the facts and telling you the choices. Nobody ever says, "you won't get your committee assignment," or "you won't get this or that." It was more getting people to see clearly what the choices would be.

By and large, leaders appeal to members' understanding of what a loss on the House floor will mean to the party. Far in advance of the vote, however, the leaders use numerous opportunities to give members a voice at the negotiating table.

The leaders meet with all combinations of members and staff. Indeed, there are so many different groupings of people who get together to discuss the issues, the long-term strategy, the short-term tactics, the communications spin, the lobbying angle, that any attempt to catalogue them would fall short. Instead, I focus on two examples of the strategy. The first—Gingrich-led task forces—occurs in the very preliminary stages of the legislative cycle. The second—Armey-style unity dinners—occurs further along in the process after factional differences have emerged within the party.

When Speaker, Newt Gingrich raised building consensus through task forces to an art form. Compared with their earlier counterparts, these working groups were more numerous, more dominated by the Speaker, and more widespread. The exact number of task forces is not known. By all accounts, there were too many to calculate. What is more, Gingrich or a loyal lieutenant was on the scene, in every case keeping a watchful eye. On occasion, even lobbyists participated. The Speaker so trusted the approach that he used task forces in his district and encouraged his colleagues to do the same. The idea, reportedly, was to bring in the best talent, cross-fertilize ideas, and produce initiatives that would win on the House floor.

As in the past, the technique provided a way for the Speaker to build support for his, and his party's, vision of good policy. Participants recall feeling a sense of ownership over the product they fashioned and expressed pride over being asked by the Speaker to get involved. Also, with committee members and staff outnumbered, task forces energized dispirited committees and overstepped rebellious ones.[7]

The second example of the strategy is Majority Leader Dick Armey's creation of unity dinners. I include this example not as evidence that Democratic leaders did not engage in such practices but rather to reveal a side of the majority leader that is seldom provided in the popular press. According to an aide who attended the meetings:

> My boss hosts weekly or biweekly *unity dinners* for members to listen to one another. The endangered species bill [is an example]. [Sherwood] Boehlert (NY: 23) (NC: 9) would present the green side of the equation, and Richard Pombo (CA: 11) would give the ranchers' side of the equation. They'd listen to each other, and the idea was to come up with something better.

Others in the room attest to the value of the meetings:

> I am incredibly impressed with the job Dick Armey did. He was in charge of the day to day management in the House. His job was to put out the fires. . . . There was a cluster of members, my boss included, who would say "no way we can do it." How the heck do you bridge them? . . . He (Armey) has a wonderful ability to bring people together.

Republicans place a lot of trust in normative approaches to coalition building. These approaches extend outward and include strategies with the media and private-sector allies.

Outreach to Grassroots Organizations and the Media

The purpose behind outreach is twofold and no doubt unchanged from previous years. Party leaders want to advance their agendas, and they want credit for the policy successes they achieve. Only when citizens perceive that it was Republicans in Congress and not the president, for example, who brought us welfare reform, will the Republican party benefit at the polls. Policy and politics are in this way inextricably connected, and it is the job of the parties' communications staff to ensure that their members look successful in the eyes of the public.

Two intermediaries help leaders convey the messages parties want believed. Lobbyists interpret Washington activities to a narrow but important set of attentive citizens—the activists most inclined to pressure their representatives and to vote on election day. The media interprets the same events, and more, to a broad cross section of citizens—a potent, albeit latent, force in American politics.

As compared with their Democratic predecessors, the new leaders introduced three changes in outreach. They formalized and made routine what had been an ad hoc coalition operation under Democratic rule. They blended interest group and media outreach by using mass media and micromedia channels of communication. And they brought into the inner sanctums of Capitol Hill a new type of advocate—antitax, profamily, and probusiness conservatives. These organizations replaced the pro-choice, proenvironment, union allies of the Democrats (Leiter 1995; Maraniss and Weisskopf 1995).

Formalizing Partnerships

During this period, every Thursday morning that the House was in session Conference Chairman John Boehner met with a dozen or so conservative lobbyists to hear how the week's activities in Washington were being received and understood by attentive citizens throughout the country. The specifics of the meetings varied with the legislative calendar, the strength of consensus within the Republican Conference, and the force of the opposition. During the Contract period, the agenda was clear, the battle lines were drawn, and commitment was strong. Everybody knew their marching orders; the lobbyists would come and report on their accomplishments over the preceding week. Typically these efforts involved masterminding the efforts and resources of an additional 50 to 500 organizations. The strategy included mobilizing their grassroots armies, mounting broad-based communications appeals, and lobbying needed officeholders one-on-one. In slow legislative periods, by contrast, group members learned what they could of unfolding events without the filter of the media. When the conservative activists feared the Republicans were compromising away too many of their principles, Boehner would explain the predicament as the leaders saw it and ask for patience. The exchange of information helped leaders monitor and respond to the restiveness of their organizational allies, sometimes winning the wiggle room that the legislators needed to work out an acceptable solution.

The Thursday Group has no direct parallel in the Democratic party's leadership apparatus. Democrats describe benefiting from their coalition partners in much the same way that Republicans do. However, they meet with allies on an ad hoc basis and reportedly leave more initiative to the lobbyists and the leadership staff.

Blending Targets

Anyone can garble the party's preferred interpretation of events. Leaders compete for news and themselves muddy the waters. Rank-and-file members lose sight of their own party's accomplishments and botch the job. Members and allies from the wings of the party openly complain about negotiated solutions and missed opportunities. These are internal sources of strife. Add as well the external challenges the leaders face—the popular and highly public president, Bill Clinton, his loyal and expert communications team, an energized and united House minority, and a corps of reporters who, although guided by professional standards of fairness, overwhelmingly vote Democrat.

According to journalists Cokie and Steve Roberts (1995, 11A), Gingrich believed "that the Washington based media are dominated by liberal elitists who will always sabotage the conservative cause if given half a chance." To avoid giving them the chance, he had for decades championed alternative methods of conveying the party's message, including newsletters, faxes, computers, and church bulletins. And this, not policy innovation, is Gingrich's true contribution. In their words, "He has been a major force in changing the way Americans learn about politics. . . . Communicate directly to the voters through a combination of new technologies—like cable TV and computers—and old ones put to new uses, like talk radio and direct mail."

Indeed, Republicans did not immediately know the full extent of their communications troubles. As a Gingrich aide recalled, "I knew there was bias. I expected it to affect the choice of story or the number of stories—that our version would be outnumbered. I never expected that the bias would include factual inaccuracies."

Staffers also expected more communications savvy from their own members, as this senior aide explains:

Most members, including members in the leadership, have no clue what communications means. To them, communications means you walk down on the triangle, and you give a press conference. Who does that touch? Nobody. It feeds the Washington beast; that's about it. They don't think of communications as being a six to eight month campaign to get a message out. They just don't think that way. Yet the most successful way to get our message out is when members carry it. When Frank Cremeans goes home and has a press conference on the telecommunications bill and explains how it's a job creator, a benefit to medicine and computerization in rural schools, that's a message that resonates. He carries it, local media cover it. It's unfiltered, and it's relating what we're doing to people's real lives.

Reportedly, too few members appreciate the value of district outreach and simple repetition.

To minimize obstruction from whatever the perceived source, press aides from various leadership offices (ComStrat) meet regularly and conference daily on the telephone. Their task, according to one Gingrich aide, was to monitor the news, fine-tune the party line, take stock of their resources (members, allies, and money), match requests for authoritative sources with articulate and knowledgeable spokespeople, and guard resources by carefully weighing how much effort to place in countering this or that negative attack.

From the start, the party blended mainstream news outlets, which reach the largest audience but over which they have the least control, with micromedia outlets, which reach narrow audiences but over which they have a modicum of control. The decision to make trusted interest groups full partners in the public relations wars over policy making was an easy transition. For decades, Republicans relied on grassroots armies to accomplish some of the campaign-related tasks that Democrats could buy with political action committee (PAC) dollars (Drew 1997). With Republicans in power, as they tell it, lobbyists from profamily, antitax, and small business organizations were working to "accomplish something positive." In the past, they had been "on the outside looking in, throwing sand in the gears" to stop legislation they disliked.

The change was exhilarating for the leaders and the lobbyists alike. The Christian Coalition, with its 1.8 million members and 12 chapters, for example, reaches a sizable audience that can put needed pressure on members of Congress (direct lobbying) as well as place timely editorials in local papers to counter negative accounts of the party's activities and accomplishments. The U.S. Chamber of Commerce is another example of a federated organization that has a "multiplier effect." Its 860,000 member executives reach many additional people. They produce a magazine *(Nation's Business)*, host debates, run morning news shows that reach 105 markets. They carry the business message to a large audience. According to Bruce Josten, "In February 1995, we hosted a town hall briefing. With 4,300 down-links, we reached numbers that would fill RFK stadium."

Beyond the leaders' formal attempts at managing the micromedia through the Thursday Group and its official offsprings (e.g., Coalition for America's Future and Coalition to Save Medicare) are other large and small liaisons working independently of but in close contact with the Republican leadership. The largest of these is the Leave Us Alone Coalition, established and chaired by Grover Norquist of Americans for Tax Reform, himself a member of the Thursday Group. Every Wednesday this group of 70 or so lobbyists meets to further their shared interests in reducing the size and cost of government. Norquist runs a fast-paced meeting with a positive message and never loses or lets his audience lose sight of the real challenge—maintaining control of the House. After hours, he is still at work, opening his Capitol Hill home to fundraisers, book signings, and party socials. He is a confidant and friend of Newt Gingrich and meets and travels with him on a regular basis. What Norquist does for the antitax community, Brian Lopina does on a smaller scale for the profamily groups. As Lopina put it, the Christian Coalition, Family Research Council, Concerned Women for America, Eagle Forum, and Traditional Values

Coalition "meet every week to plot strategies, brainstorm, and parcel out the work."

In addition to these subterranean outlets for getting out their message and mobilizing support, conference staff provide their own members numerous missives to help rank-and-file party members stay on message. In particular, the conference relies on recess breaks as a valuable time for members to go home armed with simple, catchy, usually three-word phrases that capture the party's agenda and recent accomplishments.[8]

According to Barry Jackson, staff director to the Republican Conference, the approach occasionally succeeds in overcoming distortions from the New York–based media. "We moved into Medicare June through August with the message *preserve, protect, and strengthen.* We stayed on it and were relatively successful. . . . We can get around the New York media bias. We've done it. It's hard. It takes commitment, but it can be done."

More often than not, and for different reasons, the Democrats reportedly controlled the media spin. Initially, the pace of the Contract created problems. Audiences could not keep track of events. According to one Gingrich aide, "The Democrats defined the Contract in negative terms, and it stuck, in part, because we didn't celebrate our victories along the way. Too much was happening at once." A conference staffer recalls a later period, during the flurry of activity before the 1996 elections. This time, the representatives were not keeping track. "So much was occurring so fast that if you asked anyone [Republican House members] but Armey what the party had accomplished, they couldn't tell you."

Of all the functions in which the party leaders engage, effective communications is reportedly the most elusive. It is the one leadership activity around which there exists much self-criticism and "only ifs." This statement from a senior conference staffer makes the point: "If you look at everything that we got signed into law, it's huge. But the communications element, letting people know about it, take credit for it, that has not come together."

Accounting for Changes in Governing Styles

There are many continuities in House governance. Too many conditions persist in the founders' blueprint for bicameralism to expect otherwise. The electoral connection is alive and well. Representatives get on committees, gain valuable expertise and exposure, and do what they can to succeed in Washington and take credit for it at home with their voters. The arrangement breeds a keen sense of individualism.

Over the years, party leaders have learned to build support for controversial initiatives by appealing to members' interests, one representative at a time. Republicans operate under this same constraint. The leaders must look into the hearts and minds of their rank and file and figure out what makes them tick. What argument here? What inducement there? The process is the same. Still, there is more difference to consider than is generally acknowledged. Although the new leaders describe using the same combination of power tactics that their predecessors did, they report relying more heavily on early, normative methods of influence over the utilitarian and coercive approaches that Democrats applied to great effect. The change, according to Brian Bilbray, John Boehner, and others quoted thus far, comes down to philosophical differences between the parties. There are two. One pertains to good government—a policy goal about the proper role and size of government. The other pertains to good governing—a process goal about freedom of expression and the opportunity for dissent. In what remains of this essay, I reflect on the origins and implications of each perspective as it bears on our understanding of congressional behavior.

Good Government

Republicans and Democrats see government differently. For the most part, Republicans prefer that individuals and the private sector solve social problems; they accept government intervention in special cases. Democrats, by and large, trust government solutions over market ones; they believe it is the only way to ensure fairness and equity across states with disparate economic and political circumstances. James V. Hansen (R-UT: 1) explains the difference he sees between what the two parties stand for:

> A couple of philosophies prevail around here. . . . The Democrat party is more the party of big government. . . . We believe people should work for what they get. People should pay their taxes, be good Americans, and serve their country. . . . When somebody comes up to me and says, "What can you do for me?" I always say "Nothing. I hope I can create a climate where you can get a good education. I hope I can create a climate where your entrepreneurial spirit can come out. You can turn it into something. But what can I do for you? The answer is zero.". . . And our responsibility is to sell our philosophy to the American people.

Individuals with this vision of good public policy reject some if not all of the spending that sidesteps formal authorization. The names of a dozen or so conservatives come up repeatedly for their adherence to principle over pragmatism. On the recent transportation bill (HR 2400), 54 Republicans (and 26 Democrats) voted against what was widely criticized for containing $9 billion in old-style pork (Ota 1998).

To be sure, there are dissenters from this purist, proreform mentality, and they line up for the goodies that appropriators can supply. According to a senior staffer to Majority Whip Tom DeLay, however, members and staff who assist with the whip operation must think twice about who they approach with federal programs.

A senior aide who works out of the majority leader's office describes the view that dominates: "Democrats held their coalition together by giving out all the goodies. . . . That is just raw power. . . . Money and pork was the mortar of their coalition. We can't afford that. The mortar of our coalition is ideology and principle." Even when a tiny number of Republicans can hold the rest of the party hostage, there is a wholesale distaste for manipulating successes through pork and procedures. The fiscal conservatives within the party, and there are many, justify policy and votes in terms of their effect on the budget. Members limit what they ask for, and leaders limit what they offer, all based on strong principles about cost. Each avoids the chagrin of the other because the participants in the negotiations generally value the same things. The Democratic perspective is different. For members and leaders who value government programs and serve constituents who expect more not less from their representatives in Washington, there are only costs associated with not requesting and not granting special authorizations. As a former aide to the minority leader sees it, "If the Democrats were now in the majority and you needed to do some projects to get the votes, you'd do it. The bottom line is to perform and be successful. You need to give people some stuff to get things done." Winning justifies the spending.

The parties value projects differently. And to the degree that fiscal conservatives continue to run under the Republican party label, the leaders must limit utilitarian methods of coalition building that tap the federal treasury. They continue to use selective incentives to win compliance but work to do so without compromising the budget.

Good Governing

The second distinction that nearly every Republican boasts about is the party's preference for free and open debate. All the top leaders are on record for wanting to change the culture of governing in Washington (Gimpel 1996; Gingrich 1998; Maraniss and Weisskopf 1995). These veteran members often blend their appeals for reform with criticisms toward the Democrats' old methods of management. Younger Republicans, with little or no experience in the minority, are more philosophical. They explain the leaders' tolerance toward renegade behavior in terms of freedom and fairness.

Two junior Republicans explain the philosophical distinction they see between the two parties, a view Democratic leaders would no doubt challenge. According to J. C. Watts, "Democrats operate from the top down and Republicans operate from the bottom up. Republicans do not like the leadership telling them how they should vote, or how they should act, or what they should be telling their constituents." Sue Myrick concurs: "You find there is no walking in lock step in the Republican Party the way there is in the Democrat Party. . . . We just have a different outlook. I guess the main difference is we are not trying to control everything."

Two additional comments illustrate the leadership's reported reluctance to discipline the rank and file. Each respondent claims to have witnessed the methods employed by the former majority. The first, offered by Brian Bilbray, follows his recollection of a time he bucked the leaders on a vote of major interest to his constituents. "I need to emphasize my surprise that this is not the hardball game that my cousin [a Democrat] and some of my Democratic friends said it was." Michael Oxley echoes the sentiment:

> Our side, in all honesty, has never used the kind of heavy handedness that the Democrats used over the years. I mean I was an eye witness to a lot of real arm twisting, heavy, heavy stuff under Jim Wright and Tip O'Neill. . . . There is nothing wrong in it, that was their style. They would say, "We need x number of votes, and now we're going to go out and get them. And what's this guy's hot button and that guy's weak point?" And that's what they'd go after. We're not anywhere near that in terms of being heavy-handed.

He goes on to make a point made by many veteran Republicans, who value freedom of expression, even as it extends to their adversaries on the other side of the aisle. In his view losing is an acceptable outcome if democracy is to flourish.

> These debates over rules are silly. Why don't you just use an open rule. If you want to offer the amendment, offer the amendment. If you win fine; if you lose you got your chance to offer the amendment. Sometimes we get too tied up in egos and personalities and just having to win everything. We lose sight of the fact that this is participatory democracy. And if you've got an amendment that's a good idea, you ought to be able to offer it. You know you can't be afraid to lose around here. Too many people are afraid to lose.

With the exception of most committee chairs, who want to protect their initiatives from destabilizing amendments on the floor, Republicans of all ideological stripes and seniority express their preference for openness on the floor. They strenuously object to limiting debate and manipulating votes. That the party invests so heavily in publicizing its views and educating constituents about the issues well in advance of floor votes is consistent with this "may the best bill win" mentality.

Intermingled with the party leaders' defense of opening floor debates are recollections of the bad old days in the minority. The juxtaposition suggests that something other than political ideology is involved in the Republicans' push for reforms. Their universal abhorrence for the king of the hill rule, in particular, fits with Fenno's (1986) theory about the relevance of sequencing events and Edelman's (1985) theory about the symbolic nature of politics.

Both perspectives stress the importance of history, timing, and experience. Fenno admonishes scholars to observe members of Congress in their own worlds, so what is important to them becomes important to us. The distinction is voiced again and again, as the following two comments illustrate. The first is a senior staffer to Minority Leader Richard Gephardt: "In some ways, they [Republicans] have not adapted to the majority role. They hated the king of the hill and won't use it, regardless of whether it's better for them or not. . . . They rob themselves of some extraordinarily useful tools." John Boehner provides the typical Republican response: "Getting rid of the king of the hill was probably the best thing we did for the health of the institution and the legitimacy of the legislative process in the House."

The difference expressed in these sentiments affirms Edelman's point about the symbolic content of political events and activities. Democrats view restrictive rules as an effective way of doing business. The rules themselves evoke positive images such as power and success. Members of the minority party who suffered under these rules, by contrast, attach negative meanings to them. They acknowledge the theoretical benefits of structuring choice on the House floor but dismiss the method as unfair and undemocratic.

Ronald Peters (1996) attaches more to the party's experience as a minority than to the Republicans' aversion to manipulating debates. In his view, the subservient position eventually gave way to a new set of norms that are peculiarly Republican. Individualism and the "all politics is local" mentality worked well for the party in power, not one in the minority.

Democratic speakers rose to power *within* the Democratic power structure; their path to power was to play the internal game that the Democratic regime produced (Polsby 1961 and Peabody 1975). . . . Gingrich had no path to power within the Democratic House, precisely because to work within the GOP hierarchy entailed accepting the premises of the existing order. Thus, Gingrich decided early on that his best strategy lay in fostering ideas, building ad hoc coalitions, and remolding the culture of the Republican conference.

When Republicans reject old ways of doing business, they are rejecting the Democratic culture they grew to disdain. In its place, they espouse the language of ideas, cohesion built on principle, teamwork, and outreach. Given that so many Republicans associate their 1994 victory and subsequent transition to power with these ingredients, it is no wonder that they tend to depict their style of governance and leadership in these terms and distance themselves from their predecessors.

Summary and Speculation

The recent change in party control of the House provides scholars a wonderful opportunity for reevaluating some aspects about congressional behavior. Here I focus on the consequences a change in individual preferences holds for coalition builders in the House. The two preferences that Republicans say distinguish them from Democrats are their tastes for fiscal restraint and procedural fairness. Corresponding to this reported shift in individual preferences are several new or altered approaches to governance. Republicans introduced several corporate-style management practices, including advanced strategic planning and unified team management. Coalition-building strategies also varied. Now there is reportedly less reliance on coercion (restrictive floor rules) and old-style retail politics (service to members) and more reliance on early, indirect, wholesale politics (district, grassroots, and media outreach).

Whether a coincidence or by design, Republican House governance deviates in some material ways from the familiar Democratic model. What is noteworthy is that none of the slow-acting, normative methods of influencing members and their constituents jeopardizes conservative and populist principles.

Because the Republicans are inexperienced in the majority and their inexperience coincides with a professed shift in individual preferences, we cannot verify the causal chain of events. We can test for other relationships and work at the puzzle more indirectly. In the following, I list three theoretical tenets of congressional behavior, interpret the evidence that corresponds to each, and posit a few testable propositions for further consideration.

Theory I. Alter individuals' goals and you alter behavioral outcomes (Fenno 1973; Kingdon 1989; Mayhew 1974). Republicans report that their preferences for fiscal restraint and individual liberty give rise to changes in the mix of strategies they use to build support for floor votes. There are some nettlesome problems in testing the veracity of this claim. There is no way of knowing which tactics influence which people. Nor can we determine the degree to which the new leaders have altered the overall bundle of coalition-building strategies. What we can do is systematically test the degree to which fiscal conservatives tend to defect relative to others. And we can observe evidence of fiscally neutral perks that leaders dole out and determine whether conservatives get more of these perks than nonconservatives.

Next, Republicans report operating with a "good governing" goal. As preposterous as it sounds, several members, even in leadership posts, say they value procedural fairness more than they value winning on the floor. And although they do not achieve the openness they promised at the outset of the 104th Congress, more amendments are being offered and more bills are winning by the numbers (most votes wins). The preliminary evidence suggests some testable hypotheses. Whatever the arena for investigative attention (committees or the floor), we should find evidence of more, not less, minority party involvement. Amendment activity should be more bipartisan than in the past. The duration of floor debates should increase under Republican control. These results, although conceivably the result of multiple causes, are at least consistent with the new leaders' claim that they hold different preferences on this matter than did their predecessors.

Theory II. Leaders both influence, and are influenced by, the political contexts in which they operate (Aldrich and Rohde 1997; Fenno 1986; Jones 1970). Work is well under way on two aspects of political context. Aldrich and Rohde (1995, 1997) explore conditional party government, Republican style. Evans and Oleszek (1997) connect several recent Republican congressional reforms to features external to the institution, including public opinion, organized interest groups, and the media. Peters (1996) makes a provocative argument for the connection between Republicans' current leadership style and their longtime status in the minority—the historical context. This view is consistent with Edelman's (1985) interpretation of political symbols. Republicans devalue aspects of structuring choice because they see before them only an unfair method of silencing dissent, not an agenda-setting tool to be exploited for their use.

A new line of work could focus on the parties' use of micromedia. Republicans more than Democrats report that their messages get distorted by the mass media. (Reportedly, they find electronic media worse than print media and New York outlets worse than Washington outlets.) Although both parties cleverly engage in strategies to control the spin on their activities and accomplishments, a comparative study of trade, union, and citizen group publications should reveal a disproportionately high level of Republican-inspired themes and messages.

Theory III. Politics and policy are inextricably entwined (Fenno 1991; Kingdon 1989). On this matter there is probably more continuity than change. The leaders of both parties look for issues that will help them in the next election. And both parties experience a mixed record of success. By the accounts given here, however, Republicans may face more severe challenges than their counterparts in accomplishing the leadership goal of party building (Smith 1993). Scholars could test for the implications of the parties' differential embrace of term limits. A second avenue to pursue along these lines is a test of the electoral consequences of voting rules on the House floor. We would expect more Republicans than Democrats to receive challenges that turn, at least in part, on a so-called bad vote, because their leaders provide less political cover than the Democrats were accustomed to providing.

Admittedly, this collection of propositions presents a piecemeal approach to the study of leadership. In its defense, House governance touches on an eclectic array of subfields including interest groups, the media, elections, and mass opinion.

APPENDIX

Comparison of the Study Participants Along Selected Characteristics (in percentages)

Characteristics	Republicans in House (n = 235)	Republicans in Sample[a] (n = 59)	Republicans Responding in the Study[b] (n = 41)
Median American			
Conservative Union	39.1	35.0	31.7
Men	92.7	91.5	92.7
Freshmen	30.2	36.7	39.0
Region			
Northeast	16.7	16.9	17.1
Southeast	27.8	30.5	31.7
South	10.3	11.9	7.3
Midwest	25.2	20.3	22.0
West	17.5	16.9	17.1
Northwest	2.6	3.4	4.9

Source: Barone and Ujifusa 1995.

[a]Sample is used in the analysis of Nexis and Vanderbilt Archives mentions.

[b]Sample is used in the analysis of conference materials and approaches to district visits.

NOTES

I would like to express my deep appreciation to Richard F. Fenno Jr., the conference participants, Joe Soss, and Don Wolfensberger for their criticism and encouragement. On behalf of all students of Congress, I thank the many named and unnamed representatives, staff members, and lobbyists who generously participated in this inquiry.

1. For 1 year (May 1996 through May 1997) I sat in on so-called Thursday Group meetings in which Conference Chair John Boehner met weekly with supportive lobbyists to communicate party priorities, mount grassroots support for the upcoming

agenda, and flesh out ideas for new, more distant initiatives. To witness the dynamics of the Republican leaders in session among themselves, Majority Whip Tom DeLay (TX: 22) allowed me to sit in on a meeting of his full whip team the day they discussed a strategy for responding to the president's veto of the flood relief bill (HR 1469).

2. Republicans continue to reshuffle the roles and responsibilities of party leaders vis-à-vis one another, committee leaders, and the conference. In the early days of the 104th Congress, the Contract was itself the management tool of the party. Ranking members divvied up tasks and instituted special working groups tailor-made for the times. The Speakers Advisory Group included a small number of individuals with the perspective and authority to represent various power centers within the institution. Even the Senate had a spokesman, so the chambers were aware of each other's progress. Members and their most senior staff had worked closely together for years, shared in the exuberance of their victory, and trusted one another to work as a team.

3. As recently as March 1998, well into the 105th Congress, Appropriations Committee Chairman Bob Livingston deferred, albeit grudgingly, to party leaders over adhering to budget limits.

4. According to a leadership aide to Minority Leader Richard Gephardt, the transition from majority to minority status accounts for several changes in the Democrats' management style. This is the subject of a different article.

5. Gingrich "believed that the Republican party must develop new approaches to conflict resolution precisely because it is different than the Democratic party and the Republican regime cannot rely on mechanisms the Democrats put into place" (Peters 1996).

6. These figures were provided by Bill Crosby, House Rules Committee chief council, April 15, 1998.

7. Maraniss and Weisskopf (1996, 50) connect Shuster's conversion on a 1996 budget vote to Gingrich's decision to form the Task Force on Transportation.

8. The missives range from objective fact to partisan propaganda and include "the message of the day," "talking points," "fact sheets," "suggested member activities," and a "weekend boarding pass" (a pocket-size list of recent party accomplishments).

REFERENCES

Aldrich, John H., and David Rohde. 1995. "Theories of the Party in the Legislature and the Transition to Republican Rule in the House." Working paper series of Political Institutions and Public Choice, #95-05.
Aldrich, John H., and David Rohde. 1997. "The Transition to Republican Rule in the House: Implications for Theories of Congressional Politics." *Political Science Quarterly* 112 (4): 541–67.
Barone, Michael, and Grant Ujifusa. 1995. *The Almanac of American Politics, 1996.* Washington, D.C.: National Journal.
Barry, John. 1989. *The Power and the Ambition.* New York: Vintage Books.
Birnbaum, Jeffrey, and Alan Murray. 1988. *Showdown at Gucci Gulch.* New York: Vintage Books.

Cloud, David S. 1995. "GOP, to Its Own Great Delight, Enacts House Rules Changes." *Congressional Quarterly Weekly Report,* January 2: 13–14.

Connelly, William F., Jr., and John J. Pitney Jr. 1994. *Congress' Permanent Minority? Republicans in the U.S. House.* Lanham, Md.: Rowman & Littlefield.

Deering, Christopher J., and Steven S. Smith. 1997. *Committees in Congress.* 4th ed. Washington, D.C.: Congressional Quarterly Press.

Drew, Elizabeth. 1997. *Whatever It Takes.* New York: Viking Press.

Edelman, Murray. 1985. *The Symbolic Uses of Politics.* 1967. Reprint, Chicago: University of Illinois Press.

Etzioni, Amitai. 1968. *The Active Society: A Theory of Societal and Political Processes.* New York: Free Press.

Evans, C. Lawrence, and Walter J. Oleszek. 1997. *Congress under Fire.* Boston: Houghton Mifflin.

Evans, Diana. 1994. "Policy and Pork: The Use of Pork Barrel Projects to Build Policy Coalitions in the House of Representatives." *American Journal of Political Science* 38: 894–917.

Fenno, Richard F., Jr. 1973. *Congressmen in Committees.* Boston: Little, Brown.

Fenno, Richard F., Jr. 1986. "Observation, Context, and Sequence in the Study of Politics." *American Political Science Review* 80: 3–16.

Fenno, Richard F., Jr. 1991. *The Emergence of a Senate Leader.* Washington, D.C.: Congressional Quarterly Press.

Fenno, Richard F., Jr. 1998. *Learning to Govern.* Washington, D.C.: Brookings Institution Press.

Gimpel, James G. 1996. *Fulfilling the Contract.* Boston: Allyn & Bacon.

Gingrich, Newt. 1998. *Lessons Learned the Hard Way.* New York: HarperCollins.

Jones, Charles. 1970. *The Minority Party in Congress.* Boston: Little, Brown.

Kingdon, John. 1989. *Congressmen's Voting Decisions.* 3d ed. Ann Arbor: University of Michigan Press.

Leiter, Lisa. 1995. "Interest Groups Enlist in Republican Revolution." *Washington Times,* May 25, 12.

Maraniss, David, and Michael Weisskopf. 1995. "Speaker and His Directors Make the Cash Flow Right." *Washington Post,* November 27: A01.

Maraniss, David, and Michael Weisskopf. 1996. *Tell Newt to Shut Up!* New York: Touchstone.

Mayhew, David. 1974. *Congress: the Electoral Connection.* New Haven: Yale University Press.

Ota, Alan K. 1998. "House Sets Up Battle with Senate in Passing 219 Billion Dollar Roads Bill." *Congressional Quarterly Weekly Report,* April 4: 882–88.

Owens, John. 1997. "The Return of Party Government to the U.S. House of Representatives: Central Leadership—Committee Relations in the 104th Congress." *British Journal of Political Science* 27: 247–72.

Peters, Ronald. 1996. "Newt Gingrich as Speaker in the 104th Congress." Paper presented at the annual meeting of the American Political Science Association, San Francisco, August 29–September 1, 1996.

Roberts, Cokie, and Steve V. Roberts. 1995. "The Real Conservative Revolution." *Baltimore Sun,* January 17, 11A.

Sinclair, Barbara. 1983. *Majority Leadership in the U.S. House.* Baltimore: Johns Hopkins University Press.

Sinclair, Barbara. 1995. *Legislators, Leaders, and Lawmaking.* Baltimore: Johns Hopkins University Press.

Sinclair, Barbara. 1997. "Transformational Leader or Faithful Agent? Innovation and Continuity in House Majority Party Leadership: The 104th and 105th Congresses." Paper presented at the annual meeting of the American Political Science Association, Washington, D.C., August 28–31, 1997.

Smith, Steven S. 1993. *The American Congress.* Boston: Houghton Mifflin.

Straham, Randall. 1990. *New Ways and Means: Reform and Change in a Congressional Committee.* Chapel Hill: University of North Carolina Press.

Towell, Pat. 1994. "GOPs Drive for More Open House Reflects Pragmatism and Resentment." *Congressional Quarterly Weekly Report,* November 19, 3320–21.

Republican House Majority Party Leadership in the 104th and 105th Congresses: Innovation and Continuity

Barbara Sinclair

Introduction

Newt Gingrich's phenomenal success in winning a Republican House majority in the 1994 elections and then steering the Contract with America and a balanced budget through the House had journalists and political commentators hailing him as a reincarnation of the legendary powerful Speakers of the past and a successful revolutionary leader besides—a combination of Czar Reed and Lenin.[1] Even political scientists began to question whether the discipline's prevalent conception of congressional leadership was adequate to explain the Gingrich leadership (Peters 1996; Stid 1996; Strahan 1996).

Most political scientists see congressional leaders as agents of their members; they are elected by their members and must satisfy members' expectations to get reelected (Cox and McCubbins 1993; Rohde 1991; Sinclair 1995). Those expectations are a function of members' goals and of the political and institutional context in which they attempt to advance their goals. Gingrich himself and many who have written about him see him as a fundamentally different sort of leader. He has been characterized—and has characterized himself—as a "transformational leader" whose aim is to transform how Americans think and talk about politics and thereby "transform the political alignments, institutions, and governing policies of the nation" (Blatz and Brownstein 1996, 144; Stid 1996, 1).

The change in the political context between the 104th and 105th Congresses provides something of a natural experiment. A comparison of party leadership in the 104th with leadership in the pre-104th period and in the 105th allows us to assess the adequacy of principal-agent theory for making sense of a quite complicated story and of what many see as an exceptional case.

In this essay, I assess continuity and change in the rate and type of House majority party leadership activity and in leadership strategies. If party leaders are agents of their members as posited, they will respond to changes in members' expectations. Do we, in fact, see a change in what leaders do consistent with the changes in members' expectations that, I contend, alterations in the political and institutional context brought about? As the discussion of members' expectations will demonstrate, meeting them is not straightforward. Members want legislative success, but they also want opportunities to participate fully in the legislative process. If leaders are agents, their strategies should take that into account. Are leadership strategies sensitive to this complexity? Compared with the Democratic leaderships of the late 1980s and early 1990s, does Gingrich's leadership in the 104th Congress show continuity or is it unique? To the extent that the Gingrich leadership is distinctive, can that distinctiveness be explained by changes in context that altered his members' expectations or is Gingrich, in fact, a different kind of leader? Is Gingrich the same kind of leader in the 105th as he was in the 104th? And, if not, why not? That is, to what extent does Republican leadership change from the 104th to the 105th Congress and why?

Principal-Agent Theory and Its Critics

Principal-agent theory conceptualizes leadership in legislatures as having been instituted to ameliorate problems of collective action.[2] By assumption, members of Congress want to legislate; legislating is necessary to their advancing their individual goals. Lawmaking is, however, a complex and time-consuming enterprise and one that, if successful, produces a collective good; consequently, it presents the legislature's members with collective action problems. Overcoming these collective action problems requires that members delegate powers and resources to agents. The benefits of such delegation can be great. A party leadership well endowed with powers and resources can significantly facilitate the passage of legislation that furthers its membership's policy, reelection, and power goals. It can do so by providing basic coordination services, such as legislative scheduling; by facilitating, through side payments or the coordination of tacit or explicit logrolling, for example, the passage of legislation various subgroups of its membership want; and by policy leadership— that is, using leadership powers and resources aggressively to influence the congressional agenda and the substance of legislative outputs so as to translate broadly shared legislative preferences into law. Such delegation is, however, risky for members; agents may use the powers granted them to pursue interests not those of their principal. Thus the character of the delegation and the extent to which members are willing to allow their leaders to use their delegated power and resources aggressively depend on the costs and benefits to members of strong leadership, which in turn depend on the political and institutional environment. In particular, when members are ideologically homogeneous and committed to enacting an ambitious legislative program they are most likely to expect their leadership to use its powers and resources expansively and more likely to augment the powers and resources delegated.

Some scholars and most journalists object that principal-agent theory, with its emphasis on members' expectations as the prime determinant of leadership functioning, leaves out all the richness of leaders' personality and makes them into mindless puppets. The theory does not deal with personality; in my view that is a virtue because I believe political science has little useful to say on that score. The theory does not, however, conceptualize leaders as puppets. When members perceive their leaders as both faithful and effective agents they give them considerable leeway to be creative; that is, so long as most members are convinced that the leader is furthering their goals and is skillful at doing so, those members are likely to applaud innovation on the leader's part. An elected congressional leader does not, however, have the same freedom of maneuver as is available to a member-entrepreneur who holds no position of delegated powers.

The Changing Context and Changing Expectations: 1970s to 1990s

Changes in the political and institutional context in the 1970s and 1980s altered majority party members' expectations of their party leaders. The 1970s reforms, combined with the constraints of the 1980s political environment, greatly increased the difficulty of enacting legislation, especially legislation Democrats favor. The decline in intercommittee reciprocity and the rise in floor amending activity, divided control, and the huge deficits made passing major legislation more difficult (Sinclair 1983; Smith 1989). Within that context, Democrats needed a stronger party and a more active leadership to accomplish their policy goals.

The 1970s reformers, most of them liberal Democrats, had been motivated by concerns about both policy and participation. The changes they instituted would, they believed, produce better (i.e., more representative and more liberal) policy *and* provide greater opportunities for the rank and file to participate in the legislative process. By the late 1970s many had concluded that unrestrained participation, particularly on the House floor, hindered rather than facilitated the production of good public policy. And in the more hostile political climate of the 1980s, the policy costs of unrestrained and uncoordinated legislative activism rose further.

Included in the 1970s reforms were provisions augmenting the party leadership's resources. The Speaker was given a greater say in the appointment of members to committee, more power over the referral of bills to committee, and the right to name the majority members and the chair of the Rules Committee, subject only to caucus ratification. In the mid-1970s, the Democratic membership had placed severe constraints on the leaders' uses of these new tools; both the party's ideological heterogeneity and members' desire to fully exploit their new participation opportunities limited the leaders' role. In the late 1970s and 1980s, in contrast, as legislating became increasingly difficult, members not only allowed but began to demand that their leaders aggressively employ the tools at their command to facilitate passing the legislation members wanted.

Members' willingness to have their party leaders exert stronger leadership was furthered by the decline, during this same period, in the effective ideological heterogeneity of the Democratic membership (Sinclair 1982, chap. 7–8; Rohde 1991). The Republican party became more uniformly conservative, and voting in the House became more partisan. From the mid-1950s through the mid-1960s (1955–66) about 49 percent of recorded votes saw a majority of Democrats voting against a majority of Republicans. The frequency of such party votes slumped in the late 1960s and early 1970s and then began to rise again, averaging 36 percent for the 1967–82 period. After the 1982 elections, it jumped to over half the votes and continued to rise in the late 1980s and in the 1990s. In the 103rd Congress (1993–94), 64 percent of recorded votes were party votes; in the 104th, 67 percent were.

The Leadership Response: Legislative Activity and Agenda Setting

If party leaders are agents of their members, as posited, they will respond to changes in members' expectations. As the political and institutional context changed, making legislating harder for majority party members but also increasing their ideological homogeneity, those members came to expect a higher rate of legislative activity from their leaders. They also came to expect their leaders to engage in agenda setting. When the opposition party controls the White House, the congressional majority will usually be dissatisfied with the president's agenda; as the parties became more polarized, that dissatisfaction intensified. Majority Democrats faced Republican presidents almost continuously from the early 1970s through the early 1990s. Furthermore, within the political climate of the 1980s and 1990s, House Democrats acting as solo entrepreneurs had little hope of getting their issues on the agenda; they needed help.

As predicted, the majority party leadership has become more active on major legislation since the early 1970s (see table 1).[3] Leaders more frequently involved themselves in legislative activities such as the shaping of legislation, the structuring through procedure of floor choices, vote mobilization, or other aspects of legislative strategy. The leaders of the 1980s and 1990s were more likely to involve themselves at all and in a major way than the leaders of the 1970s.

Gingrich and the rest of the new Republican majority party leadership in the 104th Congress were highly active on the legislation that made up the congressional agenda of major measures as here defined. They were at least somewhat involved in 80 percent of the measures, and their involvement was major on 63 percent. Although high, this rate of activity is by no means unprecedented; the Wright leadership in the 100th Congress was almost identically active. In terms of sheer rate of leadership activity, then, the 104th manifests continuity.

The Gingrich leadership's role in agenda setting in the 104th stands out as uniquely high. As table 2 shows, majority party leaders in the late 1960s and early 1970s really did not engage in agenda setting; over time this practice changed and the leadership increasingly took on this task. How active congressional leaders are in agenda setting is clearly related to the stage of the presidency. The data strongly suggest that during the first 2 years of their first term, presidents set the agenda; the only exception is Bush, who can be considered as serving the third term of the Reagan administration. Increasingly, however, later in a president's term the congressional majority party leadership, if of the other party, can and does compete with the president in agenda setting. Still, even in the light of this trend, the 104th Congress stands out. The Gingrich leadership dominated the agenda to nearly the same extent that presidents do at the beginning of their administrations and almost completely eclipsed the president.

The Contract with America was an innovation; although previous congressional leaders had developed agendas to guide legislative action and to enhance the credit their party could claim from legislative productivity, no leader had previously made an agenda the centerpiece of a nationalized congressional campaign. Gingrich, however, in no sense imposed the Contract on House Republican candidates or members. The Contract was put together through a highly inclusionary process (see later section). And it was done with the intention of furthering member and party goals. Thus, the Contract was an innovative response by Gingrich to his members' intense desire to become a majority. Many junior members believed with Gingrich that it would further

TABLE 1.   The Increase in Leadership Involvement on the Congressional Agenda (percentage of agenda items)

Leadership involvement	91st 1969–70	94th 1975–76	97th 1981–82	
Some	46	60	63	
Major	28	40	35	
N	50	48	49	

Leadership involvement	100th 1987–88	101st 1989–90	103rd 1993–94	104th 1995–96
Some	83	68	67	82
Major	61	53	46	64
N	41	51	54	55

See note 2 for definitions.

that collective goal; neither they nor most other members believed it would hurt them in advancing their individual goals.

Leadership Strategies

Majority party leaders, then, responded to their members' expectations by increasing their legislative activity and becoming more engaged in agenda setting. But did they go about it in a way consonant with members' expectations? Did leaders find ways to reconcile their members' desires for legislative success with their desires for meaningful participation in the legislative process? Do Gingrich's leadership strategies differ significantly from those of his predecessors and, if so, how and why?

The Strategy of Inclusion/Buy-In

For Democratic majority party leaders of the postreform era, the central leadership problem was developing strategies that minimized the conflict between members' policy and participation goals. Toward that end, including as many members as possible in the coalition-building process became a key modus operandi. This "strategy of inclusion" entailed expanding and using formal leadership structures, such as the whip system, and bringing other Democrats into the coalition-building process on an ad hoc basis—through bill-specific task forces, for example. In the postreform House, the core leadership was too small to undertake the task of successful coalition building alone; including other members provided needed assistance. At least as important, the strategy of inclusion was a way for leaders to satisfy members' expectations of significant participation in the legislative process but to do so in a manner beneficial to the party and the leadership.

Gingrich, like the Democratic leaders before him, believes that leading the postreform House requires a strategy of inclusion. Gingrich sought to involve others in his majority-building efforts, to get them to "buy in," long

TABLE 2.   The Leadership's Expanded Agenda Setting Role (Percentage of agenda items)

Administration	Nixon/Ford		Reagan		Bush	Clinton	
Congress	91st	94th	97th	100th	101st	103rd	104th
Agenda setter							
President	48	23	44	20	18	46	4
Leadership	2	17	7	28	11	NA	41
N	50	48	54	46	57	55	56

See note 2 for definitions.

before he moved into the leadership. As whip he continued that effort, reaching out to members with whom he had little in common ideologically.

The putting together of the Contract exemplifies the strategy (Koopman 1996, 142–47; Stid 1996, 6–8). In late 1993, Gingrich began to talk about holding a Capitol steps event during the 1994 election campaign. At the House Republicans' retreat in Salisbury, Maryland, in February 1994, members held intensive discussions in small groups and took the first steps toward identifying the common principles and core beliefs that would guide the drafting of the Contract. Republican incumbents and challengers were surveyed about what should be included. The leaders decided to exclude measures that were divisive within the party. When they determined the items to be included, working groups of members and leadership staff put together the actual bills. Any member who wanted to could participate, but younger activists were more likely to do so than senior committee leaders. Still, a large number of members had a hand in shaping the Contract and so felt some pride of authorship. "By the time things got to the conference, there was a great deal of buy-in already," Peter Hoekstra (R-MI), an activist member of the class of 1992, reported. "The members involved in the drafting had a great sense of empowerment and that began to run through the conference" (quoted in Stid 1996, 7).

Once in the majority, Gingrich and the Republican leadership team continued the buy-in strategy. Gingrich established numerous task forces to carry out a great variety of tasks—expediting action on Contract legislation, coming up with broad-based compromises on divisive issues, outreach beyond Congress. Inclusion—especially of junior members—was clearly an important goal (Gingrich 1995, 5). "Newt uses task forces to get people involved who have a common interest on something. To get them together. Newt's very open to new ideas," a moderate Republican explained. "He wants to let everybody do their own thing, pursue their own interests."

Gingrich also made it a point to consult and stay in regular contact with the various party subgroups. "He meets once a month with all the groups, the California delegation, the freshmen group, the sophomore group, the Tuesday lunch bunch, the Wednesday group, CATS, all these groups," a member explained. "Newt has constant meetings. Anybody can see him."

Message (as) Strategy

An aggressive attempt to participate in national discourse and to set the congressional agenda became another strategic thrust in the 1980s. Democrats clamored for their leadership to engage in agenda setting so that the president, with whom they profoundly disagreed, would not dominate the process. In addition, President Reagan taught Democrats the importance of defining issues and party images to one's benefit. House Democrats came to expect their leadership to participate effectively in national political discourse and to influence the terms of the debate so as to further Democrats' immediate legislative goals and to protect and enhance the party's image.

The primacy Gingrich places on the leader as "visionary definer, agenda setter, and value articulator" and the weight he puts on shaping the terms of the political debate lead logically to the centrality of message in his leadership strategies. Much more than for his Democratic predecessors, message becomes strategy.

Gingrich's prespeakership majority-building activities were based largely on message. The greater part of the Conservative Opportunity Society's (COS's) effort went into disseminating its message through C-SPAN (see later section). Gingrich's attack on Speaker Wright was very much a media-based effort; he used the media's interest in the story and his own greater media access that derived therefrom to convey his Congress- and Democrat-bashing message. Through his tapes and speeches, Gingrich coached Republicans in the language to use; for example, he recommended that they label Democrats as "pathetic," "sick," and, of course, "corrupt"; words such as "change," "moral," and "family" were to be associated with Republicans (Drew 1996, 42).

When Gingrich became whip, he continued to concentrate on majority building, much of it thorough message-disseminating activities. When, in 1990, he opposed the budget deal negotiated by President Bush and the bipartisan congressional leadership, it was to protect the party's antitax message he had worked to shape. The result of the first deal's defeat was a final budget package even less to the antitax Republicans' liking, as Gingrich must have known was likely. Yet he was willing to pay the policy cost to preserve the message.

The Contract with America was itself an elaborate effort to disseminate a bundle of messages about the Republican party: policy messages but also the message that, unlike the majority Democrats, the party was dedicated to cleaning up the "corrupt" Congress and prepared to stake its future on fulfilling its promises. Thus the first plank dealt with congressional reform; it was called a contract to give it an aura of legal weight, and Republicans explicitly invited voters to throw them out of office if they did not fulfill their promises. The language used to name the bills in the Contract was tested through polling and focus groups; welfare reform was named the "Personal Responsibility Act," and a cut in the capital gains tax and changes in the regulatory process aimed especially at weakening environmental regulations made up most of the "Job Creation and Wage Enhancement Act."

Message continued its primacy when Gingrich became Speaker. His media access was, however, much greater—a not unalloyed benefit, it turned out. Gingrich took advantage of the press's interest by not only granting innumerable interviews and appearing on all the interview shows but also opening the Speaker's daily press conference to television coverage. (When reporters began to

concentrate on ethics charges against him, Gingrich canceled daily press conferences altogether.) The Republican leadership insisted that each of the committees
hire a press secretary and coordinate message strategy with the beefed-up leadership press operation (Koopman 1995, 15). CommStrat, the communications strategy team of leadership press aides, talked by conference call early each morning
to discuss the message of the day (Maraniss and Weisskopf 1996, 133). The
Republican "theme teams," members organized to use the 1-minute speeches at
the beginning of a day's session to promulgate the message of the day, continued
to operate. The conference produced a "blizzard" of information, much of it
aimed at advising members about how best to talk about issues.

Although members would later bitterly criticize the leadership for not
being sufficiently effective at communication, immense effort went into
attempts to shape public perceptions of Republicans' policy proposals. Thus
special task forces put together media kits for use by Republican leaders and
rank and file on each of the major issues. On Medicare, Republicans mounted
a massive campaign that involved "polls, focus groups, corporate coalitions,
imagemakers, lobbyists, radio talk shows" (Maraniss and Weisskopf 1996,
128). Much of the most intense effort was aimed at shifting the terms of the
debate—from cutting the program to saving it by slowing the rate of increase.
"From [RNC Chair] Barbour to CommStrat to committee chairmen to House
members, the word went out that no statement or [news] story using the word
'cut' should go unanswered" (1996, 136).

In sum, Gingrich's leadership strategies as Speaker show considerable
continuity with those of recent Democratic leaderships. The buy-in strategy is the Republican version of the strategy of inclusion, an attempt to
involve a large proportion of the membership in leadership efforts and
thereby give them a stake in their success. Democrats had recognized the
importance of participating effectively in national political discourse and
had moved to increase their capabilities in the battle for public opinion;
message is even more important to Gingrich's leadership. Additionally, as
I show in a later section, Republican leaders have resorted on a regular
basis to the strategy of structuring choices through procedure, as did their
Democratic predecessors.

Gingrich's pursuit of a majority-building strategy from long before he
entered the formal Republican House leadership differentiates him from other
twentieth-century Speakers and is important enough to his leadership during
the 104th Congress that it requires examination here.

The Majority-Building Strategy

Gingrich's majority-building activities helped to shape the character of the
majority that was elected in 1994 and ensure that he would lead it. Gingrich

carried out much of this activity, especially the part of it that was most divisive within the Republican party, before he was elected to the party leadership and thus was no one's agent.

According to all accounts, including contemporaneous ones, Gingrich held the goal of winning a House majority from the beginning of his House tenure and began to do something about it almost immediately. After being involved in several precursor groups, Gingrich in 1983 formed COS, the ultimate goal of which was to elect a Republican majority to the House; the group aggressively used floor amendments and other procedural tactics and, importantly, C-SPAN (Pitney 1988). The House is a majority rule institution; the "bomb throwers" might cause the majority some annoyance and even some pain, but a reasonably cohesive majority party could always defeat them. The televising of House sessions, including special orders at the end of the day in which members can talk as long as they like on the topic of their choice, gave COS a way to reach beyond the chamber and start the task Gingrich believed so important, that of framing issues and shaping the debate.

In 1986 Gingrich became chairman of GOPAC, a political action committee founded by Pierre duPont to recruit and assist candidates for state and local offices with the aim of strengthening the Republicans' "farm team." Gingrich shifted GOPAC's emphasis from simply supplying money to supplying ideas, rationales, and motivation. Gingrich sent prospective candidates audio- and videotapes on tactics, strategy, ideas, and issues; many Republican candidates listened to those tapes and were influenced in their view of issues, and some were inspired to run for federal office (Blatz and Brownstein 1996, 144–46). By the late 1980s, most Republican House freshmen had been helped and influenced by Gingrich (Koopman 1996, 53). The big Republican classes of 1992 and 1994 consisted largely of aggressive conservatives, many of whom had received help from GOPAC.

Legislative Leadership in the 104th Congress

Gingrich's success at majority building as perceived and interpreted by his members explains much of what differentiates his leadership in the 104th from the preceding Democratic leaderships and from his own in the 105th as well. I argue that the extraordinary political context of the 104th and how it shaped members' expectations is the key determinant of Gingrich's relationships with his members and with the committees and their chairs—relationships that were extraordinary for the modern Congress. Even so, how Gingrich went about facilitating the passage of legislation shows considerable continuity with the past. Little that Gingrich did was unprecedented in kind; however, the political context allowed him to push the envelope, to exploit leadership tools more aggressively than any of his postreform predecessors.

Political Context and Member Expectations in the 104th Congress

The new Republican majority that the 1994 elections produced was unusually ideologically homogeneous and believed itself to be mandated to make far-reaching policy change. The huge freshman class—73 strong—consisted largely of true believers who were deeply committed to cutting the size and scope of government and to balancing the budget; with the sophomores, who were very similar in outlook, they made up over half of the Republican House membership. Many more senior Republican conservatives had been waiting for such an opportunity for years. Even moderate Republicans strongly agreed that, given that Republicans had run on the Contract, for the party to maintain its majority, Republicans had to deliver on their promises (Healey 1994, 3210–15).

Gingrich, in the eyes of most Republicans and the media, was responsible for the unexpected Republican victory. As a result members felt grateful to him. More important for the power and discretion they allowed him to exercise, members regarded Gingrich as a world-class, once-in-a-century political genius, an opinion reinforced in the early months by the media. Members deferred in their strategic judgments to the miracle maker who had produced a Republican majority against all expectations. Because they were convinced that Gingrich shared their policy and electoral goals and that he was politically more brilliant than anyone else, Republican members, many of whom were very junior, gave Gingrich broad latitude.

Understanding his opportunity as well as the magnitude of the task ahead, Gingrich aggressively exploited his discretion. In the days after the elections, he exercised power well beyond that specified in Republican Conference rules. He designated Republicans to serve as committee chairs, bypassing seniority in several instances. He passed over the too amiable and unaggressive Carlos Moorehead (CA) to appoint the second most senior member on Judiciary and on Commerce, both important committees with major jurisdiction over Contract items. On the Appropriations Committee, he skipped several more senior members to pick Bob Livingston (LA), a strong-minded and articulate conservative. Conservatives regarded the pragmatic, bargaining culture of that committee with deep suspicion, and, with its jurisdiction over "must-pass" spending bills, Appropriations was sure to be a major battleground. Gingrich also engineered a rules change to increase the party leadership's voice on the Committee on Committees and used that new influence to reward junior Republicans, his strongest supporters, with choice assignments.

The Democratic leadership had in the postreform years gained considerable influence over the appointment of members to committees and the Democratic Caucus had occasionally unseated sitting committee chairs or passed over the most senior member when a vacancy occurred. Although the leadership had used the requirement that the caucus approve all committee chairs in a secret-ballot vote to pressure chairs to be responsive to caucus sentiment, it had never initiated or even supported any of the efforts to bypass seniority in choosing chairs. No Democratic leader during the postreform era enjoyed the sort of political context that allowed Gingrich's actions.

Leaders and Committees

The Democratic party leadership in the 1980s and early 1990s had been actively involved in all stages of the legislative process. To meet its members' expectations of legislative outputs, leaders often found they had to take a hand well before the floor stage. Ensuring that when legislation reached the floor it was in a form that could pass the House and was satisfactory to most Democrats sometimes required leaders to intervene in committee, broker compromises after a bill was reported, or even bypass committee altogether. Committees and their leaders accepted, if not always happily, such leadership intervention because the party leaders were acting as agents of the membership.

Although informal intervention in committee, almost certainly the most frequent form of party leadership involvement, is difficult to identify consistently from the public record, the bypassing of committees and the modification of legislation after it has been reported can be counted. As table 3 shows, the frequency with which, on major legislation, either the committee was bypassed or legislation was subject to postcommittee adjustments, most often the latter, increased from the early 1980s and reached a bit over half by the early 1990s. In the 104th Congress the figure stood at 51 percent, high but not unprecedentedly so.

Yet other evidence indicates that the relationship between party and committee leaders was different in the 104th Congress; committee leaders were clearly subordinate to party leaders on Contract bills and on much of the major legislation that went into the Republicans' attempt to balance the budget (Aldrich and Rohde 1997). The party set the agenda; party leaders held the committees to a tight schedule and exerted a strong influence on the substance of legislation (Owens 1998).

When a committee was incapable of mustering a majority for legislation the party leadership and the membership wanted, the leadership stepped in and

TABLE 3.   Leadership Activism vis-à-vis Congressional Committees (percentage of major measures on which committee bypassed or there was postcommittee adjustment)

97th	100th	101st	103rd	104th
28	46	51	33	51

bypassed the committee; for example, when the Agriculture Committee refused to report the Freedom to Farm bill, which made cuts in farm programs as required by the budget resolution, the leadership inserted the language in the reconciliation bill. When the legislation a committee reported was unacceptable to a majority of the Republican membership, as on the term limits constitutional amendment, the leadership altered the language substantially after it had been reported and before it want to the floor (Sinclair 1997). On Medicare, one of the most politically sensitive issues the Republicans took on, Gingrich himself headed the "design group" that made the major substantive decisions; the group included the Republican leaders of the committees and subcommittees with jurisdiction.

Like their Democratic predecessors, the Republican leaders tried to get the belligerents in an intraparty dispute to work out their differences among themselves. However, especially in 1995, Gingrich's stature was such that he could bring more pressure to bear than his predecessors. Thus, when the Republican governors objected to provisions of the job training bill, Gingrich instructed the members of the committee to work out a deal with the governors. During one of many intraparty fights about abortion language on an appropriations bill, Gingrich threatened the combatants with a rule that would in effect gut the bill altogether if they did not resolve their differences (Maraniss and Weisskopf 1996, 93–94). When antienvironmentalism began to damage the party's image, Gingrich refused to schedule a bill that would weaken the Endangered Species Act and insisted that Commerce Committee Republicans work out a bipartisan deal on the safe drinking water bill.

The Republican leadership could act in such an assertive manner because much of the membership was ideologically committed to passing the legislation at issue and almost all were convinced that the party's fate depended on delivering on their promises. When at the beginning of the Congress Republicans revised House and party rules, they on balance strengthened the party leadership a bit vis-à-vis committee chairs, especially by imposing a three-term limit on committee chairs. A conference rule on leadership issues, although not new, took on added importance; it reads, "the Speaker may designate certain issues as 'Leadership Issues.' Those issues will require early and ongoing cooperation between the relevant committees and the Leadership as the issue evolves."

It was, however, the Republican membership's commitment to passing the Contract and Gingrich's prestige, not new rules, that allowed Gingrich to exercise such clout. Because most senior Republicans had signed the Contract, party leaders had a strong tool for persuading committee leaders to report legislation without making major changes and to do so quickly; the new Republican chairs did not all agree with all elements of the Contract, and most would have liked more time to work on their bills. The Republican party leadership could and did remind them that "we promised to do it in 100 days; we must deliver." Then and later when balancing the budget was at issue, the chairs knew that the leadership was backed by the freshmen's strong support.

Leadership-appointed task forces worked on legislative issues ranging from agriculture policy to gun control to immigration reform. These task forces provided Republicans not on the committee an opportunity to work on and influence legislation on issues they cared about. Junior members were especially heavily represented on the task forces and were thereby provided with a channel for meaningful participation in the legislative process. By and large, committees were not bypassed on those issues, but the task forces had the purpose and the effect of keeping the pressure on committees to report legislation satisfactory to the party majority and in a timely fashion.

Members' desire to accomplish quickly a mass of pent-up policy objectives led to the leadership's decision to use the appropriations process, thus bypassing the slower and more cumbersome authorizing process, the products of which the president could more easily veto. Decisions about what "riders"—policy provisions in appropriations bills—to allow were made in the majority leader's office, and he insisted that the bypassed authorizing committee leadership support the rider. Because controversial riders make appropriations bills harder to pass, many senior Republicans on the Appropriations Committee were unhappy with the strategy, but they acquiesced. Early in the year Gingrich had extracted from each of the 13 subcommittee chairs a written pledge of cooperation and commitment to the agenda. Even more important, they knew the Republican membership, especially the freshmen, strongly supported the strategy.

When the leaders were acting as agents of an intense and determined membership, the committees had little choice but to accede. But the leaders could not ignore such membership sentiment either; they occasionally found themselves forced by their members into courses of action they would have preferred to avoid. The Republican leadership brought to the floor the gift ban, lobbying reform, and campaign finance legislation only because of pressure from a determined group of mostly junior members.

In sum, party leaders played an unusually influential role in shaping legislation during the 104th Congress, but they did so as agents of a cohesive majority party that believed itself mandated to bring about major policy change. Before the budget debacle, House Republicans were convinced that Gingrich was a master strategist and they knew he shared their goals of enacting comprehensive policy change and retaining their majority—goals they believed to be linked, not conflicting. Thus they were more than willing to let him exercise great power to ensure that legislation was passed and in a form that would accomplish their objectives.

Structuring Choices

Contemporary House leaders have available much more powerful tools for structuring choices through procedure than their prereform predecessors did. Gingrich made extensive and aggressive but not particularly innovative use of these tools.

The Budget Act of 1974 provided central leaders with a powerful tool, though they were somewhat slow to recognize its potential. The act made it possible for Congress, if strongly led, to enact comprehensive policy change, always a difficult task for a decentralized institution. Reconciliation instructions that require committees to make changes in legislation under their jurisdiction give the budget act the potential of serving as such a vehicle. Reconciliation instructions were first included in the budget resolution in 1980 (Sinclair 1983, 181–90). Although the policy changes required by the 1980 budget resolution were modest by later standards, the experience demonstrated that, under certain circumstances at least, the budget process was a mechanism available to central leaders for making comprehensive policy change. By including in the budget resolution a set of instructions to make major policy changes, forcing a single vote on them as a whole, and then packaging the policy changes into one massive reconciliation bill (where again the key vote was whether to accept or reject as a whole), Reagan and his supporters in 1981 were able to achieve major policy change quickly in a system resistant to such change. Since then the budget process has become the tool of choice for those attempting to bring about comprehensive policy change.

In 1993, newly elected president Bill Clinton and the congressional Democratic majority used the budget process to enact comprehensive policy change. Enacting Clinton's economic program entailed making a number of difficult decisions. To cut the deficit by $500 billion over 5 years and increase spending on high-priority programs, Clinton proposed tax increases, which are never popular, and a cut in spending for numerous lower-priority programs. The budget process offered the best prospect of success. By wrapping the provisions into one omnibus bill, the number of battles that need to be won can be kept to a minimum—an important consideration in a system with a status quo bias. Leaders can ask members to cast a handful of tough votes, not dozens. And the stakes become so high, it is actually harder for members to vote against their party leaders. Thus, in 1993, reluctant Democrats were warned that they would bring down the Clinton presidency if they contributed to the defeat of his economic program.

In 1995, the Republicans' program entailed even more major and more painful policy change. Balancing the budget in 7 years while also cutting taxes required draconian spending cuts and the fundamental revamping of a number of popular programs, including Medicare. Like the Democrats in 1993, Republicans simply assumed they would use the budget process; it offered the only realistic hope for success.

Packaging can also be used to structure the president's choices in a way more favorable to the congressional majority. Given the frequency of divided control during the past several decades, congressional majorities often had strong incentives for trying to force the president to accept legislative provisions that, if sent to him in freestanding form, he would veto. As a new majority bent on forcing "revolutionary" policy change on a resistant president, the House Republicans made extensive use of this strategy. The Republican leadership believed that packaging the mass of major policy changes into one huge reconciliation bill made it harder for the president to veto it. For good measure they included in the reconciliation bill a must-pass provision to raise the debt limit. In a separate ploy, they loaded down must-pass legislation such as appropriations bills and legislation to raise the debt limit with provisions the president strongly opposed. However, the House Republicans overplayed their hand, and, although they won some individual policy skirmishes, they lost the war. When the president refused to cave in and vetoed the legislation and the government shut down, the public blamed the Republicans, not the president.

In the 1980s, Democratic House leaders had developed the rules that govern floor consideration into flexible and powerful tools for shaping choices. When in the minority Republicans had labeled restrictive rules dictatorial and illegitimate and had promised not to use them if they took control. The enormous usefulness of restrictive rules for promoting the party's legislative objectives largely overcame any Republican objections based on principle or the fear of seeming hypocritical. To be sure, the type of restrictions were sometimes of a different character: Republicans often limited amending activity by specifying a maximum number of hours rather than specifying the amendments that may be offered. Nevertheless, 77 percent of rules for the consideration of major measures were restrictive in the 104th—compared with 82 percent in the 103rd and 72 percent in both the 100th and 101st Congresses. On this major legislation, the restrictions by and large were more substantial than just time limits on the amending process or the requirement that amendments be "preprinted" in the *Congressional Record*; according to the Republican Rules Committee's own classification, 63 percent of the rules were either modified closed or closed.

Mobilizing Floor Majorities

Superintending the House floor and shepherding legislation to passage at the floor stage are the core of the party leadership's responsibilities as traditionally defined. In the postreform era, the leadership nevertheless became more active at this stage of the legislative process as well. Such activism continued in the 104th Congress.

The techniques that the new Republican majority leadership employed are quite similar to those their Democratic predecessors used; however, the very different political context shaped the actual operation of the techniques and their effectiveness.

Both parties have long had whip systems charged with ascertaining their members' positions on important votes and, to varying extents, with persuading members to back the party position. As members came to expect the party and its leadership to play a more active role in mobilizing votes to pass legislation on the floor, the whip systems became an essential tool.

The Republican majority party, like its Democratic predecessor, uses an elaborate whip system to count and mobilize votes on legislation of importance to the party. In the 104th it consisted of the whip, Tom DeLay, a chief deputy whip, 13 deputy whips, and 39 assistant whips. On a number of the Contract items, special task forces were set up to aid in the effort. Whips contact every member to determine his or her position; if a secure majority is not in hand, whips then attempt to persuade enough members to ensure victory.

An effective whip system needs to mirror the membership it is charged with persuading. The Republican whip system in the 104th reflected the heavily conservative cast of the party but also included a number of moderate members. Junior members, who made up a large proportion of the Republican membership, were well represented. Of the 13 deputy whips, 4 were sophomores and 3 freshmen; 29 of the 39 assistant whips were from the two most junior classes, 16 sophomores and 13 freshmen.

In the 104th Congress, the whips had the enormous advantage of working with an ideologically homogeneous membership that believed itself to be mandated to enact major policy change. The Contract itself was a key resource in holding the party together. The media amplified the leaders' emphasis on the Contract; even members who had regarded the signing as just a campaign photo opportunity realized that at minimum the party had to deliver on the promise of bringing the items to a vote; not doing so would be a disaster for the party. The leadership, of course, brought up the least contentious items first; as more and more Contract items passed, the pressure to pass the others intensified. Republicans who were less than happy with some of the bills knew that the press would have a field day if any of the items failed and that if were they responsible their colleagues would not soon forget. With the strong backing of the freshmen, Gingrich extended the Contract aura to balancing the budget in 7 years. Gingrich publicly committed the party to it, and, given the enormous media coverage he was receiving, he made the cost of failure to the party too great to bear. Thus a similar dynamic pertained during the budget battle as during the Contract period.

Republicans maintained remarkable unity on Contract items and on other measures during 1995 as well. Only 4.7 Republicans on average defected from the party position on passage votes on Contract items. During all of 1995, 73 percent of roll call votes pitted a majority of Republicans against a majority of Democrats; on those votes, Republicans on average supported their party's position 91 percent of the time.

Legislative leaders have long enlisted the aid of outside groups, especially of those generally allied with the party, in vote mobilization efforts. During the 1980s and early 1990s, House Democratic leaders had increasingly formalized such efforts and designated specific staff aides to work with groups as their primary responsibility (Sinclair 1995, 236–40).

Republicans in the 104th worked closely with their allies outside Congress when mobilizing votes. The groups Republicans consider allies differ radically from those close to Democrats, and a number of them have a social movement character. These factors gave the Republicans' joint effort a somewhat different character in the 104th Congress. The National Rifle Association (NRA), small business groups (particularly the National Federation of Independent Businesses [NFIB]), and especially the Christian Coalition had become increasingly important components of the Republican coalition in the 1990s; organized and active at the grass roots, they were key to the Republicans' victories in 1994. Many of the freshmen had strong ties to one or more of these groups. Many business groups had a major stake in the enactment of the Republican agenda as well as long-term ties to Republicans.

During the 104th Congress, the Thursday Group, a leadership-created entity consisting of lobbyists for about a dozen groups closely allied with Republicans, met weekly with Republican Conference Chair John Boehner. The invitees were chosen because of both who they were and whom they represented; many had close ties to the House Republicans, and most represented core Republican constituencies. Collectively they represented the "armies of the Republican revolution," the groups with grassroots strength.

Boehner and Whip Tom DeLay worked to orchestrate allied groups' lobbying efforts to best effect (Blatz and Brownstein 1996, 198–99; Salant 1995, 261–62). The Thursday Group functioned as an inner circle; because all the participants had multiple connections with other groups, they were expected to disseminate the message to such groups, as well as to their own members at the grass roots.

Although the character of the endeavor did not differ fundamentally from that of Democrats, the Republican efforts to maintain a united front among these groups and to enlist them in lobbying for legislation not at the top of their own priority list were unusually successful, especially during the Contract period.[4] Everyone wants to be a part of a winning team. In addition, groups such as the Christian Coalition and NFIB were more successful at mobilizing their grass roots to pressure members of Congress than most of the Democratic groups had been. Both were well organized at the local level and had been energized by their success in the 1994 campaigns.

The Republican leadership also put together and worked with single-purpose coalitions on key agenda items. Whip Tom DeLay, an avid opponent of government regulation, put together Project Relief, a coalition dedicated to regulatory relief that eventually grew to 350 industry members (Maraniss and Weisskopf 1996, chap. 2). The Coalition to Save Medicare, which consisted of Republican business allies in the health care industry and conservative senior groups, was one of nine coalitions Boehner organized.

Under the Republicans, as under the Democrats before them, if the whips and the allied interest groups are unsuccessful at cementing a firm majority to support the party position, top party leaders, including the Speaker, must get involved in persuasion. Roughly speaking, persuasion can be conceptualized as ranging from pure exhortation to the offering of material inducements. During the 104th, Gingrich himself sometimes engaged in piecemeal bargaining with members to build majorities. He seems to have done so less than his Democratic predecessors because the context made such retail politics less necessary.

On Contract items, the need and the willingness of the leadership to bargain with members for their support was very limited; almost all had signed the Contract, most genuinely supported its provisions, all were aware of the media criticism that would follow failures and even significant changes, and peer pressure was fierce.

On the myriad of complex legislation that made up the budget bill and on appropriations bills, the leadership was more willing and had more need to be flexible; the leaders attempted to give members what they needed to support the legislation. On Medicare, Gingrich himself conducted the negotiations (Hook 1995, A20). A group of rural Republicans who believed their constituencies would be unfairly hurt threatened to oppose the bill if alterations were not made. After several attempts, Gingrich came up with a revision in the payment formula for rural providers that brought the rural Republicans on board. To placate other Republicans, adjustments were made in provisions on the funding of medical education, on fraud and abuse, and on a number of other more minor issues.

The extraordinary context of the 104th Congress and the way it shaped members' expectations and perceptions proved to be a double-edged sword. In the end, Gingrich found it impossible to persuade the bulk of his membership, especially the big freshman class, that flexibility and compromise were necessary. Ideologically fervent and believing themselves mandated, junior Republicans especially remained staunchly committed to the strategy of attempting to bludgeon the president into agreeing to their policy positions by shutting the government down long after its disastrous impact on the Republican party's popularity became clear (Drew 1996, 305–75) . The context that had made possible persuading even cautious senior members to support a radical attempt to transform government's role also made it impossible to persuade the real revolutionaries to retreat and settle for half loaf.

The result of the "our way or no way" strategy was not only defeat in the public relations wars but a lackluster legislative record as well. On party agenda items, Republicans clearly won on the House floor on a phenomenal 96 percent of the cases; however, on final disposition, which is the bottom line, they won on balance (a weaker criterion) on only 39 percent, and many of the wins came after a change in strategy. They lost on balance on final disposition on 57 percent of the measures. Contrast that with the Democrats' record in the 100th Congress. On their agenda, which was ambitious, though far from as nonincremental as that of the 104th Republicans, Democrats clearly won on the House floor on 77 percent of the measures and won on balance on the rest. Thus their record in the chamber, although impressive, fell far short of that of the 104th Republicans. However, in terms of enacting their preferred policies into law, the Democrats did much better, winning on balance on 92 percent of the measures.

Leadership in the 105th Congress

I have argued that congressional leaders are best understood as agents of their members; the political context shapes members' expectations, which, along with the context directly, shape the character and exercise of leadership—what leaders try to do, how they go about doing it, and their prospects of success. This approach to understanding congressional leadership leads us to expect that, when the context changes in a major way, so should the exercise of leadership. I argue here that the political context did indeed change drastically after the budget debacle and that Republican leadership changed in response.

The disastrous government shutdowns that the budget battle led to transformed the political context. The public blamed the Republicans, and the GOP Congress's standing in the polls plummeted. With a last-minute change in tactics and enormous amounts of money, Republicans managed to hang on to a House majority in the 1996 elections, but their margin narrowed significantly and most realized they had barely escaped the fate of the two previous Republican majorities.

The calamitously unsuccessful budget fight took a severe toll on Gingrich's reputation with his members. They no longer regarded him as the world-class political genius to whose strategic judgment they could entrust their fates with total confidence. Ideological and strategic splits emerged within the party that House Republicans' sense of mandate and their confidence in Gingrich had earlier suppressed. In the summer of 1996, Republican defections led to the floor defeat of the rule for the Interior appropriations bill;

bitter intraparty factionalism produced a highly public embarrassment of the leadership and the party on campaign finance reform and a Reform Week with no bills to consider. Threats of a revolt by northeastern moderates forced the leadership to schedule a minimum wage increase that the leaders and a majority of their members strongly opposed. A majority of the membership overrode the leadership on welfare reform strategy, insisting that Medicaid changes be stripped from the bill sent to the president (Koszczuk 1997, 2019–23).

The House Republican party abandoned its "our way or no way" strategy after the budget debacle—but tentatively and haltingly. With the media pounding the Republican Congress as the least productive in history and under pressure from new Senate Majority Leader Trent Lott, Senate Republicans, and groups of their own members, the Republican House leadership began to make the sort of compromises that made possible the enactment of legislation, not just its passage in the House.

The 1996 elections sent a garbled message. A Republican party composed overwhelmingly of conservatives, with a large representation of hard-right antigovernment members, held on to its majority. Yet the margin had been reduced and was razor thin. The sense of mandate generated by the 1994 elections had completely dissipated; many Republicans had lost their sense of confidence and were no longer convinced that the public enthusiastically supported their policy goals or that they could bludgeon Clinton into acquiescence.

The party could not reach a consensus on strategy for the new Congress. The most committed Republican revolutionaries, many but not all of whom were freshmen or sophomores in the 104th, believed that the Republicans' problem had never been policy; rather, the problem was message and specifically the leadership's ineptitude in selling the Republican program to the public. Most of these members believed that Republicans should continue to pursue an ambitious agenda and simply sell it more effectively. Another and larger segment of the party consisted of conservatives who were traumatized by their near-death experience in the 1996 elections. These members, too, yearned for the good old Contract days but feared taking any actions—especially on issues such as Medicare—that Democrats and Clinton, now seen as a sort of evil genius of the public relations wars, could exploit. These members had become highly risk adverse; however, because the policies that resulted from such an approach did not measure up to their notions of good public policy, they were often at least somewhat unhappy with whatever the leadership did or refrained from doing. The moderates were more comfortable with a cautious strategy and would have been happy with bipartisan policy deals. Yet they remained a small segment of a very conservative party, and not infrequently the legislation that got to the floor of the House was too conservative to suit their policy tastes or their reelection needs. In the 105th Congress, unlike much of the 104th, they felt considerably freer to defect when confronted with such a situation.

The party leaders responded by exercising less aggressive leadership. Lacking the necessary consensus within the party, they proposed no ambitious agenda. Committees were subject to less direction from the leadership and were freer to pursue their own agendas.

This lighter leadership hand did not, however, win leaders the approbation of their members. Members complained vociferously about the lack of an agenda and the dearth of a message. Even the lack of direction to committees occasioned some dissatisfaction. Although hard-line conservatives were most unhappy, members from all segments of the party complained about aimlessness and drift. Clearly less leadership was not what members wanted. From the leaders' perspective, the problem was that no broad agreement on an achievable agenda existed within their membership.

This state of affairs led to defections and losses that would have been unthinkable in 1995. In early 1997, the rule for the resolution funding committee budgets went down to defeat on the floor when 11 junior Republicans balked at voting for an increase in funding. The Judiciary Committee was unable to report a "clean" balanced budget amendment; reelection anxiety drove a number of quite conservative Republicans to support a Democratic amendment to exempt Social Security from balanced budget calculations. The rule for the fiscal year 1998 supplemental appropriations bill that funded flood disaster aid was brought down by a combination of disparate concerns. Some Republicans voted against it because Clinton and the Democrats had been given increased funding for WIC; Democrats opposed it because of the way the WIC funding was handled; other Republicans were upset because the rule barred them from offering an amendment setting a date for the withdrawal of U.S. troops from Bosnia; still others objected to a provision concerning the supplier of paper for U.S. currency. Among the latter was Tom DeLay, the Republican whip. Moderate Republicans joined Democrats to defeat antienvironmental provisions and amendments barring affirmative action. Reformist Republicans' threat to sign a discharge petition forced the leadership to bring campaign finance reform legislation to the floor. A conflict between farm district representatives and Republican purists, who resisted any restoration of food stamps for legal aliens, led to the defeat of the rule for the conference report of an important agriculture bill in May 1998. In June, antiabortion Republicans scuttled the rule for the Treasury–Postal Service appropriations bill.

As these cases show, Republicans felt freer to defect for all sorts of ideological and parochial reasons. With the sense of mandate gone, the perception of a collective interest had weakened and so had the peer pressure to vote the party position. When the whip votes against the leadership on a procedural roll call, other members will feel little obligation to stick with the party.

The Republican leadership faced a much more difficult job in the 105th than it had in the 104th. Yet the intraparty divisions and the collective malaise did not lead to a peripheral, inactive leadership. Although there was less agreement on policy and on strategy within the party (and even within the leadership itself) and the leaders did not enjoy their members' confidence to the same extent they had in the previous Congress, members still needed an activist leadership to advance their goals. Republicans now faced an adverse climate for advancing their true policy preferences without endangering their electoral goals. They confronted an opposition-party president who had proven himself tougher and more skillful in the public relations wars than they had ever expected and an electoral imperative to avoid gridlock and produce legislative accomplishments. In this context, activist leadership might not enable members to accomplish their goals, but members knew they could not succeed as individuals.

The budget situation illustrates the problems members faced and their need for activist leadership. Republicans badly needed a budget agreement, and they needed it by the spring of 1997. The media were already pounding them as a do-nothing Congress. More serious still, Republicans desperately wanted to avoid having to propose and pass their own budget. The party's strategy had been to let Clinton go first and propose the painful cuts in popular programs then thought necessary to balance the budget by 2002; he would pay the political price and provide them with cover for unpopular decisions. When Clinton refused to oblige, Republicans were in a difficult position. Many members were unwilling to take the lead on making the unpopular decisions on programs such as Medicare; the only way of making those choices less draconian was to scale back substantially the tax cuts, a course of action anathema to many Republicans. Because Republicans could count on no Democratic votes for a partisan budget resolution and thus had to hold all but a handful of their own members, they probably could not pass a budget resolution.

Given these circumstances, a budget agreement with the president was essential, and, as past experience has demonstrated, only the party leadership could negotiate a deal. Hard-right conservatives outside the Congress were scathing in their attacks on the "timid, minimalist" deal the leaders made. Yet, although there was a good deal of private grumbling, all but the most purist of the Republican revolutionaries in the House kept quiet and all but 26 voted for the deal. (The challenge came from a different quarter. See later section.)

House majority party leadership in the 105th, then, largely conformed to what our theory would lead us to expect. The leadership did not have the same credibility with its membership as it had in the 104th and thus had less leeway to be innovative in strategy and aggressive in using its resources. Members trusted their leaders' judgment less and were more likely to second-guess their strategic decisions, to bicker among themselves about strategy and policy, and to go their own way when they disagreed with leadership decisions. Thus, the leadership had to work harder at keeping its members together even on the less difficult issues. It needed to engage in more piecemeal bargaining and in a great deal more hand-holding.

Because the Republican party leadership in the 105th was not in as strong a position vis-à-vis its members as it was in the 104th, it was not in as strong a position vis-à-vis the committees and their chairs as it had been. In response to complaints from chairs and some other members as well and because of their own weaker position and the lack of a well-defined party agenda, the leadership gave committees considerably more autonomy to set their own agendas and write their legislation without direct leadership oversight. Yet what the committees do affects the party as a whole and often requires leadership intervention on behalf of its members. When the Judiciary Committee reported a "partial birth" abortion bill that made minor concessions to opponents, the leadership substituted the tougher Senate bill, which was identical to the one Congress had passed the previous year (Langdon 1997, 706). A lack of support among their members led Republican leaders to scuttle a bipartisan State Department authorization bill reported by the International Relations Committee and substitute two "hastily drafted measures" more to the liking of conservative Republicans (Doherty 1997, 1324). The budget deal required extensive leadership oversight and a good deal of intervention to ensure that it was enacted into law in a form members would find satisfactory. When a series of big bank mergers in 1998 focused unflattering attention on Congress's inability to overhaul the outdated Glass-Steagall Act, the leadership stepped up and put together a bill. In response to pressure from deficit hawk Republicans, the party leaders instructed Appropriations Committee Chair Bob Livingston to find offsetting cuts for new spending in the 1998 supplemental appropriations bill.

Given the leadership's weakened position, committees and their chairs were more likely to take on the leadership and conflicts were more likely to become public. Thus, the 104th saw considerable tension between Appropriations Committee Chairman Bob Livingston and the leadership over riders on appropriations bills. In the 105th the tension heightened, especially with Livingston's challenge to Armey for the speakership. Transportation Committee Chairman Bud Schuster took on and almost defeated the leadership on the budget resolution that incorporated the negotiated budget deal. His substitute, which included more money for transportation and infrastructure, was a deal breaker according to the leadership and Clinton; yet it barely lost, 214–216, and only after strenuous leadership arm-twisting. Throwing down the gauntlet to the party leaders, Rules Committee Chair Gerald Solomon publicly declared that he would not write a rule for an agriculture bill if it included and protected restitution of food stamps for legal immigrants; a compromise was later worked out.

The context of the 105th made conveying a coherent and attractive message even more difficult for the leadership. House Republicans complained bitterly about the failure of the leadership's message strategy when things started going wrong in 1996. Member discontent only intensified in 1997, reaching a new high in the wake of the disaster aid disaster. The congressional leadership's perpetual problem, especially when it attempts to compete with the president in the public arena, is "getting everyone to sing from the same hymn book," so as to convey a clear message; when members are split and lack confidence in their leaders, this strategy becomes even more difficult. Yet their leaders' failures in the public relations wars did not lead members to call on their leaders to give up the attempt. Members believe a media strategy is essential to their goal advancement, and they know they cannot pursue a successful media strategy as individuals.

In sum, the party leadership in the 105th was less aggressive, less dominant, and less successful in the House than it was in the 104th, but it nevertheless remained an activist, engaged leadership. Given the context, the Republican leaders were unlikely to be able to meet their members' expectations fully, yet their attempts to do the best they could entailed the exercise of activist leadership—as has been the case for all majority party leaderships since the 1980s.

Principal-Agent Theory and Leadership Discretion

How successful is principal-agent theory at making sense of the complicated story of House majority party leadership in the postreform era and particularly of Republican leadership in the 104th and 105th Congresses? I argue that it performs well and, furthermore, that the theory in conjunction with these particular cases illuminates the thorny issue of leadership latitude. If, as I have argued, principal-agent theory does not posit leaders as puppets of their members, how much discretion do leaders have and under what circumstances? Randall Strahan (1996), whose theory of leadership is the most sophisticated of those positing, to varying extents, leader autonomy, argues that "under certain (admittedly infrequent) conditions the [leader] may act with some degree of autonomy and influence followers' preferences on questions of institutional structure and/or policy." He contends that such conditions existed in the 104th Congress and that Gingrich took full advantage of the potential the circumstances presented. My analysis of the 104th concurs but also sheds light on the character of the latitude Gingrich enjoyed and on its limits. Given members' enormous confidence in Gingrich's political sagacity and the high degree of intraparty agreement on the policy agenda, members were willing to allow Gingrich to exercise great discretion so long as they saw it as being in furtherance of their goal of delivering on their mandate. For example, Gingrich could violate seniority in picking committee chairs and override committee decisions because members, especially junior members, who made up the majority of the membership, perceived him to be doing so to advance their goals. In any case, junior members, by and large, did not have well-formed preferences on many of the matters of institutional structure or normal procedure at issue. However, when Gingrich exercised discretion in furtherance of an objective the members did not share, he soon found he was limited; this limitation existed even in early 1995 when the conditions seemed most conducive to leader autonomy. Thus when Gingrich attempted to exercise leadership in favor of the Mexican bailout, he quickly discovered that his members refused to follow and he had to retreat. More serious, of course, was members' unwillingness to grant him discretion to compromise sufficiently to get a budget deal. For a great many members, doing so would have entailed selling out their policy principles, and that they were unwilling to do.

Under more normal circumstances, the character of leaders' latitude is quite different. When the majority is even moderately ideologically heterogeneous, leaders must decide what policy positions to promote and how vigorously; whatever their decisions, not all their members will be satisfied. When the political context is such that, for some significant proportion of their membership, policy goals and reelection needs dictate different legislative strategies, leaders are again confronted with choices; again, however, whatever they do, they are likely to leave some members at least somewhat dissatisfied. (Although, through clever use of procedural strategies, leaders can sometimes ease the problem for members, especially if members' expectations are not excessively high.) Under such circumstances, leaders have less discretion to innovate boldly and use their resources aggressively. However, the configuration of preferences among their members provides them with latitude and, in fact, forces choices on them; they are confronted with the necessity of balancing their members' conflicting preferences in such a way that most of their members are not too dissatisfied. They can be sure that, no matter what they do, some level of dissatisfaction will exist. Such was the situation facing Republican leaders in the 105th Congress. However, setting the 105th apart, a considerable proportion of the Republican membership consisted of self-styled revolutionaries committed to nonincremental policy change and most had experienced the heady 104th. Thus the balancing job confronting leadership under normal circumstances was much more difficult and the level of dissatisfaction higher.

NOTES

1. In addition to the sources cited, this essay is based on interviews I conducted. Unattributed quotations are from those interviews. I delivered a previous version at the 1997 annual meeting of the American Political Science Association, August 28–31, Washington, D.C.

2. See Sinclair (1995) for an elaboration of the argument in this section. A fuller version of the discussion of Democratic majority party leadership presented later can also be found in that work.

3. The congressional agenda is defined as *Congressional Quarterly*'s list of major legislation, augmented by those measures on which key votes occurred (again according to *Congressional Quarterly*). The list produced thus includes legislation considered major by very close contemporary observers. The data for the 91st and the 94th Congresses are not strictly comparable to the data for later Congresses because only House key vote measures were added, whereas for the later Congresses Senate key vote measures were also added. The president's agenda is here defined as those items mentioned in the state of the union address or its equivalent and in special messages of some prominence. Majority party leadership agenda setting, if it occurs, will become manifest in the Speaker's speech on being elected to his or her office at the beginning of a session of Congress, the party's reply to the president's state of the union address, the leadership's reply to special presidential addresses, or major news conferences.

Two measures of leadership involvement were constructed. The first measure, intended to distinguish some involvement from none, is based on answers to the following questions: (1) Was the bill a part of the leadership's agenda? (2) Did the Speaker or the majority leader advocate passage during floor debate? (3) Did *Congressional Quarterly*'s account report the leadership as being involved? If any one of the answers is *yes,* the leadership is considered to have been involved. A second, more refined measure distinguishes major from minor involvement on the basis of the mode or modes of involvement reported by *Congressional Quarterly*. Four modes are distinguished: (a) the leadership uses its control over scheduling, the Rules Committee, or other procedure to advantage the legislation; (b) the leadership is involved in a floor vote mobilization effort; (c) the leadership is centrally involved in some other aspect of legislative strategy; or (d) the leadership participates in shaping the content of the legislation by talking or negotiating with or among the committee(s) or with the Senate or with the president. Major leadership involvement is defined as engaging in (d), shaping legislation, or in any two of the other activities (e.g., 1, 2, a, b, or c).

4. Republicans seem to have given affected interest groups a considerably greater role in drafting legislation than the Democrats ever did. See Drew (1996, 116–17).

REFERENCES

Aldrich, John, and David Rohde. 1997. "Balance of Power: Republican Party Leadership and the Committee System in the 104th House." Paper presented at the annual meeting of the Midwest Political Science Association, April 10–13, Chicago.
Blatz, Dan, and Ronald Brownstein. 1996. *Storming the Gates: Protest Politics and the Republican Revival.* Boston: Little, Brown.
Cox, Gary, and Mathew McCubbins. 1993. *Legislative Leviathan: Party Government in the House.* Berkeley and Los Angeles: University of California Press.
Doherty, Carroll. 1997. "GOP leaders Scuttle Bipartisan Bill in Nod to House Conservatives." *Congressional Quarterly Weekly Report,* June 7, 1325–27.

Drew, Elizabeth. 1996. *Showdown: The Struggle between the Gingrich Congress and the Clinton White House*. New York: Simon & Schuster.

Gingrich, Newt. 1995. "Leadership Task Forces: The 'Third Wave' Way to Consider Legislation." *Roll Call*, November 16, 5.

Healey, Jon. 1994. "Jubilant GOP Strives to Keep Legislative Feet on Ground." *Congressional Quarterly Weekly Report*, November 12, 3210–15.

Hook, Janet. 1995. "Budget Battle Forces Gingrich into the Trenches." *Los Angeles Times*, October 21, A20.

Koopman, Douglas. 1995. "The House of Representatives under Republican Leadership: Changes by the New Majority." Paper presented at the annual meeting of the American Political Science Association, August 30–September 3, Chicago.

Koopman, Douglas L. 1996. *Hostile Takeover: The House Republican Party 1980–1995*. Lanham, Md.: Rowman & Littlefield.

Koszczuk, Jackie. 1997. "For Embattled GOP Leadership, a Season of Discontent." *Congressional Quarterly Weekly Report*, July 20, 2019–23.

Langdon, Steve. 1997. " 'Partial Birth' Ban Passes House with Veto-Proof Vote Margin." *Congressional Quarterly Weekly Report*, March 22, 706–7.

Maraniss, David, and Michael Weisskopf. 1996. *Tell Newt to Shut Up!* New York: Touchstone.

Owens, John. 1998. "From Party Responsibility to Shared Responsibility, from Revolution to Concession: Institutional and Policy Change in the 104th Congress." In *The Republican Takeover on Capitol Hill*, ed. Dean McSweeney and John E. Owens, 33–70. London: Macmillan.

Peters, Ronald. 1996. "The Republican Speakership." Paper presented at the annual meeting of the American Political Science Association, August 29–September 1, San Francisco.

Pitney, John. 1988. "The Conservative Opportunity Society."

Rohde, David. 1991. *Parties and Leaders in the Postreform House*. Chicago: University of Chicago Press.

Salant, Jonathan D. 1995. "Alliance of Private Groups Pushes GOP 'Contract.' " *Congressional Quarterly Weekly Report*, January 28, 261–62.

Sinclair, Barbara. 1982. *Congressional Realignment*. Austin: University of Texas Press.

Sinclair, Barbara. 1983. *Majority Leadership in the U.S. House*. Baltimore: Johns Hopkins University Press.

Sinclair, Barbara. 1995. *Legislators, Leaders, and Lawmaking*. Baltimore: Johns Hopkins University Press.

Sinclair, Barbara. 1997. *Unorthodox Lawmaking*. Washington, D.C.: Congressional Quarterly Press.

Smith, Steven. 1989. *Call to Order: Floor Politics in the House and Senate*. Washington, D.C.: Brookings Institution Press.

Stid, Daniel. 1996. "Transformational Leadership in Congress?" Paper presented at the annual meeting of the American Political Science Association, August 29–September 1, San Francisco.

Strahan, Randall. 1996. "Leadership in Institutional and Political Time: The Case of Newt Gingrich and the 104th Congress." Paper presented at the annual meeting of the American Political Science Association, August 29–September 1, San Francisco.

Can Advisory Committees Facilitate Congressional Oversight of the Bureaucracy?

Steven J. Balla and John R. Wright

Introduction

The pursuit of a successful legislative career leaves little time for attention to the details of policy implementation. Except for members of the House Appropriations Committee, who are expected by their colleagues to monitor the bureaucracy (Fenno 1966), oversight of federal agencies is not one of the principal goals of elected representatives (Fenno 1973b). Reelection and legislating are the central, interconnected components of legislative careers (Fenno 1978, 1991), and thus members of Congress have little incentive to engage in bureaucratic oversight (Fenno 1973a).

The lack of legislative interest in oversight, together with the superior policy expertise of federal agencies, make congressional control of the bureaucracy highly problematic (see, e.g., Bibby 1968; Dodd and Schott 1979; Lowi 1979). Scholars have increasingly recognized that Congress cannot control agencies sufficiently through costly hearings and investigations, and thus recent research has investigated the extent to which Congress controls the bureaucracy through less direct and less costly methods. McCubbins and Schwartz (1984) observe that legislators establish rules and procedures that enable interested parties to examine agency actions and alert Congress about noncompliant bureaucratic behavior. Similarly, McCubbins, Noll, and Weingast (1987, 1989) argue that members of Congress manipulate agency structure and process so that bureaucratic decisions closely resemble those that legislators would have made in the absence of delegation.

We follow this general vein of research that investigates unobtrusive and inexpensive methods of congressional oversight. We propose that Congress can use federal advisory committees to oversee agencies in an efficient and effective manner. Congress has created advisory committees (defined and described later in this essay) in numerous statutes. Many of these statutes not only require agencies to consult with advisory committees when making policy but also mandate that committees be composed of representative cross sections of the parties who hold a stake in agency decisions. We argue that advisory committees can best facilitate congressional oversight under two conditions. First, advisory committees must actually be composed of representative cross sections of stakeholders (i.e., they must not be biased in favor of particular constituencies). Second, advisory committee members must be well informed about agency policy choices and their likely consequences. Under these conditions, advisory committees can reduce the information asymmetry between Congress and agencies, which in turn can reduce the distance between agency policies and congressional preferences.

We develop our argument by first presenting an overview of the advisory committee system and a review of the scholarly conclusions about the composition and operation of advisory committees. Next, we provide an intuition for, and illustration of, our perspective on advisory committees and congressional oversight. We then examine the plausibility of this perspective as applied to three advisory committees: the National Drinking Water Advisory Council of the Environmental Protection Agency, the National Advisory Committee on Meat and Poultry Inspection of the Department of Agriculture, and the Advisory Committee on Student Financial Assistance of the Department of Education. These cases illustrate that Congress often has a preference for well-informed, heterogeneous advisory committees and that agencies vary in the extent to which they assemble heterogeneous committees and provide them with information about agency decision making. We conclude by discussing the implications of our perspective and case studies for legislative-executive relations and suggesting directions for future research.

What are Advisory Committees?

As defined in the Federal Advisory Committee Act (FACA) of 1972, an advisory committee is

> any committee, board, commission, council, conference, panel, task force, or other similar group, or any subcommittee or other subgroup thereof . . . , which is—(A) established by statute or reorganization plan, or (B) established or utilized by the President, or (C) established or utilized by one or more agencies, in the interest of obtaining advice or recommendations for the President or one or more agencies or officers of the Federal Government, except that such term excludes . . . any committee which is composed wholly of full-time officers or employees of the Federal Government.

Clearly, advisory committees vary in numerous respects, and the formal definition of advisory committees covers many that are not designed for congressional oversight of the bureaucracy. We focus here only on advisory committees that Congress creates to advise federal agencies over time on national policy making. Hence, several types of advisory committees fall outside our perspective, including presidential advisory committees (e.g., President Clinton's Advisory Commission on Consumer Protection and Quality in the Health

Care Industry), advisory committees created to address a particular problem (e.g., the Technical Study Group on Cigarette and Little Cigar Fire Safety), advisory committees that provide expert, nonpolitical advice (e.g., the science advisory boards of several agencies), advisory committees designed to provide citizen input into the management of local affairs (e.g., the Department of the Interior's Sleeping Bear Dunes National Lakeshore Advisory Commission), and advisory committees established by agencies and operating outside congressional authority.

Even excluding these types of committees, many can potentially provide an oversight function. Of the 963 advisory committees in existence in 1997, 652 were authorized or mandated by Congress, and many, although certainly not all, of these advisory committees are charged with advising agencies over time on national policy making.[1] For example, the Commercial Fishing Industry Vessel Advisory Committee (CFIVAC), established by the Commercial Fishing Industry Vessel Safety Act of 1988, possesses the authority to "advise, consult with, report to, and make recommendations to the Secretary [of the Department of Transportation] on matters relating to the safe operation of vessels," "review proposed regulations," and "make available to Congress any information, advice, and recommendations that the Committee is authorized to give to the Secretary." The act mandates that the CFIVAC be composed of members of the commercial fishing industry, naval architects, marine surveyors, equipment manufacturers, educational or training professionals, underwriters, and representatives of the general public.

What Do We Know about Advisory Committees?

Scholars have long studied advisory committees of the federal government. Leiserson (1942) traces the evolution of advisory committees. Truman (1951) points out that advisory committees can help legislatures and agencies develop constituencies. McConnell (1966) highlights the importance of business-dominated advisory committees in the policy-making process. Wolanin (1975) provides an overview of presidential advisory committees. Fritschler (1989) describes advisory committee participation in the regulation of smoking in the 1960s. It was not, however, until passage of FACA, which instructed the executive branch "to institute a comprehensive review of the activities and responsibilities of each advisory committee," that it became possible to analyze committees in a systematic manner (Bybee 1994; Kerwin 1994).

The FACA provision that has stimulated the most research is the balance requirement. FACA stipulates that any legislation that authorizes or mandates an advisory committee "require[s] the membership of the advisory committee to be fairly balanced in terms of the points of view represented and the functions to be performed by the advisory committee." Pika (1983) suggests that this provision was motivated by public interest groups, which had proliferated in the 1960s without achieving proportionate access to bureaucratic policy making. He also notes a "wide gap between the stated goals of FACA and compliance with the mandated procedures" (1983, 309). Some agencies, for example, created new committees to accommodate public interest groups but gave these committees little responsibility. As a result, agencies achieved balance in membership across committees but not within committees.

Schlozman and Tierney (1986) describe the widespread, although not necessarily balanced, participation of groups in the advisory committee system. Three-quarters of the groups that they surveyed (95 percent of those from unions, 74 percent of those from corporations, and 67 percent of those from public interest groups) serve on advisory committees. Corporations, however, are more likely than unions or public interest groups to serve on multiple committees, so that the total volume of corporate participation is higher than that of other constituencies.

Petracca (1986) expands on this theme. He asserts that that FACA's balance requirement "remains, for the most part, an unfulfilled statutory goal" (1986, 92). He maintains that "considerable discretion remains in the selection of members for most advisory committees," and "the data reveal a striking imbalance in the representation of diverse interests on most committees" (1986, 95). He assumes that "where there are larger concentrations of interests, those interests are more likely to exercise greater influence" (1986, 97). In other words, the implied consequence of an imbalance in representation is an imbalance in influence. The favored interests are business interests, which "serve on committees without balanced representation and with broad jurisdictional mandates" (Petracca 1986, 104).

Gais, Peterson, and Walker (1984) and Priest, Sylves, and Scudder (1984) provide additional support for this conclusion. Gais, Peterson, and Walker report that citizen groups are less likely than occupational groups to serve on advisory committees or otherwise possess institutionalized access to bureaucratic decision making. Priest, Sylves, and Scudder examined corporate participation between 1973 and 1977. They found a slight decrease in corporate participation but nevertheless observed substantial participation throughout this period.

In sum, existing research on advisory committees suggests that committees are not balanced and that business interests dominate the system. This research, however, has generally been conducted at a high level of aggregation, so that its conclusions pertain to specific types of advisory committees but not to particular committees. It also raises the following question: Why would Congress prefer unbalanced advisory committees when it has mandated that committees be composed of representative cross sections of the constituencies holding a stake in agency policies?

Congressional Oversight through Advisory Committees

We develop our hypothesis about the oversight capabilities of advisory committees in this section by way of a hypothetical example. Simply stated, our argument is that if Congress creates advisory committees for purposes of bureaucratic oversight, then Congress will prefer advisory committees that are not only balanced but also well informed about agency policies and their likely consequences. We begin by noting that legislation is generally the product of compromise among competing interests. When making social policy, for example, legislators frequently balance the costs borne by industry (e.g., compliance with environmental mandates) with the benefits derived by the general public (e.g., cleaner air and water). Because much legislation delegates policy-making authority to the bureaucracy—environmental statutes, for example, typically instruct the Environmental Protection Agency (EPA) to develop numerous regulations—delegation raises the possibility that bureaucratic decisions upset the delicate political balance struck by Congress. Hence, EPA regulations, for example, may be less stringent than envisioned by the legislative coalition. This deviation may occur because bureaucratic preferences differ from congressional preferences or because agencies acquire information during the regulatory process that was unavailable to Congress.

The following hypothetical example illustrates how agency policies can stray from those favored by Congress. Suppose that Congress enacts a statute that mandates the identification and removal of various contaminants found in the nation's drinking water. The statute calls for the establishment of maximum contaminant levels that provide "an adequate standard of safety" and grants the EPA the authority to determine these levels. Environmentalists prefer higher safety standards (i.e., lower contaminant levels) than Congress, Congress prefers higher standards than the EPA, and the EPA prefers higher standards than the drinking water industry. During rule making, the agency commissions a study that finds the health effects of many contaminants to be less severe than Congress had believed when it enacted the statute. The EPA's scientists evaluate this study and discover that its conclusions are likely erroneous, but agency officials do not report this discovery to Congress. Congress is therefore aware of the study and its conclusions but is not informed that the study may be misleading.

Should the EPA reveal all it knows about the new study? What contaminant levels should the EPA propose? Should Congress accept the EPA's proposal, or should it revisit the issue and set contaminant levels itself? The answers to these questions depend critically on what Congress believes about the health effects of contaminants. If Congress believes that the study is sound, then the EPA can propose contaminant levels higher (i.e., less restrictive) than those originally intended by Congress and more in line with those preferred by the agency. In other words, by not divulging the erroneous conclusions of the study, the EPA can claim that if it sets contaminants at the levels implied by the statute, the resulting safety standards would actually be *higher* than those preferred by Congress, resulting in overregulation of drinking water. In contrast, if Congress views the study with appropriate skepticism, then it would be difficult for the EPA to make a convincing case that contaminant levels should be relaxed. The EPA would need to establish contaminant levels consistent with the enacting legislation to generate congressional support and to forestall congressional involvement in the rule-making process.

This example implies that the EPA has an incentive to suppress information to prevent Congress from discovering the truth about the study. Even though Congress may recognize this incentive, it cannot be certain that it properly gauged the severity of the health effects of contaminants when it drafted the statute. Thus, confronted by an agency with divergent preferences and superior information, Congress is vulnerable to manipulation. To prevent manipulation, Congress must acquire additional policy expertise about the true health effects of contaminants.

When seeking policy expertise, Congress can turn to a variety of sources, some of which are more costly than others. Interest groups are one of the least costly sources (Wright 1996), but, as the present example illustrates, groups do not necessarily provide the requisite information. Scientists affiliated with the drinking water industry have no more incentive than does the EPA to acknowledge the flawed nature of the study. Furthermore, if the EPA stonewalls requests for additional information about the study, then scientists affiliated with environmental groups will not be able to assess fully the EPA's claims about the relatively low health effects of contaminants. Congress could, of course, compel the agency's scientists to testify under oath or commission yet another study, but these strategies are costly and must be employed selectively.

The major impediment that Congress faces in this example—an impediment that we think Congress frequently confronts—is access to information about agency policy choices and their likely consequences. If environmentalists were able to evaluate the EPA's study and report their assessment to Congress, then Congress would be more confident about the congruence between its preferences and the contaminant levels selected by the EPA. Given that environmentalists prefer lower contaminant levels, they have an incentive to reveal the EPA's attempt to suppress information about the inaccuracy of the study and, in the process, to deter the EPA from promulgating contaminant levels that deviate substantially from those preferred by Congress. Hence, one way for Congress to reduce its informational disadvantage is to provide environmentalists with access to EPA decision making.

We suggest that Congress routinely establishes access of this sort through advisory committees.[2] In our view, a principal function of advisory committees is to provide competing interest groups with institutionalized access to agency policy making. In the present example, Congress could oversee the setting of contaminant levels by mandating that both the drinking water industry and environmentalists have access to the EPA information. For example, Congress could require the agency to consult with these interests when developing regulations. Because environmental groups have a keen interest in assessing the plausibility of the EPA's assertions about the relatively low health effects of contaminants, Congress could rely on these groups to uncover the EPA's efforts to misrepresent its information.

Thus, the requirement that advisory committees be balanced has direct bearing on the utility of committees as instruments of oversight. We argue, in contrast to previous research on advisory committees, that the motivation for achieving balance is more profound than placating public interest groups. If advisory committees are to serve an informational purpose, then balance is essential, because the relative preferences of Congress and agencies change across issues and over time (e.g., when elections alter the occupancy of the White House or the partisan composition of Congress). In the present example, the EPA is aligned with the drinking water industry. It is, however, just as plausible for the EPA to be aligned with environmentalists, in which case Congress's informational disadvantage could be best alleviated by industry groups.

The creation of balanced advisory committees, however, may not be enough to facilitate oversight. Agencies typically possess the authority to appoint advisory committee members, and they largely control the access of members to agency decision making. Agencies can use these mechanisms to lessen the efficacy of advisory committees as instruments of oversight. They can, for example, appoint individuals who have little experience or expertise in the matters under advisory committee jurisdiction. They can also constitute advisory committees that are biased in favor of particular constituencies. Finally, they can use advisory committees in a perfunctory manner, by limiting committee access to and influence over agency decision making.

With these possibilities in mind, we suggest that two conditions must be met for advisory committees to facilitate congressional oversight: (1) committees must be heterogeneous in their composition and (2) committee members must have access to agency information. The first condition implies that Congress can identify at least one member to serve as a reliable informant about agency policy making (i.e., a member whose preferences, like those of environmental groups in the present example, are biased against the agency). The second condition implies that informants can provide Congress with information about the outcomes that will likely follow from agency policies.

In the remainder of this essay, we "soak and poke" among three advisory committees to gain some preliminary evidence for or against our hypothesis.

The advisory committees we examine are located within diverse bureaucracies (a long-standing cabinet department, a relatively recent addition to the cabinet, and an independent agency) and have jurisdiction over diverse policy areas. Our analysis focuses on four central questions: Did Congress establish an advisory committee composed of a representative cross section of parties who hold a stake in agency policies? Did Congress provide advisory committee members with the access necessary to develop expertise regarding the relationship between agency proposals and policy outcomes? Did the agency, to the extent that it possessed the authority to appoint members, assemble a heterogeneous advisory committee? How much influence over policy making did the agency grant to the advisory committee?

Case Studies

The advisory committees on which we focus are the National Drinking Water Advisory Council (NDWAC), the National Advisory Committee on Meat and Poultry Inspection (NACMPI), and the Advisory Committee on Student Financial Assistance (ACSFA). We collected information about our cases from a variety of sources. We attended advisory committee meetings. We also interviewed individuals familiar with the history and operation of the advisory committees, including agency personnel, former congressional and agency officials, and interest group representatives. Finally, we assembled documents from the advisory committees, the agencies of jurisdiction, the *Federal Register,* and the committee management secretariat of the General Services Administration.

By way of preview, we find that in each instance Congress expressed a preference for an advisory committee composed of a representative cross section of stakeholders and assigned members a variety of policy-making responsibilities. Nevertheless, the advisory committees varied cross-sectionally and over time in the extent to which they were heterogeneous in composition and possessed the access necessary to alleviate Congress's informational disadvantage. These differences are in part the result of variance in Congress's willingness to enforce its statutory mandates and in agency compliance with these mandates. Together these cases suggest that advisory committees can facilitate congressional oversight and that both Congress and agencies play an important role in determining which committees operate in such a manner.

The National Drinking Water Advisory Council

Legislative History of Drinking Water Policy
State governments were historically responsible for regulating drinking water. The Safe Drinking Water Act of 1974 transferred this authority to the EPA and

charged it to set maximum levels for contaminants found in drinking water (Mathiasen 1975). By the mid-1980s, however, the EPA had regulated "only about two dozen of more than 600 contaminants" (Cohen 1987, 134). Congress strengthened the act in 1986 by requiring the EPA to establish maximum levels for 83 contaminants within 3 years and 25 contaminants in each subsequent 3-year period. This ambitious approach turned out to be problematic in that the EPA did not have the resources necessary to establish regulatory priorities; as a result, it left unregulated many dangerous contaminants, including cryptosporidium, which was responsible for more than 100 deaths in Milwaukee during a 1993 outbreak (Freedman 1996).

Congress amended the act once again in 1996 (Hosansky 1996). It loosened the act's timetable and provided the EPA with the flexibility to focus its regulatory program on contaminants that have known adverse health effects and that are present in drinking water at levels that threaten public health. It also eased the regulatory burden placed on state regulators, most of whom have the authority to make drinking water policy within broad parameters established by the EPA. The drinking water industry supported these changes, in part because utilities would no longer be required to monitor contaminants not likely to be present in their systems (Freedman 1996). Although environmentalists opposed these changes, their acquiescence was garnered through several concessions, such as requirements that water systems notify the public about contaminants and their health effects and that water system operators receive government certification.

Congress and the Creation of the NDWAC
Congress mandated the creation of the NDWAC in the Safe Drinking Water Act of 1974, which charged the NDWAC to "advise, consult with, and make recommendations" to the EPA in the area of drinking water policy. Congress delegated to the EPA the authority to appoint the NDWAC's 15 members. It also established the following membership categories:

> Five members shall be appointed from the general public; five members shall be appointed from appropriate State and local agencies concerned with water hygiene and public water supply; and five members shall be appointed from representatives of private organizations or groups demonstrating an active interest in the field of water hygiene and public water supply.

By allocating membership rights in this manner, Congress articulated a preference that the NDWAC be composed of a representative cross section of the parties who hold a stake in drinking water policy.

The History of the NDWAC

Throughout much of its history, the NDWAC played a marginal role in the making of drinking water policy. It was perceived in many quarters as a rubber stamp for EPA decision making that exerted little independent influence over implementation of the act. Although some of its members were representatives of key stakeholders (e.g., water utilities, state regulators, and environmentalists), others had little connection to drinking water and owed their appointment to White House and congressional connections.

The NDWAC's role has changed dramatically since the 1996 amendments. The EPA has authorized the NDWAC to work closely with the agency in establishing priorities for the drinking water program and developing policy in areas such as consumer confidence reports, operator certification, and source water protection. For example, the EPA drafted regulations to govern the information that water systems must provide to consumers. This draft left unresolved a variety of important issues (e.g., the level of information about sources of contamination that should be included in consumer reports). The NDWAC studied and debated these issues extensively and ultimately provided the EPA with policy recommendations.

Interest Group Mobilization

The interest group community has also changed dramatically since the act's initial passage. In the 1970s, environmentalists actively sought to place authority over drinking water policy in the hands of the federal government. In the 1980s, they lobbied for more stringent standards and regulatory timetables. During these years, the drinking water industry was, in the words of one official, "asleep at the wheel." For example, the American Water Works Association (AWWA), the oldest and largest organization of drinking water professionals, did not open a government affairs office until the mid-1980s. By the 1990s, however, the drinking water industry had mobilized, perhaps in response to the environmentalism of the 1986 amendments. In addition to the AWWA, the National Association of Water Companies (NAWC), which represents large, privately owned utilities, and the National Rural Water Association (NRWA), which represents rural, public utilities, are active participants in the making of drinking water policy. As a result, the policy area is now characterized by numerous interests with diverse preferences.

The Appointment of NDWAC Members

Interest groups and other stakeholders are generally quite interested in serving on the NDWAC. The EPA appoints NDWAC members in the following manner: Each fall, the agency publishes a *Federal Register* request for nominations. Its Office of Ground Water and Drinking Water processes these nominations and proposes candidates for membership. Its proposal is forwarded to the assistant administrator of water, who, after consultation with political appointees inside and outside the EPA, officially determines the composition of the NDWAC.

In recent years, individuals nominated for NDWAC membership have generally possessed distinguished drinking water credentials. For example, one candidate was the deputy general manager of the Metropolitan Water District of Southern California, a public utility that provides water to millions of consumers. Another candidate was the chief of Michigan's Division of Water Supply. This candidate also served as the vice president of the Association of State Drinking Water Administrators (ASDWA), an organization that consists of the lead drinking water official of each state and territory. Finally, one candidate was a senior attorney at the Natural Resources Defense Council (NRDC), the environmental group most active in the area of drinking water policy.

Many nominees received support from legislators and interest groups. Congressional support usually occurred on behalf of constituents. In 1996, for example, Senator Feinstein (D-CA) and three members of Congress from California wrote letters backing the candidacy of the general manager of the Contra Costa Water District, a public utility that serves more than 400,000 Californians. Interest group support was typically oriented toward securing representation on the NDWAC for constituencies with a stake in drinking water policy. Major stakeholders have generally fared well in the appointment process. In recent years, the EPA has selected individuals who were endorsed by interest groups representing the drinking water industry (e.g., the AWWA, the NAWC, and the NRWA), state regulators (e.g., the ASDWA), and environmentalists (e.g., the NRDC).

Assessing the NDWAC
Congress established the possibility of a well-informed, heterogeneous advisory committee by granting broad authority to the NDWAC and mandating that its members be drawn from the constituencies with a major stake in drinking water policy. This possibility was not fully realized until two decades later, after the mobilization of the drinking water industry and passage of the 1996 amendments. The NDWAC is currently composed in large part of representatives of the interest groups that are most active in drinking water policy. These groups' preferences vary quite extensively, from environmentalists, who favor stringent maximum contaminant levels, to the drinking water industry, which favors a more flexible regulatory program. The NDWAC's members are well informed about implementation of the amendments; they play an important role in setting rule-making priorities, drafting regulatory proposals, and assessing EPA policies at various stages of development.

The National Advisory Committee on Meat and Poultry Inspection

Background on Food Safety and Inspection

Legislation to address food safety and inspection dates back to the turn of the century. These laws (e.g., the Meat Inspection Act of 1890) charge the U.S. Department of Agriculture (USDA) with "regulating the meat, poultry, and egg products industries to ensure that meat, poultry, and egg products moving in interstate commerce or exported to other countries are safe, wholesome, and accurately labeled" (U.S. Department of Agriculture 1997, 4-3).

The USDA's traditional approach to inspection was grounded in organoleptic, or sensory, inspection. Agency personnel, in other words, conducted inspections by looking at, smelling, and touching products. Over time, this system was increasingly criticized, in part because it could not adequately detect "hazards such as pathogenic microorganisms that can cause foodborne illness" (U.S. Department of Agriculture 1997, 4-3). A fatal *E. coli* outbreak in 1993 brought widespread attention to the inadequacies of organoleptic inspection.

In part as a reaction to this outbreak, the USDA embraced a new approach—the Pathogen Reduction/Hazard Analysis and Critical Control Point (HACCP) regulatory program. The HACCP program focuses on points in the "farm-to-table" continuum that pose the greatest risk to safety and uses monitoring to determine whether microbiological hazards are present at these points. Under the HACCP program, plants are required to identify control points (e.g., slaughter procedures), establish limits regarding parameters such as time and temperature, implement procedures designed to monitor compliance with these limits, and take corrective action when limits are exceeded. The USDA's responsibilities include ensuring that plants' programs conform to regulatory requirements, documenting that plants are carrying out their programs, and imposing penalties on noncompliant plants.

Congress and the Creation of the NACMPI

Congress established the NACMPI in 1971 under the authority of the Federal Meat Inspection Act of 1906 and the Poultry Products Inspection Act of 1957. Both statutes require the secretary of agriculture to "consult with an advisory committee before issuing product standards and labeling changes or on matters affecting federal and state program activities" (National Advisory Committee on Meat and Poultry Inspection 1998). According to its charter,

> [NACMPI's] membership shall be drawn from representatives of government, industry, trade associations, the scientific community, and consumer organizations, and shall be composed of individuals with diverse capabilities distinguished by their knowledge and interest in meat and poultry inspection and other FSIS [Food Safety and Inspection Service] responsibilities.

In sum, Congress has assigned a broad advisory function to the NACMPI, which is designed to be heterogeneous in composition.

The History of the NACMPI

Throughout much of its history, the NACMPI possessed two basic characteristics. First, it did not play an important role in the making of meat and poultry inspection policy. Although it assembled once a year to react to USDA policies, its recommendations generally exerted little influence over agency decision making. Second, the NACMPI was dominated by industry interests. In 1990, for example, the U.S. Meat Exporters Federation, the American Association of Meat Processors, and firms such as Veribest Cattle Feeders, Inc., and George A. Hormel and Company were represented on the NACMPI. No NACMPI member, however, was affiliated with a consumer organization.

The Farm Bill

The Federal Agriculture Improvement and Reform Act of 1996, more commonly known as the farm bill, precipitated changes in both of these characteristics (Austin 1997). Dissatisfied with the fact that the NACMPI was unbalanced and uninfluential, Congress mandated the creation of a new advisory committee—the Safe Meat and Poultry Inspection Panel. The panel was to be composed of seven members, at least five of whom represented the food, meat, and poultry science professions. Individuals were to be nominated by the National Institutes of Health and the Federation of American Societies of Food Animal Science and to be selected by the secretary of agriculture. The act charged the panel with reviewing and evaluating inspection procedures and regulations with regard to their "adequacy, necessity, safety, cost-effectiveness, and scientific merit."

After passage of the farm bill, Congress and the USDA struck a deal. Congress did not appropriate any funding for the panel, over which the USDA was to have relatively little control. In return, the USDA agreed to reconstitute the NACMPI by making its membership a more representative cross section of stakeholders and granting it a central role in the making of food safety and inspection policy.

The Composition of the NACMPI

One result of this deal is that the USDA now explicitly assigns membership rights to a variety of constituencies with a stake in food safety and inspection policy. It has stated that the NACMPI is to consist of 16 members, 4 representing state inspection programs, 4 representing meat and poultry processors, 1 representing meat and poultry product distributors, 2 representing industry meat associations, 3 representing consumer interest groups, 1 representing ranchers, and 1 representing technology consulting firms.

In 1997–98, the first term of the reconstituted NACMPI, its membership reflected this increased emphasis on heterogeneity. Although industry groups such as the National Meat Association and the National Pork Producers were still well represented, consumer groups such as the Safe Food Coalition and the Center for Science and the Public Interest were better represented than in the past. Other NACMPI members were drawn from the state inspection programs of New York, South Carolina, Texas, and Wisconsin and from technical organizations such as ABC Research Corporation.

NACMPI's Influence

Another result of the deal between Congress and the USDA is that the NACMPI now exerts influence over the policy-making process. For example, it plays an important role in the setting of the Food Safety and Inspection Service's regulatory agenda. Of the 18 issues considered to be on the agenda in 1998, the NACMPI raised 10, despite, in some instances, opposition on the part of the USDA. In addition, the agency, according to a USDA official, is reluctant to make policy choices without the "blessing" of the NACMPI, or at least an adequate airing of the advisory committee's dissatisfaction. For example, the USDA recently launched a controversial pilot program in which plants, under agency supervision, conduct their own inspections. In the past, the USDA's approach would have been to establish the program and then solicit the NACMPI's reaction. In this instance, the NACMPI has played a major role not only in evaluating the program but in designing it as well.

Assessing the NACMPI

The NACMPI was neither heterogeneous nor an important player in the making of food safety and inspection policy for the first 25 years of its existence. In 1996, in response to congressional pressure, the USDA reconstituted the NACMPI by making its membership more heterogeneous and by increasing its authority. NACMPI members are now drawn from industry groups, consumer groups, state government departments, and other organizations with a major stake in food safety and inspection policy. These members possess more information about USDA policies than their predecessors, because they play a role in setting the regulatory agenda, drafting proposals, and evaluating USDA decisions at a variety of stages of the policy-making process.

The Advisory Committee on Student Financial Assistance

An Independent Advisory Committee

Congress established ACSFA in the Higher Education Act Amendments of 1986 and charged it to advise Congress and the Department of Education on student financial aid policy. The ACSFA consists of 11 members, 3 of whom are appointed by the House of Representatives, 3 of whom are appointed by the Senate, and 5 of whom are appointed by the Department of Education. The act does not specify a precise balance in the composition of the ACSFA, although it states that members should be drawn from constituencies such as "States, institutions of higher education, secondary schools, credit institutions, students, and parents."

Congress has assigned the ACSFA a wide variety of specific responsibilities and tasks. The act gives ACSFA jurisdiction over issues such as the "maintenance of access to postsecondary education for low- and middle-income students" and simplification of student loan programs (e.g., paperwork reduction, standardization of procedures, and changes in the repayment process). In 1989, legislators requested that the ACSFA "assist the Congress in identifying and discussing issues that should be considered by the Congress" during the 1992 reauthorization of the act (Advisory Committee on Student Financial Assistance 1997, 3.1.2). The Student Loan Reform Act of 1993 instructed the ACSFA to conduct a 3-year evaluation of the Federal Family Education Loan Program and the Ford Federal Direct Loan Program.

Although the ACSFA is located within the Department of Education, it is independent of the agency in many respects. The ACSFA controls its budgetary, personnel, procurement, and other administrative and management decisions. It is not required, although it is permitted, to submit its recommendations to the Department of Education before submission to Congress. In contrast, the act instructs the ACSFA to make "special efforts" to keep legislators apprised of its activities. Not surprisingly, individuals familiar with the ACSFA indicate that it works closely with Congress and communicates sporadically with the Department of Education.

The Politics of Higher Education and the Origin of the ACSFA
The ACSFA's independence must be understood in the context of the acrimony that existed between Congress and the Department of Education in the 1980s (Hook 1986a, 1986b, 1986c). The Reagan administration repeatedly proposed major cuts in education spending. These cuts targeted higher education programs, a reflection of the administration's preference for spending on elementary and secondary education. In 1986, for example, the administration favored reducing the budget of the Department of Education by 15 percent. These savings were to be generated in part by decreasing the number of postsecondary students who received federal aid by more than 1 million.

Although the 1986 amendments included provisions favored by the administration (e.g., a tightening of eligibility for guaranteed student loans), they represented a bipartisan rejection of substantial spending cuts. They also reflected a deep distrust between Congress and the Department of Education. For example, legislators limited the authority of the Department of Education to write rules governing need analysis, which is used to determine the financial resources of aid applicants. In fact, an early House version had restricted this authority completely and placed it solely in the hands of Congress.

The creation, structure, and process of the ACSFA were a product of this tension. Private educational institutions, and other parties who had fared well when need analysis was under the jurisdiction of the Department of Education, opposed Congress's assumption of greater authority over student financial aid policy. Congress sought to diffuse this opposition by creating the ACSFA, which provided interested parties with a forum for advising Congress on need analysis and other issues. Congress, which anticipated that the agency would be predisposed to undermine an advisory committee oriented toward assisting Congress in expanding its policy-making authority, designed the ACSFA to be independent of the Department of Education. According to a former congressional staffer, the ACSFA has emerged as an important source of information and guidance, although (as discussed later) in a manner not anticipated at its creation.

The Appointment of ACSFA Members.   The ACSFA's members include university presidents and financial aid officers, representatives of organized interests, and members of private firms that are active in the area of higher education policy. Unlike many advisory committees, ACSFA vacancies are not announced in the *Federal Register*. Appointments are made by high-level officials—House and Senate leaders and the secretary of education. For example, the chair of the ACSFA's 1997–98 term, the chancellor of the University of Mississippi, was appointed by Senate Majority Leader Trent Lott (R-MS). Officials have at times assigned a low priority to their appointment responsibilities. William Bennett, the secretary of education under President Reagan, opposed the creation of the ACSFA and initially refused to make appointments. One of President Bush's appointees was a relative who, after learning about the ACSFA and its duties, was disinterested enough to decline the appointment. The Clinton administration's early appointments were more a reflection of political debts than qualifications, although some of its recent appointees are highly regarded in the higher education community. According to an official at the Department of Education, the agency is endeavoring to become better informed about ACSFA activities and recommendations and views the appointment of prominent experts as an integral part of this process.

ACSFA's Staff.   The key feature of the ACSFA that makes it a valuable resource for Congress is not its membership but its staff. Many advisory committees are staffed only by a designated federal officer, an agency official who provides administrative and logistical support for committee activities. The ACSFA, in contrast, has a six-person staff, including a staff director with a doctorate in education in policy research and a staff economist, both of whom have been with the ACSFA since it began operating in 1988. These individuals' activities greatly exceed those of a designated federal officer and include substantive, policy-oriented responsibilities.

The ACSFA's staff, for example, regularly communicates with legislators and congressional staffers, to both receive tasks and deliver recommendations. It also gathers the technical information (e.g., data on various aspects of student loan programs) necessary to fulfill its congressional mandates. By controlling this information, the staff exerts substantial influence over the substance of the ACSFA's policy recommendations. According to an individual familiar with this process, the staff presents technical information to ACSFA members in ways that favor recommendations consistent with staff preferences.

Congress did not anticipate the emergence of an informative staff, which was the product of the staff director, who possesses both policy expertise and political savvy. Congress nonetheless works closely with the ACSFA's staff, which has carved out a unique niche in the making of student financial aid policy. In fact, some of the ACSFA's recommendations are not subject to the approval of its membership, nor are they discussed at meetings. For example, during the 1998 reauthorization of the act, legislators requested that the ACSFA provide a detailed comparison of the House and Senate bills and make recommendations about reconciling the differences. The ACSFA's staff performed this comparison and forwarded its recommendations to Congress without seeking the advice or approval of ACSFA members.

Assessing the ACSFA

The ACSFA plays an important role in providing Congress with information about the making of student financial aid policy, although not in a manner anticipated when it was created. As a product of the distrust that existed between Congress and the Department of Education in the 1980s, Congress makes decisions regarding issues such as need analysis itself rather than delegating this authority to the Department of Education. In this policy-making environment, Congress has a need for independent information about student financial aid (i.e., information that is not provided by the Department of Education). The ACSFA provides such information through the expertise of its staff, which has evolved into a small research organization that works closely with Congress, despite the fact that it is located within the Department of Education.

Discussion

Our aim in this essay has been to explore the possibility that advisory committees facilitate congressional oversight of the bureaucracy. We have argued that

Congress is often at an informational disadvantage relative to the agencies to which it delegates policy-making authority. If Congress does not reduce this asymmetry, then policy outcomes may not reflect the bargains struck by legislative coalitions, particularly when agency preferences diverge substantially from coalition preferences. Our perspective suggests that advisory committees can operate as instruments of oversight when they are heterogeneous in composition and when their members have access to agency decision making.

Two of our cases—the NDWAC and the NACMPI—currently meet these conditions. In both instances, Congress articulated a preference for advisory committees composed of representative cross sections of stakeholders. This goal, however, has been realized only in recent years, despite the fact that these advisory committees have been in existence since the early 1970s. Neither the EPA nor the USDA demonstrated a willingness to assemble heterogeneous, well-informed advisory committees until the passage of statutes that fundamentally altered their policy-making environments and increased the attractiveness of complying with earlier congressional mandates.

Our third case—the ACSFA—illustrates that Congress can use advisory committees for informational purposes other than bureaucratic oversight. Congress makes many decisions regarding student financial aid policy itself, in part because of its historically acrimonious relationship with the Department of Education. As a result, its most pressing need is not for information about agency policy choices but for technical information about issues such as need analysis. It receives this information from the advisory committee's staff, which over time has developed a reputation for working closely with Congress and providing a source of expertise that is independent of the Department of Education.

Together these cases suggest that advisory committees evolve during the course of their existence. Each of the three advisory committees is more useful to Congress now than when it was created. For the NDWAC and the NACMPI, new statutes have provided the EPA and the USDA with the impetus to enhance the representativeness of the advisory committees and to increase the role that they play in the policy-making process. For the ACSFA, entrepreneurial behavior by its staff has transformed the advisory committee into a reliable, independent source of information about student financial aid policy.

In sum, this research indicates that advisory committees can facilitate oversight by reducing the information asymmetry between Congress and bureaucratic agencies. Given its exploratory nature, the research also raises several questions that merit further attention. First, why does congressional enforcement of statutory mandates vary? Even though Congress may express a preference for heterogeneous, well-informed advisory committees, it does not necessarily take steps to ensure the realization of this goal, as it did when it used the 1996 farm bill to pressure the USDA into reconstituting the NACMPI.

Second, why do agencies vary in the extent to which they comply with statutory mandates? Agencies may naturally be predisposed against advisory committees, which enhance external participation in internal decision making and therefore can limit bureaucratic discretion. Despite these considerations, the EPA elevated the role of the NDWAC in 1996 to make it an important institutional actor in the area of drinking water policy.

Third, does interest group mobilization affect the utility of advisory committees as instruments of oversight? One explanation for the changes in the composition and operation of the NDWAC and the NACMPI is the mobilization of the drinking water industry and food safety groups, respectively. It may be that as the interest group environment increases in its complexity, it becomes feasible to constitute heterogeneous advisory committees, which can then provide Congress with reliable information about agency policy making. Fourth, what role are advisory committees playing in the current movement toward consultative rule making? As Kerwin (1994) points out, negotiated rule making and other approaches designed to enhance the quality of external participation are increasingly being used to complement and supplement traditional approaches that typically limit access to agency information (e.g., notice and comment rule making). Fifth, what impact do heterogeneous, well-informed advisory committees exert over bureaucratic policy making? Existing research is based on the notion that advisory committees are biased in favor of interests such as business and therefore suggests that committees provide policy benefits to particular constituencies. If, however, advisory committees are heterogeneous and have access to agency decision making, then they may steer agencies toward policies favored by Congress, which are often the product of compromise among competing interests.

We presented a previous version of this essay at the 1998 annual meeting of the American Political Science Association, in Boston. We thank Bill Gormley and Carolyn Wong for comments on that version.

1. The committee management secretariat of the General Services Administration provides detailed information about the advisory committee system on-line (http://policyworks.gov/org/main/mc/linkit.htm).

2. Advisory committees are certainly not the only instruments through which Congress can facilitate external participation in agency decision making. For example, notice and comment rule making provide interested parties with opportunities to comment on proposed regulations. We focus on advisory committees not only because they have largely been ignored by scholars of legislative-executive relations but also because they differ from other instruments in two potentially important respects. First, advisory committees provide members with privileged access to agency decision making. Advi-

sory committees generally have a relatively small number of members (i.e., 15 to 20). In contrast, agencies routinely receive dozens or hundreds of comments on proposed regulations. Second, advisory committees provide members with access to numerous facets of agency decision making. Some advisory committees, for example, play a major role in setting regulatory agendas and drafting proposed regulations.

REFERENCES

Advisory Committee on Student Financial Assistance. 1997. *History of the Advisory Committee.* Washington, D.C.: Advisory Committee on Student Financial Assistance.
Austin, Jan, ed. 1997. *Congressional Quarterly 1996 Almanac.* Washington, D.C.: Congressional Quarterly Press.
Bibby, John F. 1968. "Congress' Neglected Function." In *The Republican Papers,* ed. Melvin R. Laird, 477–88. New York: Anchor Press.
Bybee, Jay S. 1994. "Advising the President: Separation of Powers and the Federal Advisory Committee Act." *Yale Law Journal* 104: 51–128.
Cohen, Mary W., ed. 1987. *Congressional Quarterly 1986 Almanac.* Washington, D.C.: Congressional Quarterly Press.
Dodd, Lawrence C., and Richard L. Schott. 1979. *Congress and the Administrative State.* New York: Wiley.
Fenno, Richard F., Jr. 1966. *The Power of the Purse: Appropriations Politics in Congress.* Boston: Little, Brown.
Fenno, Richard F., Jr. 1973a. *Committee Organization in the House.* Vol. 2. panel discussions before the Select Committee on Committees. 93rd Cong. 1st sess. Washington, D.C.: Government Printing Office.
Fenno, Richard F., Jr. 1973b. *Congressmen in Committees.* Boston: Little, Brown.
Fenno, Richard F., Jr. 1978. *Home Style: House Members in Their Districts.* Boston: Little, Brown.
Fenno, Richard F., Jr. 1991. *The Emergence of a Senate Leader: Pete Domenici and the Reagan Budget.* Washington, D.C.: Congressional Quarterly.
Freedman, Allan. 1996. "The Politics of a Popular Bill." *Congressional Quarterly Weekly Report,* July 13, 1954.
Fritschler, A. Lee. 1989. *Smoking and Politics: Policy Making and the Federal Bureaucracy.* 4th ed. Englewood Cliffs, N.J.: Prentice Hall.
Gais, Thomas L., Mark A. Peterson, and Jack L. Walker. 1984. "Interest Groups, Iron Triangles, and Representative Institutions in American National Government." *British Journal of Political Science* 14: 161–85.
Hook, Janet. 1986a. "Congressional Resistance Strong: Deep New Cuts in Social Spending Proposed." *Congressional Quarterly Weekly Report* February 8, 222–25.
Hook, Janet. 1986b. "Higher Education Bill Ready for Final Action." *Congressional Quarterly Weekly Report* September 20, 2217–20.

Hook, Janet. 1986c. "Student Loan, Grant Provisions Settled: Conferees Reach Agreement on Higher Education Measure." *Congressional Quarterly Weekly Report* September 13, 2124.

Hosansky, David. 1996. "Highlights of the Drinking Water Bill." *Congressional Quarterly Weekly Report* August 3, 2180.

Kerwin, Cornelius M. 1994. *Rulemaking: How Government Agencies Write Law and Make Policy.* Washington, D.C.: Congressional Quarterly Press.

Leiserson, Avery. 1942. *Administrative Regulation: A Study in Representation of Interests.* Chicago: University of Chicago Press.

Lowi, Theodore J. 1979. *The End of Liberalism: The Second Republic of the United States.* 2d ed. New York: Norton.

Mathiasen, Carolyn S., ed. 1975. *Congressional Quarterly 1974 Almanac.* Washington, D.C.: Congressional Quarterly Press.

McConnell, Grant. 1966. *Private Power and American Democracy.* New York: Vintage Books.

McCubbins, Mathew D., Roger G. Noll, and Barry R. Weingast. 1987. "Administrative Procedures as Instruments of Political Control." *Journal of Law, Economics, and Organization* 3: 243–77.

McCubbins, Mathew D., Roger G. Noll, and Barry R. Weingast. 1989. "Structure and Process, Politics and Policy: Administrative Arrangements and the Political Control of Agencies." *Virginia Law Review* 75: 431–82.

McCubbins, Mathew D., and Thomas Schwartz. 1984. "Congressional Oversight Overlooked: Police Patrols versus Fire Alarms." *American Journal of Political Science* 28: 165–79.

National Advisory Committee on Meat and Poultry Inspection. 1998. *Handouts: Part One.* Washington, D.C.: National Advisory Committee on Meat and Poultry Inspection.

Petracca, Mark P. 1986. "Federal Advisory Committees, Interest Groups, and the Administrative State." *Congress and the Presidency* 13: 83–114.

Pika, Joseph. 1983. "Interest Groups and the Executive Presidential Intervention." In *Interest Group Politics,* ed. Allan J. Cigler and Burdette A. Loomis, 298–323. Washington, D.C.: Congressional Quarterly Press.

Priest, T. B., Richard T. Sylves, and David F. Scudder. 1984. "Corporate Advice: Large Corporations and Federal Advisory Committees." *Social Science Quarterly* 65: 101–11.

Schlozman, Kay Lehman, and John T. Tierney. 1986. *Organized Interests and American Democracy.* New York: Harper & Row.

Truman, David B. 1951. *The Governmental Process: Political Interests and Public Opinion.* New York: Alfred A. Knopf.

U.S. Department of Agriculture. 1997. *Strategic Plan 1997–2002: A Healthy and Productive Nation in Harmony with the Land.* Washington, D.C.: U.S. Department of Agriculture.

Wolanin, Thomas R. 1975. *Presidential Advisory Commissions: Truman to Nixon.* Madison: University of Wisconsin Press.

Wright, John R. 1996. *Interest Groups and Congress: Lobbying, Contributions, and Influence.* Boston: Allyn & Bacon.

Representation, Careerism, and Term Limits: A Simulation

Linda L. Fowler and Brian Frederking

The debate in the political arena over legislative term limits parallels a long-standing argument in the academy over career-minded representatives' fidelity to their constituents' interests. At issue for both advocates and scholars is how the desire for reelection affects the principal-agent problems inherent in representation. Does it promote greater accountability, as Schlesinger (1966) argues, or undermine popular control, as Mayhew contends (1974)? On the one hand, legislators who desire reelection appear to work hard at winning the trust of their constituents and anticipating voters' policy preferences in order to retain their positions (Arnold 1990; Fenno 1978; Kingdon 1989). On the other hand, lawmakers seem to develop an increased propensity for shirking—indulging their own ideology instead of attending to citizens' views—the longer they are in office (Davis and Porter 1989; Kalt and Zupan 1990; Lott and Davis 1992; Reed and Schansberg 1995).

The arguments about the impact of careerism on representation are largely speculative (see Benjamin and Malbin 1992; Will 1992). Some scholars have attempted to forecast the likely composition of the legislature if term limits were adopted (Mondak 1995; Opheim 1994; Reed and Schansberg 1995), and others have examined changes in electoral competition in states such as California, in which restrictions on legislative tenure have become law (Daniel and Lott 1997). Yet the more fundamental question of how legislators will make policy decisions once they are subject to term limits remains a puzzle, one we cannot answer without some understanding of the reaction of interest groups, challengers, and constituents to the new institutional arrangement. Whatever the rules, interest groups will have the capacity to reward their friends and punish their foes, while ordinary citizens will suffer from a lack of information and organization. This asymmetry in the ability to hold lawmakers accountable is compounded when an opponent is too weak to make an issue of the representative's record. Quite simply, lawmakers have a great deal of leeway—regardless of their tenure—when strategically placed groups control the campaign environment and when inexperienced and underfunded challengers offer minimal competition.

The consequences of introducing these other actors into the principal-agent relationship are substantial. Theorizing about representation expands beyond the disparities in information between lawmakers and constituents that so muddle legislative accountability (Bianco 1994; Lupia and McCubbins 1998) to encompass the political context in which they interact with each other. In effect, the voters (principals) and the agents (incumbents) become imbedded

189

in a multiplayer signaling game, and this game evolves strategically over many iterations. Measuring representation, too, becomes more complex. Scholarly efforts to estimate the effects of legislative tenure on lawmakers' positions, as we outline later in this essay, are already fraught with serious problems of measurement error and selection bias, and the introduction of additional sets of preferences only makes a bad situation worse.

In this essay, we present a dynamic model of representation involving a vote-maximizing lawmaker, a disciplined interest group, and a disorganized majority that traces the evolution of a lawmaker's policy stance and electoral fortunes over the course of his or her career. We introduce challengers of varying quality and manipulate the strategies of groups, as well as the attentiveness of the public, to map the electoral gains and losses to lawmakers as they cast successive roll call votes. We test the model with computer simulations of a legislator's choice of policy positions in a variety of scenarios involving these actors. Our results reveal the short-term pull of interest groups on legislators, just as advocates of term limits have contended, yet they also demonstrate an increased threat over time of majority reprisal as a representative's rate of defection grows. The incidence of shirking is most pronounced very early in a lawmaker's career, which indicates that most of the damage to a constituency's interests has been done by the time term limits would compel a lawmaker to leave office. In addition, strong challengers and attentive publics within the constituency elevate the risks of shirking to the lawmaker. Thus, when these forces are absent, term limits are ineffectual in protecting the interests of the constituency majority; when they are present, term limits are unnecessary.

Careerism and Representation

Careerism creates two different and conflicting packages of incentives for lawmakers: the desire for reelection simultaneously induces lawmakers to please the constituent majority and to court interest groups to appease potential opponents and obtain vital campaign resources. Foremost among the scholars who frame the desire for reelection in a positive light is Richard Fenno (1978) in his classic study of legislative home styles. For Fenno, the ingredients of accountability lie in the perpetual uncertainty with which House members view their electoral fortunes—no matter how secure they may seem to outside observers. In addition, he depicts the day-to-day workings of representation as focused on the building of constituent trust through the presentation of self and through explanation. Fenno recognizes that once senior lawmakers complete the expansion of their reelection constituency, they risk becoming less attentive to changes within the district. But his study (1978) indicates that most representatives endeavor to anticipate constituent preferences and avoid "getting too far away from the district" because they never know when voters will demand an accounting on a particular vote.

John Kingdon's legislators (1989) also respond most frequently to the perceived desires of the constituency. When interviewed in Washington immediately after they had cast a vote, House members repeatedly invoked potential constituent reaction and actively avoided what they nervously termed "a string of wrong votes" (Kingdon 1989).

Arnold (1990), too, focuses on the legislator's uncertainty about constituent reaction and endeavors to specify the conditions under which voters are likely to hold lawmakers responsible for policy decisions. These conditions include early-order effects rather than delayed consequences, proximity of citizens to the outcome, identifiable government action traceable to the legislator's decision, and entrepreneurship by a challenger to make these circumstances salient to the electorate. Arnold concedes that relatively few roll calls in Congress meet all these requirements and, therefore, relies on legislators' calculation of constituents' potential policy preferences and the likely traceability of future policy consequences as the primary source of constraint on representatives.

The subjective nature of the relationship between legislators and constituents outlined earlier inhibits empirical testing. In observing representatives' behavior, scholars can never be sure whether lawmakers deviate from their constituents' preferred policies intentionally or simply make a mistake. Moreover, studies of representation based on lawmakers' perceptions have never been attempted on a nationwide scale nor covered more than a few points in time, which limits their generalizability. Although the logic undergirding a positive view of careerism is compelling, the evidence is not likely to change the minds of reformers pushing for term limits.

Mondak (1995) offers an alternative perspective on legislative turnover by focusing on the capacity of citizens to process information about incumbents over time. Employing a simulation with hypothetical proportions of excellent, good, fair, and poor representatives, he demonstrates that even under conditions of very minimal information, voters eventually filter out the lower-quality lawmakers. Consequently, if citizens have fewer elections to screen legislators, they will be less accurate in finding the good ones. Indeed, Mondak (1995, 717) estimates that a legislature elected with what he terms unrestricted screening will have a greater proportion of excellent and good lawmakers (40 percent) than a legislature that has a fixed number of filtering opportunities (30 percent).

The political economists who adapt principal-agent models to the question of legislative shirking have produced a number of statistical studies that measure tenure effects on legislators' responsiveness to their constituents. Their findings, however, lead to conflicting conclusions about the value of term limits in promoting greater accountability and suffer from serious problems of measurement.

Of greatest interest to the whole term limit debate is work on the last period problem—the term right before retirement when the desire for reelection ceases to constrain roll call behavior and lawmakers are free to sell government benefits to competing groups (Barro 1973; Ferejohn 1986) or pursue their own ideology (Lott and Reed 1989). This literature strongly suggests that low voluntary turnover is highly desirable in a legislature because it minimizes the number of members who know they are in their last term,[1] but subsequent studies have produced inconsistent results. Some studies have reported a positive relationship between retirement and ideological shirking (McArthur and Marks 1988; Reed and Schansberg 1995; Zupan 1990), whereas others have uncovered little connection between the two variables (Lott 1987; Lott and Davis 1992; Vanbeek 1991). A key variable omitted from these analyses, however, is the ambition for higher office among retiring members, which seems to reduce shirking (Carey 1996, 176).

Of greater comfort to proponents of term limits are the studies that link length of service to the likelihood of ideological shirking, either because lawmakers become more inclined to consume policy benefits for their own satisfaction as their tenure increases (Davis and Porter 1989) or because they develop brand-name recognition that discourages opponents (Kalt and Zupan 1990). Reestimation of the equations in the latter article challenges this conclusion (Lott and Davis 1992), however, and additional work by Reed et al. (1998) on the connection between tenure and support for government spending also raises questions about the impact of long service on lawmakers' policy positions.

A serious criticism of this type of analysis concerns measurement error in the dependent and independent variables (Lott and Davis 1992). Most important, the distortion in the data created by sorting effects (Lott and Reed 1989) raises questions about whether the analyses are correctly tapping behavior that is linked to length of service. Because lawmakers who deviate from their constituency preferences are more likely to suffer electoral defeat over time, legislators with "tenure-related characteristics" will be overrepresented in the legislature and, therefore, will yield "biased predictors of how the legislature would perform" if length of service were altered (Lott and Reed 1989, 80).

In the end, however, none of this literature is directly relevant to the term limits debate because it does not control for the fact that internal institutional arrangements in legislatures are often tied to seniority, such as the selection of party leaders and committee chairs. Most commentators believe that the rules of the game over competition for leadership slots will change when the percentage of senior lawmakers drops, and this shift will make past behavior connected with tenure an unreliable predictor of future action.[2] Altered incentives are probably most problematic for estimating the relationship between tenure and career decisions or policy preferences for Republican legislators, who had higher than average retirement rates from the House during the 1970s and 1980s because of their frustration with their permanent minority party status.

These problems notwithstanding, the public choice literature on tenure effects suffers most from the absence of challengers, interest groups, and attentive publics in estimates of lawmakers' roll call strategies. We know that high-quality opponents increase the intensity and salience of election campaigns for voters (Jacobson 1992; Westlye 1992) and that organized interests persuade lawmakers to defect from the majority preference in their district regardless of legislators' tenure (Kalt and Zupan 1990). We also have evidence from a variety of studies that legislators' roll call positions are broadly reflective of constituency preferences (Jackson and King 1989; Overby et al. 1992; Peltzman 1984, 1985). Estimating the linkages between careerism and tenure without controlling for such factors leads to misspecified models.

The model we propose explicitly incorporates these actors into a theory of representation. We use computer simulations to estimate the policy response of lawmakers to the strategic opportunities and pitfalls inherent in balancing the competing interests of organized groups and disorganized majorities under various conditions of electoral competition. Although we recognize the very real limitations of simulations, we believe that this approach enables us to clarify the structure of the relationships among legislators, groups, and constituents; to trace the evolution of these relationships over time; and to readily modify assumptions about the various actors' behaviors. Given the formidable problems inherent in measuring representation outlined previously, focusing on the underlying dynamics of legislative careerism makes a good deal of sense.

A Theory of Representation: Legislators, Challengers, Constituents and Groups

The common starting point in the literature on representation is a paradox: ignorant voters who have difficulty in both assessing their own interests and judging the performance of elected officials nevertheless must exercise control over legislators' decisions.[3] We begin with this dilemma and add the additional wrinkle of collective action. In other words, even if voters adopt various heuristic devices to compensate for their ignorance, they still have the problem of acting on their information in a coordinated fashion; in the United States, that capacity is contingent on the behavior of organized groups and the appearance of competitive challengers. Similarly, career-minded lawmakers are not simply in the business of pleasing or deceiving a constituency but also must contend with the demands of interest groups and the appeal of a potential opponent.

Let us assume that a legislator seeks to maximize his or her reelection vote. He or she has two constituent groups: a large, unorganized group of citizens of size s_1 and a small, organized group of size s_2. Group 1 is much larger than Group 2 and is decisive in each election. The size of the group is relevant in terms of the number of votes and its ability to deliver those votes but is not relevant to either group's desired policy benefits.

A policy index ranging from 0 to 1 represents the amount of the legislator's and constituent groups' support for a particular set of policy positions. A value of 0 represents no support for the policy, and a value of 1 represents full support for the policy. The index may be multidimensional, although we consider only the case of a single dimension here.

Suppose that for each constituent group the marginal loss in utility of additional support of the issue increases linearly (i.e., total costs rise at an increasing rate). Also, suppose that marginal benefits in utility decline over time (i.e., total benefits rise at a decreasing rate). Assume that policy gains and losses are uniformly distributed within each group and that net benefits to each group are maximized when marginal costs equal marginal benefits. Net benefits thus rise at a decreasing rate, reach a maximum, and then fall at an increasing rate. Group 1 receives maximum net benefits equal to B_1, and Group 2 receives maximum net benefits equal to B_2.

Each group casts its votes for the legislator in proportion to the net benefits resulting from the policy stance it *believes* he or she takes. For example, if members of Group 1 believe that the legislator will support the policy that delivers B_1, they will cast all of their votes for him or her. Thus,

$$V_{1,t} = \max [0, 1 - (P^*_{1,t} - B_1)^2/d_1]$$

and

$$V_{2,t} = \max [0, 1 - (P^*_{2,t} - B_2)^2/d_2] \tag{1}$$

where $P^*_{1,t}$ and $P^*_{2,t}$ are the opinions regarding the legislator's policy stance, P_t, at time t of Group 1 and Group 2, respectively. The groups' perceptions of the legislator's positions will change over time with the legislator's successive policy stances and the information the groups obtain about these positions. But at time t, the vote the legislator receives from each group is proportional to its perceived policy benefits.

The parameters d_1 and d_2 reflect the rate at which each group's vote proportion declines as the legislator deviates from its most preferred position. The proportion of votes delivered thus can fall off quite rapidly or quite slowly, depending on the alternatives available to the groups, notably the challenger. Total votes obtained by the legislator when no challenger is present at time t are

$$V_t = s_1 V_{1,t} (P^*_{1,t}) + s_2 V_{2,t} (P^*_{2,t}) \tag{2}$$

Before each roll call the legislator announces a platform, w, that he or she thinks will maximize his or her votes. He or she delivers on these promises and does not change positions until the next roll call so that

$$P_t = w_t \tag{3}$$

Because the small group, Group 2, is organized, it can monitor the legislator's behavior, determine his or her policy stance, and communicate this information to its members. Thus, Group 2's opinion about the legislator's current policy position after T elections, P_T, is

$$P^*_{2,T} = P_T = w_T \tag{4}$$

With the certainty of perfect information over time, the group can react to the legislator's position and deliver its vote as a direct function of the legislator's policy stance.

In contrast, the large group, Group 1, is not organized and therefore can neither monitor the legislator's record directly nor mobilize its members to vote responsively. Instead, Group 1 must estimate the legislator's cumulative record over T roll calls, U_T, which it does by averaging its past estimate of the legislator's positions with his or her current platform, w_t. Thus, Group 1's evaluation of the legislator's voting record is

$$U_T = [1 / (T-1)] \quad \sum_{t=1}^{T-1} w_t \tag{5}$$

The expected value of the legislator's voting record for Group 1 after $T - 1$ roll calls is

$$E[U_T] = E[(1 / (T-1)) \sum_{t=1}^{T-1} w_t] = [1 / (T-1)] \quad \sum_{t=1}^{T-1} P_t \tag{6}$$

After the election, the winning legislator's platform is w_1, which is the only source of information either group has about how the legislator will behave. Therefore, the opinions of both groups are the same, and because the legislator votes in accord with his or her announced platform,

$$P^*_{1,1} = P^*_{2,1} = w_1 \tag{7}$$

The value of w_1 that maximizes the legislator's total vote is obtained by substituting both constituent groups' opinions (equation 1) into the vote function (equation 2) and differentiating the vote function with respect to w_1. To find this value, assume for convenience and without loss of generality that

$$B_1 < B_2 \qquad (8)$$

Under these conditions the legislator's optimum policy position lies between B_1 and B_2, such that

$$dv_1/dw_1 = [(s_1/d_1)(w_1 - B_1) + (s_2/d_2)(w_2 - B_2)]2 = 0 \qquad (9)$$

if

$$\frac{s_1 / d_1}{s_2 / d_2} = \frac{B_2 - w_2}{w_1 - B_1} \qquad (10)$$

If s_1 is relatively large, then, the legislator will locate relatively close to B_1, depending on the values of d_1 and d_2, which signify the rate of decline in support as the legislator deviates from each group's position.

On the second roll call, Group 2, the small, organized group, can approach the legislator and communicate its preferences. It also is able to deliver all of its votes to the legislator if he or she takes its preferred policy stance. However, Group 2 recognizes the constraints imposed on the legislator by the presence of the large, decisive Group 1, so it delivers its votes on a schedule proportional to how closely the legislator matches its preference. The schedule is simply its vote function, $V_2 (P^*_{2,2})$. Because Group 2 knows the legislator's record, $P^* = P$.

The large, unorganized Group 1 is unable to approach the legislator or to discern his or her true position. It consequently delivers its vote to the legislator on the basis of its opinion of his or her current platform, w_2, and its perception of his or her cumulative voting record, U_1. Thus, after the legislator has begun to cast roll calls, the opinions of the two groups diverge.

The structure of the model is illustrated by an example in which there is no challenger (i.e., $d_1 = d_2 = 1$) and for which Group 1 and Group 2 are at opposite ends of the policy index (i.e., $B_1 = 0$ and $B_2 = 1$). Let us suppose that Group 1 is three times the size of Group 2, such that $s_1/s_2 = 3$. Under these conditions, the legislator would find it optimal to begin his or her career by locating relatively close to Group 1 and choosing $w_1 = 0.25$, a position that nets him or her 81 percent of the total vote. But after one iteration the legislator's optimal point for w_2 is 0.46, and he or she receives 83 percent of the vote. The percentage increases because Group 1 deals with its uncertainty by including the legislator's initial position in its schedule, arriving at an estimate $P^*_{1,2}$ of 0.36, whereas Group 2 delivers its votes solely on the basis of w_2. In this way, the legislator picks up some votes, even though he or she has moved away from the position of the large, decisive group.

Because the large group puts as much weight on past positions as on the current platform, w_t, the legislator's present stance becomes relatively less important in Group 1's calculation of $P^*_{1,T}$. In effect, Group 1 assumes it is observing independent and identically distributed outcomes as it develops a sense of the legislator's overall record. It does not assign much weight to a single vote but rather constructs a running average of the lawmaker's overall position. The legislator can exploit this imperfect information by moving closer and closer to Group 2. After the Tth iteration, the opinions of the two groups are

$$P^*_{1,T} = (1 - 1/T)U_{1,T} + (1/T)w_T$$

and

$$P^*_{2,T} = w_T \tag{11}$$

Both the legislator's voting record and past platform positions have an expected value of $\sum_{t=1}^{T-1} P_t$, and we substitute the past platform positions for his or her prior voting record. Group 1's estimate therefore is

$$P*_{1,T} = (1 - 1/T)\sum_{t=1}^{T-1} w_t + (1/T)w_t$$
$$= (1/T)\sum_{t=1}^{T} W_t \tag{12}$$

The legislator's voting function with respect to policy positions thus becomes

$$V_T = s_1(1 - [(1/T)\sum_{t=1}^{T} w_t - B_1]^2)/d_1 + s_2(1 - [(w_T - B_2)]^2)/d_2 \tag{13}$$

Differentiating this function with respect to w_T and iteratively solving for w_t, one finds that the legislator moves closer and closer to the preferred position of the small, organized Group 2, at first gaining votes and then gradually losing votes, until eventually he or she loses.

The Simulation

The simulation traces the evolution of a legislator's policy positions over a series of roll call votes in which the legislator attempts to maximize electoral support while balancing the conflicting preferences of a small, organized group and a large, disorganized majority. It incorporates informational and organizational asymmetries, which tend to favor the small group in seeking the legislator's defection from the majority. It also makes explicit provision for the strength of a challenger.

The Constituency Majority

We start with the constituency majority, Group 1, which is large enough to be decisive in terms of electoral votes but is also disorganized because of high transaction costs in processing information and coordinating its actions. We model the lag effects caused by the large group's uncertain perceptions and disorganization as a running tally in which voters average the legislator's most recent policy stance into his or her past record.[4] Group 1 then delivers its support to the legislator in proportion to the benefit obtained from his perceived position. In effect, constituents fall short of the exact position at any given point in the roll call sequence, which captures the majority's inefficiency in rewarding or sanctioning the legislator's decisions.

    The running tally differs from other retrospective voting schemes in that constituents judge legislators on an accumulated record rather than on their total utility at the end of the term (Ferejohn 1986) or the overall state of the country (Fiorina 1981). Moreover, it contrasts with Bianco's (1994) method of modeling representation in that it does not require constituents to predict the outcome of a policy or the degree of common interest between the constituency's view and the lawmaker's position. Finally, it differs from the prospective voting calculus of Lott and Reed (1989), in which voters base their estimate of a legislator's defection at $N + 1$ on the level of defection at $N - 1$, by allowing voters to learn over time. In sum, our approach makes legislators individually accountable for decisions rather than results, and it renders them personally responsive to their own constituencies rather than collectively responsible for the performance of the government. We doubt that voters keep score in precisely this way, but we believe our approach serves as a useful heuristic device that captures the essence of Fenno's (1978) writings about representation.

The Small, Organized Group

Opposing the majority is a small group, Group 2. The intense preferences that drive citizens into organized groups and the organizational resources that maintain the group enable its members to monitor the legislator's decisions and to coordinate their actions. Thus, for any roll call the legislator's position and Group 2's perception of it are equivalent. Group 2's organizational advantage means that it can match the legislator's policy choices in direct proportion to the actual benefit received. Although Group 2 could store information about the legislator's past behavior, it has no incentive to keep such a tally. If it used the averaging technique of the majority, Group 2 would dilute its support for the legislator and diminish his or her incentives to deviate from the majority. Thus, because of its small size, Group 2 must deliver support when the legislator has earned it, and it must react immediately to punish any backsliding. In this model, the only medium of exchange between Group 2 and the lawmaker is votes. Presumably, if we included campaign contributions or other resources at an organized group's disposal, the incentives for collaboration between the two would be even greater. We do not need to further complicate the simulation, however, to establish the fundamental point regarding the disparities between Group 1 and Group 2 in administering electoral rewards and sanctions.

The Legislator

It is customary in spatial models to assume that legislators maximize votes, whereas in principal-agent models it is the practice to assume that they maximize utility. The difference is significant on two counts: first, vote maximization privileges the majority by giving weight to sheer numbers, and, second, it removes lawmakers' personal preferences from the analysis and emphasizes the strategic aspect of policy over its substance. We opt for vote maximization as the basis of legislative behavior because we subscribe to the view held by many political scientists that whatever goals legislators have—the pursuit of influence or policy outputs, for example—they first need to earn reelection to achieve other ends.

Despite the numerical weight of the majority, legislators are susceptible to the pressures of small groups to achieve their electoral aims. The efficiency of organized interests in processing information is something that lawmakers ignore at their peril. Nevertheless, as a practical matter lawmakers do not necessarily find interest groups to be as unforgiving as we have portrayed Group 2. Groups organized around value issues, such as the environment or abortion, are notoriously quick to punish their legislative friends for straying from the path of truth, although many groups strive to develop long-term relationships with legislators and tolerate the occasional deviation from their preferred positions.

The Challenger

In a world of perfect information and policy mobility, any incumbent who deviated from the position of the median voter would lose an election. But in the real world of congressional elections, challengers face barriers to entry so that electoral competition is not guaranteed. Prospective challengers may be unable to raise money because of biases in the campaign finance systems, or they may be unable to develop solid credentials because of weaknesses in the party system of recruitment. Moreover, they may be unable to overcome the inertia of the incumbent's initial election until the majority has had sufficient time to process and respond to the incumbent's cumulative record. Given the many reasons why challengers may refuse to run against incumbents or may be unattractive to voters when they do enter a contest, we construct several different simulations and set different values for the rate at which the incumbent's support declines because of the challenger's appeal.

Our model treats the challenger as a parameter rather than as an additional actor, which differs from the way opposing candidates figure in Downsian models of party competition. With this approach, we are able to focus on the expected value of a challenger (or potential challenger) in the groups' evaluations of the lawmaker's position. The construction of separate w, P, P^*, and V values for a challenger at each iteration would make the simulation hopelessly unwieldy and is unnecessary to make the basic point about the role of electoral competition in constraining a legislator's roll call decisions.

Time

The lawmaker has no control over the frequency of roll call votes relevant to Group 2 because committees and party leaders set the legislative agenda. An issue may require many votes over the course of the authorization and appropriation process, particularly if amendments are numerous, and it may recur over many sessions of the legislature. The uncertainty of the policy agenda creates two strategic problems for the legislator. First, its cumulative effect on the majority means that the legislator cannot undo a series of votes that favor Group 2 simply by siding with the majority at election time. In other words, the inertia built into Group 1's running tally not only gives the lawmaker leeway to court organized interests but also impedes his or her ability to reverse course quickly. Second, periodic elections punctuate the legislator's sequence of policy decisions. The elections themselves operate according to a fixed timetable, but they cut into the policy stream at indeterminate points. In effect, the lawmaker must reconcile two separate but interdependent time sequences—the roll call calendar and the electoral calendar.

We deal with the complexities of the legislator's dual calendar by simulating the evolution of the policy sequences over time. We then examine the electoral consequences of the legislator's record at various points in the iteration (e.g., if the election occurred at the 10th iteration, the 20th, and so forth).

Simulation Results

We begin with the legislator's first roll call on taking office and assume that Group 1 and Group 2 have a preferred position on a policy index, with Group 1 at 0 and Group 2 at 1. For each iteration, t, all possible values for the legislator's position, w, were calculated and the one that produced the most votes for that particular time was selected as the legislator's position. Recollect that Group 2's perception and the legislator's policy stance are equivalent, but Group 1's perception is an estimate based on the average of the lawmaker's past policy positions. However, both groups have the same information about the legislator's initial policy position at the start of his or her term. At each roll call, the legislator announces a position that will maximize his or her total vote and adheres to it until the next iteration. Group 1 and Group 2 deliver their support to the legislator in proportion to their perceived benefit, which in Group 1's case is an estimate and in Group 2's case is accurate. In all of the tables in this essay, the meaning of t is undefined and is addressed in the text.

In table 1, we present the simulation results for groups of different sizes; the majority group, Group 1, ranges in size from 3 to 10 times larger than the small group. The legislator's position is P, which is also equal to the small group's perception, P_2^*, so we do not report the latter value. The large group's estimate of the lawmaker's position is represented by P_1^*, and the total vote for the legislator is shown as V. In this first example, we assume that both groups are indifferent between the incumbent and challenger, so that only the incumbent's policy stance is relevant in calculating the values of P, P^*, and V.

The difference in group size influences the legislator's initial position, P, because as Group 1 becomes larger, the lawmaker starts his or her term in office closer to Group 1's preferred position of 0. Group size also affects Group 1's ability to sanction the legislator for siding with the small group. The larger the group, in fact, the more iterations are required for the incumbent to finally lose because it takes longer for the large group to incorporate information about the legislator's deviation into P_1^*. Indeed, a legislator with a very large, disorganized constituency in which the ratio is 10:1 will not lose until he or she has taken more than 50 positions. This pattern occurs in part because the lawmaker starts out closer to the large group and because his or her early shifts in position are not picked up as quickly. At the same time, the legislator does not move quite as close to the small group's preferred point before he or she is caught and thrown out of office.

What is instructive about this example is that each position maximizes the legislator's total vote for that iteration but gradually leads to a loss of votes over time, even when a challenger is not a factor in either group's perception of the incumbent. Such perverse consequences are not uncommon in rational choice models, in which an optimal choice can actually make the actor worse off. It is also noteworthy that once the incumbent gets too far from the constituency, it is not easy to repair the damage. In the case in which the ratio of group size is 3:1, an incumbent who stops siding with the small group just before the 35th iteration will lose anyway. This outcome occurs because the small group will withdraw votes when the legislator shifts course in direct proportion to the benefit lost, whereas the large group rewards the shift in direction only partially because of the inertia of the past record. Indeed, once the lawmaker gets close to 50 percent of the vote, the only salvation is to shift radically back to the large group's preferred position and hold it for several iterations while making a deal with the small group to continue its support during this transition period despite its loss of policy benefits.

A basic question arises, then, about how myopic and how risk averse lawmakers are in choosing their optimal position at each iteration. If legislators focus on the immediate benefits associated with a particular roll call, they set

TABLE 1.   The Effect of Group Size on a Legislator's Vote Total Ratio of Large Group (S_1) to Small Group (S_2)

	Group size								
	Ratio = 3.1			Ratio = 5.1			Ratio = 10.1		
Time (t)	P	$P_1{}^*$	V	P	$P_1{}^*$	V	P	$P_1{}^*$	V
1	.25	.25	.81	.17	.17	.86	.09	.09	.91
2	.46	.36	.83	.35	.26	.87	.22	.16	.92
3	.57	.43	.82	.46	.33	.86	.31	.21	.92
4	.64	.48	.79	.53	.38	.84	.38	.25	.91
5	.69	.52	.77	.58	.42	.82	.43	.29	.90
6	.72	.56	.75	.62	.45	.81	.47	.32	.88
7	.75	.58	.73	.66	.48	.79	.51	.34	.87
8	.77	.61	.71	.68	.51	.77	.54	.37	.86
9	.79	.63	.69	.71	.53	.75	.57	.39	.85
10	.81	.65	.68	.73	.55	.74	.59	.41	.83
15	.86	.71	.62	.79	.62	.67	.67	.49	.77
20	.89	.75	.57	.83	.67	.62	.73	.54	.72
25	.91	.78	.54	.86	.71	.58	.77	.59	.68
30	.92	.80	.51	.88	.73	.55	.79	.62	.65
35	.93	.82	.49	.89	.76	.52	.82	.65	.62
40				.90	.77	.50	.83	.67	.59
42				.91	.78	.49	.84	.68	.58
45							.85	.69	.57
50							.86	.70	.55

Note: P, legislator's position; $P_1{}^*$, large group's estimate of that position; and V, total vote received from the large group plus the small group. In this example there is no challenger.

themselves up for electoral defeat. Suppose, however, that they can forecast the likely consequences of siding with the small group or that they are vote satisficers rather than vote maximizers. In both cases, the lawmaker would be cautious about moving too far away from the constituency majority—just as Fenno, Kingdon, and Arnold predict.

Ultimately, the implications of these results for the term limit debate depend on how we interpret the iterations—the meaning of t. If we assume that each t is equivalent to an election, such that Group 1 and Group 2 calculate their support for the legislator only once during the legislator's term, then the case for term limits is very strong. It also becomes more compelling as the disparity increases in size between the disorganized majority and the organized minority. For example, when the groups are at a 3:1 ratio, the simulation predicts that the legislator does not appear vulnerable until more than 15 elections have taken place. The legislator does not actually lose until t is at 35, which in the case of U.S. House members represents 70 years in office!

Yet the six-term limits proposed for Congress and most states' legislatures turn out to offer the majority relatively little protection from the legislator's defection. If we look at the values for the legislator's position, P, in all three scenarios, the rate of defection toward the small group is most rapid between the first and second terms and between the second and third terms. By the end of the fifth term, in fact, the rate of movement toward the small group has slowed dramatically, after which point Group 2 gets only incremental endorsement of its demands. In sum, defection from the majority's preferred policy is so rapid that restrictions on tenure fail to prevent the most damaging policy shifts, unless lawmakers are prohibited from seeking reelection altogether. This restriction, of course, would trigger the last period problem, which Barro (1973) has indicated is most severe when turnover is at 100 percent.

Other interpretations of t are less alarming in terms of majority control over legislators' policy decisions. If elections were to take place, say, after every five roll calls, then the legislator who consistently moved toward the small group would lose office when t equals 35, which would be at seven terms. Elections at intervals of 10 roll calls would send a very clear signal of voter disapproval to the legislator after three terms and lead to defeat by the fourth term. In these cases, term limits would be unnecessary because the lawmaker would be removed anyway through the electoral process.

The ambiguity surrounding t highlights several important aspects of the debate over legislative tenure. Clearly, legislators' defection from the majority is not simply a function of the length and number of terms in office. Equally important is the frequency with which they vote on issues salient to small, organized interests. In short, legislators could inflict considerable damage on the majority whenever the legislative agenda required numerous votes on special interest legislation, regardless of limits on tenure. Interest groups, presumably, would understand this dynamic and attempt to pack the legislative calendar with as many proposals as possible. If staff members become more influential or committees and party leaders less capable of managing the flow of legislation—two developments about which opponents of term limits worry—organized interests might be quite successful with such a ploy in frustrating the intent behind the term limits proposal.

The meaning of t is also pertinent to how the legislator interprets the gradual erosion of support that takes place from accommodating organized groups. As noted earlier, legislators may not be myopic vote maximizers. Presumably, a career-minded legislator could anticipate the sequence of iterations and recognize that siding with Group 2 leads to a slippery slope that eventually produces defeat. Similarly, a legislator with a long career horizon would be more risk averse when his or her margin slips below 60 percent and might take steps to reverse the pattern of support for Group 2 much earlier than a legislator who was less concerned about long service. In the former case concern for the constituency would arise when t is at 15, but in the latter case it might not kick in until t equals 30.

Adding an appealing challenger to the simulation cuts the number of iterations before the incumbent is defeated dramatically. In table 2, we hold group size constant at a ratio of 5:1, and in the left-hand columns we present examples in which the challenger appeals to the majority group, either weakly or very strongly. In the former case, the weak challenger is only modestly influential in helping the majority assess the record of the incumbent; that is to say, the incumbent loses at the 29th iteration instead of at the 42nd iteration. But in the latter case, the strong challenger makes a very big difference, driving the incumbent into retirement on the 17th iteration.

Three aspects of the challenger's impact are particularly important. First, the presence of the appealing challenger forces the legislator to take an initial stance that is extremely close to the majority's preference. Second, the shift in the majority's perceptions of the lawmaker's position occurs much more rapidly. Third, the incumbent loses on the basis of a policy position that is just slightly past the midpoint on the policy index. Without the challenger, as shown in table 1, the incumbent had moved much closer to the policy preference of the small group.

Paradoxically, a strong challenger who appeals from the start to the small group does the most damage to the legislator's electoral fortunes and causes him or her to lose on the seventh iteration. This result occurs because the presence of a challenger who caters to the organized group compels the legislator to take an initial stance that is quite far from the preference of the majority and pulls him or her very quickly toward the small group's ideal point of 1. Given both the weight that the initial position occupies in the large group's perceptions of the legislator's position and his or her rapid movement, the majority requires very little time to figure out what is happening and responds accordingly. This situation is analogous to the problem incumbents face from a primary challenge.

Again, the meaning of *t* is critical to interpreting these results but less so than in the first example. In the presence of a strong challenger who appeals to the large group, one need only interpret *t* as representing the end of a legislative session to end up with an electoral loss at the end of six terms. In the case of the strong challenger who appeals to the small group, treating *t* as equivalent to a session gets rid of the legislator in three terms. These results are instructive because they suggest that when incumbents face strong competition, voters do not need the arbitrary constraint of term limits either to keep legislators from straying too far from the majority preference or to punish them for defection.

TABLE 2.   The Effect of a Challenger on Legislator's Vote Total with Group Size Held Constant at a Ratio of 5:1

	Strength of challenger										
	Weak			Strong			Weak			Strong		
	Group 1			Group 1			Group 2			Group 2		
Time (t)	P	P_1*	V	P	P_1*	V	P	P_1*	V	P	P_1*	V
1	.14	.14	.86	.04	.04	.84	.20	.20	.83	.50	.50	.58
2	.30	.22	.87	.10	.07	.84	.40	.30	.85	.70	.60	.63
3	.41	.28	.86	.16	.10	.84	.51	.37	.84	.78	.66	.60
4	.48	.33	.84	.21	.13	.83	.58	.42	.81	.82	.70	.56
5	.53	.37	.82	.24	.15	.81	.63	.46	.79	.85	.73	.54
6	.58	.41	.80	.28	.17	.79	.67	.50	.77	.87	.75	.51
7	.61	.44	.78	.31	.19	.77	.70	.53	.75	.89	.77	.49
8	.64	.46	.76	.34	.21	.74	.72	.55	.73			
9	.66	.48	.74	.37	.23	.72	.75	.57	.71			
10	.69	.50	.72	.39	.24	.69	.76	.59	.70			
15	.76	.58	.64	.48	.31	.55	.82	.66	.63			
17	.78	.60	.61	.51	.33	.49	.84	.68	.61			
20	.80	.63	.58				.86	.71	.58			
25	.83	.67	.53				.88	.74	.54			
29	.85	.69	.49				.89	.77	.51			
33	.91	.78	.49									

Note: P, legislator's position; P_1*, large group's (Group 1) estimate of that position; and *V*, total vote received from the large group plus the small group. The left-hand columns contain the results for equations when the challenger is appealing to the large group, and the right-hand columns represent the results for equations when the challenger is appealing to the small group.

With these basic results in mind, we consider additional examples with more complex assumptions about the way voters process information, the possible alternative strategies the incumbent might use, and the configuration of small group preferences. For each of these scenarios we present two possible cases: the presence of a weak challenger and the presence of a strong challenger. In the interest of simplicity, we omit the legislator's positions at each iteration and simply present a plot of the lawmaker's total vote at each point in time.

Assumptions about How Citizens Process Information

The literature on congressional elections is rich in findings that show voters like incumbent legislators (see Jacobson 1992). We build this bias into the equation in a curvilinear fashion—assuming that it is lowest at the beginning and end of a career and peaks at roughly the midpoint, which we set at $t = 25$.

In figure 1, it is quite clear that a bias toward the incumbent, produced by whatever means, provides him or her with the kind of leeway to cater to a special interest group that many reformers have surmised. Indeed, with a weak challenger the legislator does not begin to slip into the marginal category in terms of the total vote until the 38th iteration and still does not lose. With the addition of a strong challenger, however, the situation is quite different. The incumbent loses by the 20th iteration, before the hypothesized bias has even reached its maximum.

A very different situation arises for the legislator when an attentive constituency is present in the district. In this case, we assume that an attentive group of citizens has the same preference as the disorganized majority but is able to process information about the legislator's position with the same efficiency—in terms of both knowledge and adjustment of support—as the small, organized group. In this situation, the incumbent starts very close to the majority preference and stays there throughout the entire period. The result is continuous reelection with extremely high vote totals (see fig. 2). A strong challenger makes a small difference in preventing deviations from the majority preference but is not at all influential in this particular case.

Finally, we consider the case in which voters sample the lawmaker's positions at random and act together on the information they obtain. Instead of simply keeping a running tally, they periodically obtain perfect information about a particular position and act directly on these data from the legislator's record. The results are difficult to present graphically, but in effect they reveal that an incumbent is very vulnerable to majority retribution whenever disorganized voters can obtain accurate information, even on a random basis. The incumbent is vulnerable regardless of whether the challenger is strong or weak, because the legislator's defeat is contingent on the randomness of the exercise and when voters pick up a true reading of the legislator's position.

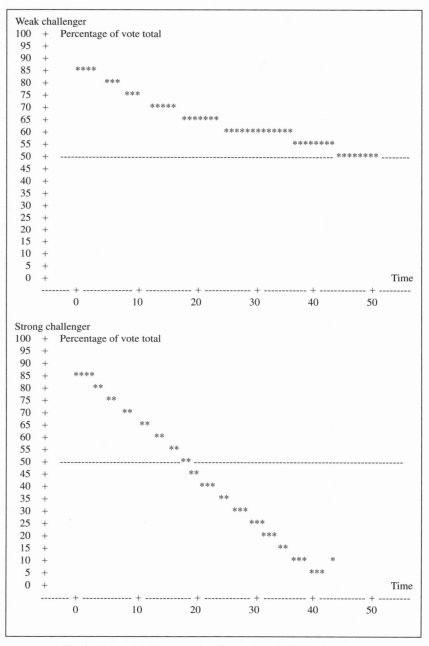

Fig. 1. **Incumbent's percentage of vote, time, and incumbent bias**

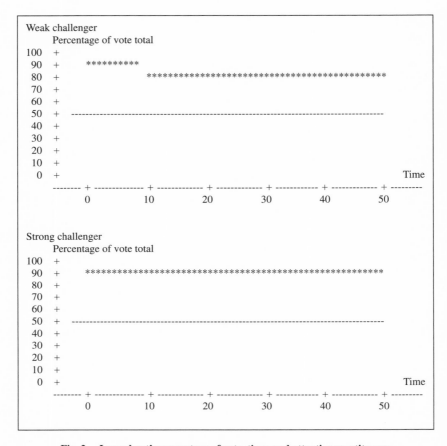

Fig. 2.   Incumbent's percentage of vote, time, and attentive constituency

Assumptions about How Incumbents Choose Positions

Given an incumbent's need to court an organized group not just for votes but for the resources it can provide during a campaign, is there any strategy that a lawmaker could use to satisfy this group without eventually antagonizing the disorganized majority? In figure 3, we show that such a strategy is feasible, but only if the incumbent can be sure of a weak challenger.

Here the legislator flip-flops on his or her positions, first siding with the large, disorganized group and then pleasing the small group on the next roll call. In effect, we have a 0, 1, 0, 1, . . . sequence in which the legislator alternates between the ideal points of both groups. This approach works quite well in the absence of a challenger because it periodically costs the legislator votes

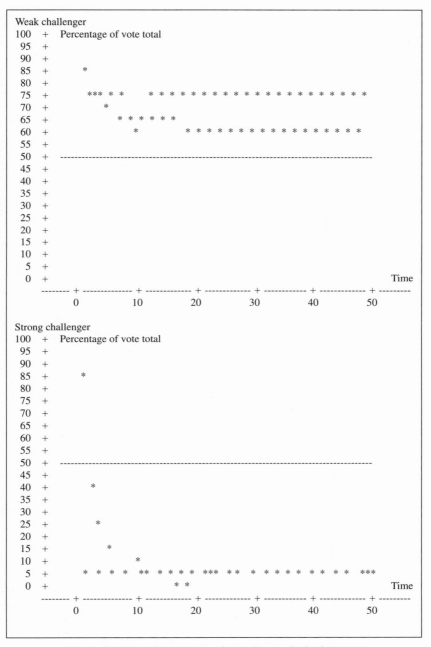

Fig. 3. Incumbent's percentage of vote, time, and mixed strategy

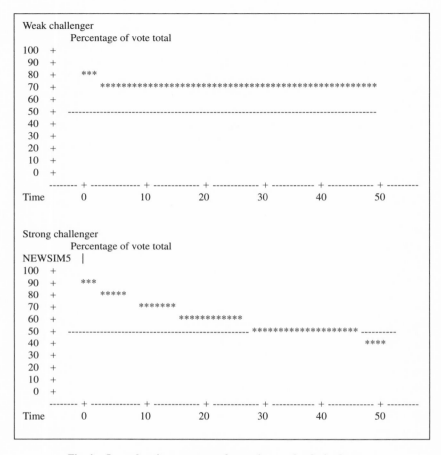

Fig. 4.   Incumbent's percentage of vote, time, and polarized groups

but never leads to defeat. However, when a strong challenger is on the scene, the legislator loses almost immediately as a result of having given full support to the small group.

Assumptions about Small Group Preferences

Lastly, we consider the impact of more than one small, organized group on the legislator's policy stance. Although multiple groups of intense constituents may lessen the probability of a legislator's reelection (Fiorina 1974), their presence can also permit the legislator to play one off against the other and thereby diminish constituent control (Ferejohn 1986). In figure 4, we present two different scenarios: one in which the legislator tries to appeal to both groups and one in which he or she courts only one group and ignores the preferences of the other. We assume for purposes of illustration that the large group is still a majority but that this time its most preferred position is at 0.5.

When the legislator tries to be evenhanded between the two small, organized groups, the position that maximizes the total vote is midway between the two groups, which also coincides with the preference of the majority. The legislator takes this position, never deviates from it, and never loses more than a few votes from the small groups. This relationship holds regardless of the strength of the challenger's appeal to the large group.

However, when the legislator decides to favor one small group over the other and a strong challenger who appeals to the slighted group appears, the legislator eventually ends up in electoral trouble. This result occurs because the challenger pulls the lawmaker closer and closer to one of the small groups— a shift that is finally perceived and punished by the disorganized majority.

Conclusion

Legislative reformers turn out to be correct in worrying about the ability of small, organized interest groups to obtain policy benefits disproportionate to their numbers and that this relationship grows more detrimental to the constituency majority over time. Popular control over elected representatives turns out to be episodic and inefficient, and it allows legislators a great deal of leeway to pursue nonmajoritarian interests. Unresponsive lawmakers get called to account by the disorganized mass public, but numerous iterations are often required before they are punished for their behavior. Long tenure, however, is not necessarily the obstacle to greater constituency control that reformers fear. Depending on how one chooses to interpret t, electoral sanctions may take a very long time to operate or they may kick in after several terms, but they eventually remove an incumbent who has moved too close to an organized group. The key factors in the ability of voters to hold legislators accountable turn out to be a strong challenger, an attentive constituency, a habit among voters of sampling the legislator's true position at random, or countervailing power between opposing groups. When one of these conditions is met, other mechanisms of popular control are not needed.

Furthermore, term limits are not necessarily a mechanism for making legislators more responsive to the majority. Legislators have the greatest incentive to seek the support of an organized group early in their tenure, and they make the largest policy shifts between the first and third iterations. The worst damage to the majority's interest takes place, therefore, well before the typical restriction of six terms would take effect. Moreover, under term limits groups would undoubtedly endeavor to pack the legislative agenda so that they could squeeze the maximum advantage out of junior lawmakers.

Finally, once legislators begin to seek interest group support, their personal career horizons affect how far they are willing to shift positions. Those who desire a legislative career are likely to be risk adverse and would probably reverse course when they slipped below 60 percent of the total vote, even if it cost them votes in the short run. They would certainly not push to the very brink of electoral defeat, as noncareerists would, before modifying their stance. Again, depending on the interpretation of t, the careerist's goal of reelection might constrain his or her behavior sooner or later, but it would constrain it eventually. Overall, the simulation results strongly suggest that term limits are neither necessary nor sufficient for legislative accountability.

This simulation rests on a particular set of assumptions about how legislators, organized groups, and disorganized majorities behave. Whether they are plausible, of course, determines how seriously one credits the results. Nevertheless, our simulation imparts a powerful lesson about the effects of tenure on legislative performance because it demonstrates that the effects of long service are not independent but vary with the political context in which legislators operate. How we control for such factors is a matter of considerable uncertainty, but we believe neither scholars nor reformers can ignore them.

A corollary follows naturally from this conclusion: that several different options are available for enhancing majority control over elected representatives. Reformers could restrict interest group access to legislators through a variety of institutional reforms, or they could reduce legislators' dependence on interest group support through campaign finance reform or stronger political parties. Similarly, they could devise ways to improve the capacity of voters to reward and sanction lawmakers through the electoral process. Most important, reformers could endeavor to improve the competitiveness of election contests, through either eliminating partisan gerrymandering, subsidizing challengers' campaigns with public funds, or improving the capacity of parties to identify and groom promising candidates. All of these proposals are presently under consideration in Congress and state legislatures in some form or other, and their adoption might well eliminate the need for further discussion of term limits.

Viewed from this perspective, the current debate about term limits seems very much beside the point. The real issue is not length of service, per se, but its influence within the political environment in which legislators operate—the leverage of interest groups, the voters' capacity to evaluate incumbents, and the deterrent effect of seniority on prospective opponents. Advocates of term limits assume that restricting tenure will have a beneficial effect on all three components of the legislative context, but they have offered little evidence to support such assumptions. Unless they address the full spectrum of factors that influence representation, term limits are bound to fail in producing a more accountable legislature.

NOTES

We wish to thank John Aldrich for his helpful comments regarding revisions to this manuscript.

1. Obviously, lawmakers who are defeated do not suffer from the last-period problem unless they know in advance they are going to be beaten.

2. See the commentary in *Social Science Quarterly* on Reed and Schansberg's (1995) forecast of the changes in the composition of the House by Greene (1995), Jacobson (1995), Oppenheimer (1995), and Upshaw (1995).

3. We wish to acknowledge Nabeel Alsalom, formerly of the Department of Economics at the University of Rochester, who formalized this conception of representation.

4. An alternative way to treat voter uncertainty is through polling devices. In an imaginative refinement of the spatial modeling literature, McKelvey and Ordeshook (1986) relax the assumption of perfect information. Instead, they assume that voters take cues from published opinion polls to estimate the relative positions of the candidates and their approximate distance from the voters' ideal point. After a succession of polls, the voters will have enough information to choose the candidate closest to them, even though they do not know his or her exact position. Candidates will move to the median voters' preference if such polls are in use even though they recognize that their exact position remains obscure to the electorate.

REFERENCES

Arnold, R. Douglas. 1990. *The Logic of Congressional Action.* New Haven: Yale University Press.

Barro, R. 1973. "The Control of Politicians: An Economic Model." *Public Choice* 14: 19–42.

Benjamin, Gerald, and Michael J. Malbin, eds. 1992. *Limiting Legislative Terms.* Washington, D.C.: Congressional Quarterly Press.

Bianco, William T. 1994. *Trust: Representatives and Constituents.* Ann Arbor: University of Michigan Press.

Carey, John M. 1996. *Term Limits and Legislative Representation.* New York: Cambridge University Press.

Daniel, Kermit, and John R. Lott Jr. 1997. "Term Limits and Electoral Competitiveness: Evidence from California's State Legislative Races." *Public Choice* 90: 369–86.

Davis, M., and P. Porter. 1989. "A Test for Pure or Apparent Ideology in Congressional Voting." *Public Choice* 60: 101–11.

Fenno, Richard F., Jr. 1978. *Home Style: House Members in Their Districts.* Boston: Little, Brown.

Ferejohn, John. 1986. "Incumbent Performance and Electoral Control." *Public Choice* 50 (1): 5–25.

Fiorina, Morris P. 1974. *Representatives, Roll Calls, and Constituencies.* Lexington, Mass.: D. C. Heath.

Fiorina, Morris P. 1981. *Retrospective Voting in American National Elections.* New Haven: Yale University Press.

Greene, Jay P. 1995. "Term Limits: A Measure of Our Ignorance." *Social Science Quarterly* 76: 717–19.

Jackson, John E., and David C. King. 1989. "Public Goods, Private Interests, and Representation." *American Political Science Review* 83: 1143–64.

Jacobson, Gary C. 1992. *The Politics of Congressional Elections.* 3rd ed. New York: HarperCollins.

Jacobson, Gary C. 1995. "The House under Term Limits: A Comment." *Social Science Quarterly* 76: 720–24.

Kalt, Joseph P., and Mark A. Zupan. 1990. "The Apparent Ideological Behavior of Legislators: Testing for Principal-Agent Slack in Political Institutions." *Journal of Law and Economics* 33: 103–31.

Kingdon, John W. 1989. *Congressmen's Voting Decisions.* 3rd ed. Ann Arbor: University of Michigan Press.

Lott, J. R., Jr. 1987. "Political Cheating." *Public Choice* 52: 169–86.

Lott, J. R., Jr., and M. Davis. 1992. "A Critical Review and an Extension of the Political Shirking Literature." *Public Choice* 74: 461–84.

Lott, J. R., Jr., and W. Reed. 1989. "Shirking and Sorting in a Political Market with Finite-Lived Politicians." *Public Choice* 6 (1):75–96.

Lupia, Arthur, and Mathew D. McCubbins. 1998. *The Democratic Dilemma: Can Citizens Learn What They Need to Know?* New York: Cambridge University Press.

Mayhew, David R. 1974. *Congress: The Electoral Connection.* New Haven: Yale University Press.

Mondak, Jeffrey J. 1995. "Elections as Filters: Term Limits and the Composition of the U.S. House." *Political Research Quarterly* 48: 701–27.

McArthur, J., and S. Marks. 1988. "Constituent Interest versus Legislator Ideology: The Role of Political Opportunity Cost." *Economic Inquiry* 26: 461–70.

McKelvey, Richard D. and Peter C. Ordeshook. 1986. "Sequential Elections with Limited Information: A Formal Analysis." *Social Choice and Welfare* 3: 199–211.

Opheim, Cynthia. 1994. "The Effect of U.S. State Legislative Term Limits Revisited." *Legislative Studies Quarterly* 19: 49–60.

Oppenheimer, Bruce I. 1995. "House Term Limits: A Distorted Picture." *Social Science Quarterly* 76: 725–29.

Overby, L. Marvin, Beth M. Henschen, Michael H. Walsh, and Julie Strauss. 1992. "Courting Constituents? An Analysis of the Senate Confirmation Vote on Justice Clarence Thomas." *American Political Science Review* 86: 997–1003.

Peltzman, Sam. 1984. "Constituent Interest and Congressional Voting." *Journal of Law and Economics* 27: 181–210.

Peltzman, Sam. 1985. "An Economic Interpretation of the History of Congressional Voting in the 20th Century." *American Economic Review* 75: 656–75.

Reed, W. Robert, and D. Eric Schansberg. 1995. "The House under Term Limits: What Would It Look Like?" *Social Science Quarterly* 76: 717–40.

Reed, W. Robert, D. Eric Schansberg, James Wilbanks, and Zhen Zhu. 1998. "The Relationship between Congressional Spending and Tenure with an Application to Term Limits." *Public Choice* 94: 85–104.

Schlesinger, Joseph A. 1966. *Ambition and Politics: Political Careers in the United States.* Chicago: Rand McNally.

Upshaw, Everett. 1995. "An Economist's View of Research on Term Limits." *Social Science Quarterly* 76: 730–33.

Vanbeek, J. 1991. "Does the Decision to Retire Increase the Amount of Political Shirking?" *Public Finance Quarterly* 19 (4): 444–56.

Westlye, Mark C. 1992. *Senate Elections and Campaign Intensity.* Baltimore: Johns Hopkins University Press.

Will, George. 1992. *Restoration: Congress, Term Limits, and the Recovery of Deliberative Democracy.* New York: Free Press.

Zupan, Mark A. 1990. "The Last Period Problem in Politics: Do Congressional Representatives Not Subject to a Reelection Constraint Alter Their Voting Behavior?" *Public Choice* 65: 167–80.

Understanding Presentation of Self

William T. Bianco

Goffman's work on presentation of self provides an important foundation for Fenno's *Home Style,* because it describes how a member of Congress influences constituent impressions of the member's personal characteristics (Fenno 1978). Drawing on research in Bianco (1997), this essay characterizes the factors that influence a voter's search for and reaction to new information about a candidate, including a description of how initial impressions, beliefs about sincerity, and search costs enter into voters' calculations.

In developing these findings, the larger goal is to build on one of the signal strengths of *Home Style,* its depiction of members of Congress (and by extension constituents) as purposive actors whose decisions reflect goals, beliefs, and expectations about others. Fenno's treatment of this assumption as an integral part of a coherent vision of legislator-constituent relations was an important milestone in convincing mainstream legislative politics scholars to take seriously purposive behavior models.

Even so, contemporary critics of the rational choice enterprise persist in arguing that these models embody unrealistic assumptions about real-world decision making and that maximizing behavior, characterized by thorough consideration of all available information, is a real-world exception rather than the rule.[1] As Tversky and Kahneman (1986) conclude, "the logic of [rational] choice does not provide an adequate foundation for a descriptive theory of decision making. We argue that the deviations of actual behavior from the normative model [rational choice] are too widespread to be ignored, too systematic to be dismissed as random error, and too fundamental to be accommodated by relaxing the normative system" (1986, 68).

An analysis of a legislator's presentations to constituents is an ideal venue to address this debate between rational choice and political psychology. Of the three elements comprising Fenno's definition of home style—allocation of resources, presentation of self, and explanations of Washington activity—presentation is the only one that does not have a clear link to the rational choice literature. Many scholars have described resource allocations in terms of a cost-benefit analysis; explanations have been modeled using the technology of signaling games (Austen-Smith 1992; Bianco 1994). However, no one has offered a game-theorem analysis of presentation of self. Moreover, the concept has its roots not in economics but in Goffman's seminal book and in related work on impression formation in psychology, anthropology, and sociology.

Supporters of the views expressed by Tversky and Kahneman would probably argue that the relative lack of attention to presentation is no accident. Rational choice models, they would say, with their stress on systematic calculation and unbiased consideration, cannot capture presentation of self, which involves the invocation of complex beliefs and symbols, factors that stem from deep cultural, ethnic, or religious ties between a representative and his or her constituents.

My previous work (Bianco 1997) engages this debate by comparing predictions derived from two models of impression formation. The first model is drawn from the psychology literature: a voter, a motivated tactician in the sense of Fiske (1993), forms impressions of a candidate according to the continuum model (Fiske and Neuberg 1990). The second model captures the behavior of a rational actor, who forms impressions as part of equilibrium behavior in a signaling game.

The analysis shows that the two models yield the same predictions about impression formation. That is, given the same situation (i.e., an initial impression, beliefs about context, and new information), motivated tacticians will reason to the same conclusions about a candidate as their rational actor counterparts. This essay summarizes these findings and uses them to offer three new results about presentation of self: how initial impressions influence the success of presentational efforts, how beliefs about a candidate's sincerity influence voters' reactions to presentations, and how search costs influence the search for new information.

Representatives, Constituents, and Presentation

Impressions underlie interpersonal interactions—as Goffman (1959) puts it, they "define the situation, enabling others to know in advance what [an individual] will expect of them, and what they may expect of him" (1959, 1). In the context addressed here, Goffman's definition can be operationalized by assuming that a voter's impression is relevant to his or her choice in the next election. That is, the voter has some conception of what a good representative would be and (all else equal) is more likely to vote for a candidate who resembles this ideal type over one who does not. Thus, the problem for the voter is to develop an accurate impression of the candidates running for office.

Candidates, of course, have a somewhat different perspective: "when an individual appears in the presence of others, there will usually be some reason for him to mobilize his activity so that it will convey an impression to others which it is in his interest to convey" (Goffman 1959, 4). Thus, while voters want to hold accurate impressions, the problem for each candidate is to shape voter impressions so as to increase his or her chances of winning an election.

This description makes clear that presentation of self is a core feature of the relationship between politicians and their constituents. By virtue of their interest in what government does, constituents want a "good" representative;

by virtue of their interest in staying in office, representatives want to look "good" to as many constituents as possible. Fenno's observation of members of Congress confirms that members are well aware of the need to influence what voters think; voters in turn are well aware that there is value in knowing what candidates are about. Fenno's work on presentation of self has spawned a vast and fruitful literature, and I do not propose to review it here. Instead, I focus on three questions about presentation that this literature does not address.

First, what factors determine the success or failure of a representative's presentational efforts? For example, suppose a candidate claims an affinity with voters, saying or doing something that suggests "I am one of you." When is this assertion taken seriously, in the sense that it creates or reinforces a belief among voters that the candidate shares their values and policy preferences? Presumably some claims—implicit or otherwise—are more credible than others; credibility is also likely to vary across representatives. However, although the literature on campaigns contains many examples of both successful and unsuccessful efforts by candidates to shape what voters think, it has relatively little to say about what factors drive the success or failure of presentation.

The literature on the impact of racial and gender-based stereotypes on voter perceptions provides a good example of this problem. Some analyses of campaigns by female or minority candidates (e.g., Huddy and Terkildsen 1993; Kahn 1992; McDermott 1997; Paolino 1995; Sigelman et al. 1995) suggest that these candidates are prisoners of stereotypes, unable to alter the belief that they are out of touch with district majorities. However, other studies (e.g., Carsey 1995; Sonenshein 1990; Swain 1993) point to cases in which such candidates have managed to evade politically damaging labels. Taken together, these studies suggest a question: When is it possible for such candidates to say or do things that cause voters to look beyond their initial impressions to a more information-rich picture?

A second, related question is how voters account for the possibility that a candidate's actions are strategic rather than sincere. Given an interest in reelection, candidates have an obvious incentive to say or do things that generate favorable impressions. Suppose a voter observes a candidate action that ostensibly signals agreement with the voter's concerns. Does this action reflect a true underlying agreement, or is it a political gesture designed to shape the voter's impression and thereby win his or her support? Insofar as voters discount behavior that might be strategic, a candidate's agreement with constituent concerns can only be signaled by actions whose implications can be independently verified or factors that are not subject to manipulation. Yet the literature on presentation, *Home Style* included, provides many examples of situations in which candidates shape impressions and win support with behavior that might be strategic. Clearly, voters do not totally ignore possibly strategic actions, and it strains credibility to assume that they take everything a candidate does at face value. Thus the question: How do beliefs about sincerity enter into voters' calculations about impression formation?

A third question about presentation concerns the impact of search costs: To what extent are voters likely to seek out new information given that the search is costly? Fenno (1978) points out that candidates spend much time and effort seeking out voters and determining their concerns. Voters face a similar problem: the information needed to form impressions may not be available as a matter of course. Moreover, given that for most voters, "politics is a sideshow on the circus of life" (Fiske 1990, 20), significant search costs may deter voters from moving beyond initial impressions. Insofar as they do, all of a candidate's efforts at presentation will be for naught—the candidate may be talking and acting, but these efforts will have no impact on voter perceptions.

Questions about search costs are central to the debate over the quality of vote decisions in contemporary American elections. Many analysts (most notably, Popkin [1991]) argue that opportunity costs constrain information search, leading voters away from a detailed appraisal of a candidate's record and toward impressions derived from casual observation of the characteristics, such as age, gender, race, or ethnicity. However, *Home Style* provides numerous examples of voters seeking out additional information about candidates—and candidates acting to put information before the electorate. Both observations suggest that the impact of search costs hinges on other factors, such as the quality of a voter's initial impressions. Although search costs are likely to be an important influence on impression formation, they are unlikely to be decisive for all voters.

Modeling Impression Formation: Continuums and Signals

In this section I describe two models of impression formation: the continuum model of Fiske and Neuberg (1990) and a signaling game. The goal is to develop and compare predictions from each game about the content of a voter's impressions of a candidate as a function of initial impressions, search costs, the candidate's actions, and the voter's beliefs about the candidate's willingness to behave strategically.

Psychological Models of Impression Formation

This essay's specification of psychological models of impression formation draws on the motivated tactician literature, research in which "the perceiver is no longer a cognitive miser mainly concerned with conserving scarce mental resources, but instead a motivated tactician choosing among a number of possible strategies, depending on current goals" (Fiske 1993, 172). In the work of Fiske and others (e.g., Cheng and Holyoak [1985]), motivated tacticians are purposive actors who build perceptions and consider alternatives with an eye toward making good choices—choices in line with their goals—while balancing the benefits from a good choice against decision costs. Thus, motivated tacticians "evaluate potential officeholders in much the same manner as they appraise the other people they encounter in their daily lives" (Rahn 1993, 472–73).

More specifically, the analysis operationalizes Fiske and Neuberg's (1990) continuum model of impression formation, which posits a five-step path to impressions. The first is initial categorization, a snap judgment about a target's unobserved characteristics based on some immediately apparent feature. The second step, attention, is the decision to gather additional information about a target. The third and fourth steps, confirmatory categorization and recategorization, involve consideration of whether new information confirms the initial impression or suggests a new categorization.

The final step, piecemeal integration, occurs when a perceiver's initial categorization is inconsistent with the new information, and new information does not suggest an unambiguous new category. In this case, a target's characteristics are "averaged or added" (Fiske and Neuberg 1990, 8) to arrive at an impression. Fiske (1990, 12) argues that piecemeal integration comes closest to matching the process envisioned by rational choice models of candidate evaluation.

Signaling games constitute the game-theorem representation of impression formation. A signaling game captures a situation of asymmetric information between two or more players. One player has private information—information known only to the player—that is relevant for a decision made by a second player. The second player's decision influences both players' payoffs. Before the second player decides, the first player has the opportunity (or is forced) to make some sort of signal. The signal can be a direct statement or an action that reveals information indirectly. By sending appropriate signals (taking different actions), the first player can influence the second player's beliefs and thereby influence the second player's choice. Of course, the first player may have an incentive to reveal false information or to avoid revealing any information at all. The second player must take these possibilities into account when deciding how to respond to ostensibly informative signals.

These descriptions reveal numerous parallels between signaling games and the continuum model. For one thing, both models describe perceivers as essentially goal-driven purposive actors. The specification of motives often differs, but assumptions about motivation are, as Fiske (1990, 12) notes, empirical questions. The two models also specify the same distinction between initial impressions arising from a largely automatic process and subsequent impressions developed from attention to new information.

Where the two models diverge is in their description of how perceivers react to new information. The fundamental precept of rational action is full consideration of all information. Motivated tacticians approach this ideal only in cases of surprises—when new information is inconsistent with previously held beliefs.

To appreciate the significance of this distinction, consider how rational actors and motivated tacticians account for strategic behavior. When assessing an opponent's action in a signaling game, a rational actor considers whether the action, or signal, is a valid indication of type or an attempt to bias the receiver into a false inference. In contrast, the description of confirmatory categorization suggests that as long as a target's behavior confirms the initial categorization, the motivated tactician will not consider whether these actions are sincere or deceptive. Based on Fiske and Neuberg's (1990) description, a full accounting for strategic behavior may not arise until piecemeal integration, the final stage in their model. The question is, do these differences in process generate differences in impressions? That two models differ in structural or cognitive assumptions does not imply that they yield different predictions about impressions.

Formalizing the Continuum Model and the Signaling Game

A full description of the two models of impression formation is contained in Bianco (1997); this section lays out the overall structure and important points of comparison. It is important to understand that the two analyses capture the same situation: the motivated tactician and the rational actor have the same goals and constraints and the same quantity and kinds of information. The differences lie in the techniques the players use to form impressions.

Both models begin with two players: a candidate and a voter.[2] The voter's impression formation task is to infer the candidate's type—some aspect of the candidate's policy preferences or other unobserved characteristic. There are two possible candidate types, α and $\sim\alpha$; the voter is an α. The voter prefers to vote for a candidate whose type agrees with his or her own and to vote against candidates whose types differ. By extension, then, the voter prefers to form an accurate impression of the candidate's type. The candidate, however, prefers that the voter make a politically beneficial impression, concluding that the candidate's type is the same as the voter's.

Before forming an impression, the voter first observes a visible feature of the candidate, which allows the voter as motivated tactician to form an initial impression—an initial categorization for the voter as motivated tactician or prior beliefs for the voter as rational actor. In addition, the voter can, if he or she chooses, observe an action taken by the candidate, a_1 or a_0, which provides a basis for additional cognition. At the margin—ignoring the impact on the voter's impression—α candidates prefer to take action a_1 rather than a_0, while $\sim\alpha$ candidates prefer a_0 over a_1.

The candidate's willingness to reveal information through actions (equivalently, to behave strategically) is specified as an additional aspect of type: some candidates will take their preferred action regardless of the consequences, whereas others are willing to take whatever action is needed to ensure a favorable impression. The candidate is aware of both aspects of his or her type; the voter holds beliefs about these factors.

The player's motivations and payoffs are simple. The voter wishes to form an accurate impression of the candidate and receive a higher payoff if he or she does. The voter also incurs a cost if he or she gathers additional information about the candidate (i.e., observes the candidate's action). The candidate receives a higher payoff if the voter concludes that the candidate's type matches the voter's. The candidate also receives a payoff from his or her action; for candidates who are unwilling to behave strategically, these payoffs are sized such that they are unwilling to take a less preferred action as a means of generating a favorable impression. Candidates who are willing to behave strategically have payoffs that allow them to take whatever action triggers a favorable impression from the voter (i.e., the costs of misrepresentation are not prohibitive).

Two Analyses of Impression Formation

In this section I develop predictions about impression formation based on the continuum model and the signaling game. These predictions specify the content of the voter's impression of the candidate as a function of the voter's initial impression, the voter's beliefs about the candidate's sincerity, and search costs.

Bianco (1997) characterizes the voter's path to impression formation in each game. Analysis of the signaling game develops predictions using sequential equilibrium analysis. In a sequential equilibrium for this game, the candidate's strategy maximizes this player's expected payoff given the voter's strategy; the voter's strategy maximizes the voter's expected payoff given the candidate's strategy, and the voter's beliefs about the candidate's type are calculated using Bayes' rule whenever possible.

Analysis of the continuum model follows the discussion in Fiske and Neuberg (1990). The voter begins with an initial categorization (here based on exogenous information about the candidate's type), decides whether to gather additional information (i.e., observe the candidate's action), then moves to either confirmatory categorization, recategorization, or piecemeal integration depending on whether inferences drawn from the action are compatible with the initial categorization or with other possible categorizations.

The first result is detailed in Bianco (1997) and will simply be stated here: the two models make the same predictions about the content of impressions.

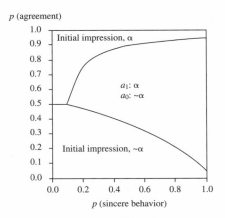

p (agreement)

Fig. 1.   Initial impressions and the reaction to new information

This similarity of predictions is a general result; it does not depend on the magnitude of search costs or on any other parameter specified here. Simply put, although the continuum model and the signaling game of impression formation differ in their internal workings, they make the same predictions about impression formation given the same initial assumptions about motivations, information, and costs.

Figure 1 plots the voter's impressions as a function of initial beliefs about the candidate, expectations about the candidate's sincerity, and an assumed value for search costs, .05.

When *p* is high (the top of the y-axis), the voter's initial beliefs are that the candidate is more likely to be type α rather than type $\sim\alpha$; low values of *p* (bottom of the y-axis) imply the candidate is probably type $\sim\alpha$. High values of *q* (right-hand side of the x-axis) imply that the candidate's actions are probably sincere; low values (left-hand side) imply that the candidate is willing to be strategic (take actions that misrepresent type) if needed.

First consider the left-hand regions in the figure (the large triangle in the bottom half and the irregular shape in the top half), which correspond to situations in which the gain from additional information is relatively small. Here the voter does not gather additional information and judges the candidate based on an initial impression. In particular, when *p* > 0.5 the voter concludes that the candidate is type α; when *p* < 0.5, the voter concludes that the candidate is type $\sim\alpha$.

In the right-hand region of figure 1, the voter gathers information (observes the candidate's action); his or her reaction hinges on its content. When the candidate takes action a_1 (suggesting that the candidate shares the constituent's type, α), the voter will conclude that the candidate is type α. If the candidate takes action a_0, suggesting that his or her type differs from that of the constituent, the voter will respond by revising his or her initial impression and concluding that the candidate is type ~α.

Figure 1 reveals an asymmetry in a voter's decision to search for additional information about a candidate. In general, a voter who holds favorable initial impressions is more likely to seek out and respond to new information than a voter whose initial impressions are unfavorable; note that the region in which attention occurs is much larger given $p > 0.5$ than p 0.5.

Next, figure 2 shows the impact of search costs by plotting constituent behavior given three values for search costs: 0, .05 (as in fig. 1), and 0.3.

The middle plot in figure 2 replicates figure 1, or a situation in which search costs equal .05. The top plot shows the voter's impressions when search costs equal 0—where information gathering is a nondecision. Here a voter's reaction to the candidate's actions hinges on the content of his or her initial impressions. Voters with favorable initial impressions always respond to actions as though they were sincere behavior. Voters who hold unfavorable initial impressions behave similarly given a high enough probability of strategic behavior and sufficient uncertainty about the candidate's type. However, given a wide range of beliefs, unfavorably disposed voters will gather new information and ignore it; regardless of how the candidate acts, the voter will stick with his or her initial impression.

The bottom plot in figure 2, in which search costs equal 0.3, show that the asymmetry in a voter's decisions about new information decreases as search costs increase. To see this relationship, note first that the region in which attention occurs is much smaller when search costs are higher. Moreover, the region is roughly symmetric, about $p = 0.5$. In substantive terms, as search costs increase, voters with favorable initial impressions are just as reluctant to gather additional information as their unfavorably disposed counterparts. If costs increase further, at some point the two types of voters behave identically: neither search for new information, and both judge the candidate based on their initial impressions.

Discussion

This essay has modeled impression formation as a means of understanding how legislators present themselves to constituents. Regardless of whether this behavior is modeled using a signaling game or a psychology-based approach, the central insight is that a voter's search for and response to new information hinges on both the quality and content of the voter's initial categorization, on the compatibility of this categorization with new information, and on beliefs about the sincerity of the candidate's actions.

More specifically, the analysis shows that voters who are favorably disposed to a candidate—whose initial categorization suggests that the candidate

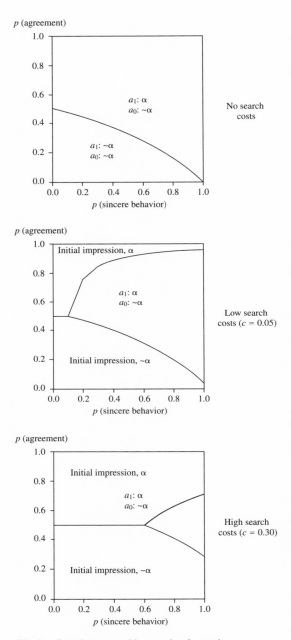

Fig. 2. Search costs and impression formation

shares their type—are in general receptive to new information about the candidate. Assuming that such voters gather information, their inferences will be relatively insensitive to beliefs about the candidate's sincerity; they will use new information even if chances are good that the actions constitute strategic behavior. In contrast, when voters are unfavorably disposed to a candidate, their reaction to new information hinges on beliefs about sincerity. A voter who holds these perceptions will consider actions taken by a candidate if they are perceived to be sincere. When sincerity is in doubt, the response to new information depends on a straightforward interaction between beliefs about sincerity and the quality of the voter's initial categorization: as quality declines, the voter will consider actions given higher probabilities that they are strategic in nature.

When Does Self-Promotion Work?

What kinds of constituents react favorably when a legislator claims that he or she shares their interests? In the context of this analysis, self-promotion implies a situation in which both the probability of sincere behavior and search costs are low. The analysis here suggests that this activity is more useful as a means of reinforcing positive evaluations than as a way of converting opponents into supporters. Figure 2 shows that self-promotion is more likely to influence constituents whose initial impressions are favorable than those whose initial impressions are unfavorable. Favorably disposed voters will always respond positively to self-promotion; the only question is whether search costs deter the gathering of additional information. In contrast, even when search costs are nonexistent, voters with unfavorable impressions are likely to ignore a legislator's actions; they prefer impressions based on factors that the legislator cannot manipulate.

It should be noted that this asymmetry in the response to good news about a candidate does not exist for the response to bad news. The analysis here predicts that, regardless of initial impressions, voters will have the same response to actions that suggest that a legislator's type differs from their own: they will take the action seriously and conclude that the legislator is indeed not their type. In both cases, this response is driven by the same strategic calculation: because all legislators, regardless of their type, prefer that constituents form favorable impressions, actions that suggest the opposite conclusion can never reflect an attempt at manipulation.

These results also confirm the intuition that minority candidates can become prisoners of stereotypes: given nonzero search costs and initial impressions that are sufficiently negative, voters will not gather additional information about a candidate, even given a high probability of sincere behavior. Thus, the problem for these candidates is not that the cost of becoming well informed deters voters from moving beyond stereotypes. Nor is the search for new information necessarily hindered by a belief that the candidate's actions misrepresent his or her true preferences. Rather, the problem is that the voter's incentive to search is also related to the content of his or her initial impressions. Sufficiently negative impressions deter information search, regardless of other factors.

How Do Voters Account for Strategic Behavior?

The analysis highlights a sharp asymmetry in how beliefs about a candidate's sincerity influence reaction to new information. These beliefs have no effect on voters who hold favorable initial impressions. Assuming that search costs are not prohibitive, these voters will always gather information supplied or signaled by a candidate and incorporate it into their evaluations, regardless of the probability that this information reflects strategic behavior. In contrast, beliefs about sincerity loom large in the calculations of voters whose initial impressions are unfavorable. The impact is straightforward: when a candidate is thought to be sincere, the voter will revise impressions based on what the candidate says or does. However, given a substantial probability of strategic behavior, compounded by even small search costs, voters whose initial impressions are negative are likely to ignore a candidate's actions.

These results suggest a new interpretation of anecdotes in which voters judge candidates on the basis of what the candidates say or do, ignoring the possibility that these behaviors result from the candidate's interest in reelection, rather than the candidate's policy goals or other substantive motivations. Some would say that these stories reflect an inability or unwillingness on the part of constituents to think through the implications of their candidate's behavior. However, the analysis here suggests a more benign interpretation of the constituents' reaction. Simply put, the decision to ignore the possibility of strategic behavior by a candidate is not inconsistent with the rational use of information. In particular, we should expect voters who hold favorable initial impressions to take seriously virtually everything they learn about a candidate, even when the sincerity of a candidate's actions is in doubt.

The Impact of Search Costs

The analysis also identifies an asymmetry in how search costs influence information search. These costs are more likely to deter information gathering when the voter's initial categorization is favorable than when it is unfavorable. Sympathetic voters are more likely to see a candidate's actions as sincere signals; thus, search costs loom large in their decisions about attention. Disgruntled counterparts, in contrast, are driven away from attention by concerns about sincerity; thus, high search costs are less likely to alter their decision. This asymmetry decreases as search costs increase: given moderate to high costs, there is little difference in the information-gathering strategies of favorably and unfavorably disposed voters.

This finding implies that a candidate's ability to push information—lower the search costs for interested voters—is more valuable as a means of reinforcing favorable impressions than as a way of converting unfavorable impressions into favorable ones. Voters who already like a candidate are essentially spring-loaded to consider additional information; if search costs can be reduced sufficiently, they will always modify their impressions in light of new information. Thus, one way for a candidate to shape voters' impressions is to ensure that they are exposed to new, favorable information about the candidate. In contrast, voters who hold unfavorable impressions are far less motivated to consider new information. Even if search costs are reduced to 0, these voters may ignore new information because they favor impressions developed from nonstrategic indicators. The only exception is if their impressions are relatively imprecise and they assess a high probability of sincere behavior. Thus, candidates who wish to convert opponents into supporters must do more than simply expose these voters to new, favorable information; conversion will occur only among some opponents and only if these voters discount the possibility of strategic behavior by the candidate.

NOTES

For their comments on this paper and the larger project that it is drawn from, I thank John Aldrich, Bob Bates, John Brehm, Bruce Bueno de Mesquita, Dick Fenno, Susan Fiske, Skip Lupia, Kathleen McGraw, Bob O'Connor, Dave Rohde, Ken Shepsle, and, especially, Jim Kuklinski and Phil Paolino for their extremely helpful comments, admonitions, and generally well-deserved, unbridled criticisms.

1. See Hogarth and Reder (1986), Cook and Levi (1990), and the 1995 special issue of *Critical Review*.

2. The results do not appear to be sensitive to the number of voters, because the candidate's strategy is weakly dominant and independent of the constituents' policy preferences.

REFERENCES

Austen-Smith, David. 1992. "Explaining the Vote: Constituency Constraints on Legislative Strategy." *American Journal of Political Science* 36: 68–95.

Bianco, William T. 1994. *Trust: Representatives and Constituents.* Ann Arbor: University of Michigan Press.

Bianco, William T. 1997. "Different Paths to the Same Result: Rational Choice, Political Psychology, and Impression Formation in Campaigns." *American Journal of Political Science* 42: 1062–81.

Carsey, Thomas. 1995. "The Contextual Effects of Race on White Voter Behavior: The 1989 New York City Mayoral Election." *Journal of Politics* 57: 221–28.

Cheng, Patricia W., and Keith J. Holyoak. 1985. "Pragmatic Reasoning Schemes." *Cognitive Psychology* 17: 391–416.

Hogarth, Robin M., and Melvin W. Reder, eds. 1986. *Rational Choice: The Contrast Between Economics and Psychology.* Chicago: University of Chicago Press.

Fenno, Richard. 1978. *Home Style (House Members in Their Districts).* Boston: Little, Brown.

Fiske, Susan T. 1990. "The Motivated Tactician in Models of the Presidency." Paper presented at a University of Colorado conference on studying the presidency, Boulder.

Fiske, Susan T. 1993. "Social Cognition and Perception." *Annual Review of Psychology* 44: 155–94.

Fiske, Susan T., and Steven L. Neuberg. 1990. "A Continuum of Impression Formation, from Category-Based to Individuating Processes." Vol. 23 of *Advances in Experimental Social Psychology*, ed. M. P. Zanna. San Diego: Academic Press.

Goffman, Erving. 1959. *The Presentation of Self in Everyday Life.* New York: Doubleday.

Cook, Karen Schweers, and Margaret Levi, eds. 1990. *The Limits of Rationality.* Chicago: University of Chicago Press.

Huddy, Leonie, and Nayda Terkildsen. 1993. "Gender Stereotypes and the Perception of Male and Female Candidates." *American Journal of Political Science* 37: 119–47.

Kahn, Kim F. 1992. "Does Being Male Help? An Investigation of the Effects of Candidate Gender and Campaign Coverage on Evaluations of U.S. Senate Candidates." *Journal of Politics* 54: 497–517.

McDermott, Monika L. 1997. "Voting Cues in Low-Information Elections: Candidate Gender as a Social Information Variable in Contemporary United States Elections." *American Journal of Political Science* 41: 270–83.

Paolino, Phillip. 1995. "Group-Salient Issues and Group Representation: Support for Women Candidates in the 1992 Senate Elections." *American Journal of Political Science* 39: 294–313.

Popkin, Samuel L. 1991. *The Reasoning Voter.* Chicago: University of Chicago Press.

Rahn, Wendy M. 1993. "The Role of Partisan Stereotypes in Information Processing about Political Candidates." *American Journal of Political Science* 37: 472–96.

Sigelman, Carol, Lee Sigelman, Barbara Walkosz, and Michael Nitz. 1995. "Black Candidates, White Voters: Understanding Racial Bias in Political Perceptions." *American Journal of Political Science* 39: 243–65.

Sonenshein, Raphael J. 1990. "Can Black Candidates Win Statewide Elections?" *Political Science Quarterly* 105: 219–41.

Swain, Carol M. 1993. *Black Faces, Black Interests: The Representation of African-Americans in America.* Cambridge: Harvard University Press.

Tversky, Amos, and Daniel Kahneman. 1986. "Rational Choice and the Framing of Decisions." In *Rational Choice: The Contrast between Economics and Psychology*, ed. Robin M. Hogarth and Melvin W. Reder, 67–93. Chicago: University of Chicago Press.

Member Goals and Party Switching in the U.S. Congress

David Castle and Patrick J. Fett

Introduction

Seven congressional Democrats switched parties after the 1994 elections that gave Republicans control of both the House and Senate for the first time in 40 years. The party switches by five House members and two senators in the 104th Congress were the largest number for any Congress in this century and brought the total number of former Democrats to 19 in the House and 8 in the Senate.

Party switching of this magnitude suggests partisan realignment. Many of the party switchers in the 104th Congress were southerners who had switched parties during the 1980s, prompting scholars to note the link between party switching and realignment (Canon and Sousa 1992; King and Benjamin 1985; Rothenberg 1985). Others (Burnham 1995; Caldwell 1995) see the congressional party switches that followed the 1994 elections as a continuation of a partisan realignment in American politics.

Party switching has almost invariably been studied in the context of realignment. Party switching by campaign activists (Clark et al. 1991; Kweit 1986; Nesbit 1988; Stone 1991) and voters (Dyer, Vedlitz, and Hill 1988; Erickson and Tedin 1981) has produced state-level realignment, which has in turn helped lead to party switching by prospective congressional candidates (Castle and Fett 1994).

More comprehensive (Aldrich 1995) and theoretical (Aldrich and Bianco 1992) studies, however, demonstrate that party switching by congressional incumbents should be seen as individual goal-directed behavior for which ongoing partisan realignment is but a crucial part of the environment in which party switching takes place. Richard F. Fenno Jr. has shown that members of Congress work to further their political goals through committee activity. We suggest that members of Congress might switch parties for the same reasons.

Fenno (1973, 1) notes that "a member of the House is a congressman first and a committee member second" and that "he will act on his committee in ways calculated to achieve such goals." Following Fenno, we posit that a member of Congress is an incumbent first and a member of a political party second. Members will act in ways calculated to achieve political goals, even switching parties if necessary to attain those goals.

Fenno finds that the most widely held goals of House members are reelection, influence within the institution, and good public policy. The pursuit of these goals might lead some incumbents to switch political parties. Members of Congress may thus calculate that switching parties will help their reelection prospects, particularly if their districts or states are undergoing partisan realignment. Legislators might increase their influence within the institution by switching to the majority party or by switching in return for better committee assignments. And policy disagreements with fellow party members can be resolved by switching parties. We test hypotheses about party switching as the pursuit of individual political goals in a study of congressional incumbents during the period 1960–95.

Data and Measures

Sampling Procedures

An empirical study of congressional party switching requires data on both party switchers and members of Congress who did not switch parties. Our data include all representatives and senators who switched parties while serving in Congress during the years 1960–95. The year 1960 was selected as the starting point of the study because of evidence of the beginnings of a partisan realignment in the South during the 1960s (see Lamis 1988). Because our focus is on party switching by congressional incumbents, we exclude those who switched parties before their election to Congress.

A total of 18 members of Congress switched parties during the 1960–95 period (see appendix). The party switchers are identified through biographical information published in *Congressional Quarterly Weekly Report, The Almanac of American Politics,* and *Politics in America.* We include only individuals who switched from one of the two major parties to the other. Sixteen of the major party switches were to the Republican party, whereas only two congressional incumbents switched to the Democratic party. Both Republican-to-Democrat switches occurred in the early 1970s.

The population of congressional party switchers is supplemented by a random sample of 10 percent of the nearly 2,000 persons who served in Congress during the 1960–95 period and who did not switch parties during their congressional service. The sampling of nonswitchers was accomplished through a two-stage procedure: (1) random four-digit numbers were used to select 195 individuals from the sampling frame of 1,943 persons who served in either the House or the Senate between January 1960 and December 1995 and (2) random two-digit numbers were then generated to select particular years of service for the individuals randomly selected in the first stage. For example, the first-stage random number results in the selection of Carroll Campbell, a Republican House member from South Carolina, from the list, and the second-stage sampling selects 1984 as Campbell's particular year of congressional service to be analyzed in this essay.

The purpose for combining the population of congressional party switchers with a random sample of nonswitchers is to see whether the two groups exhibit different behavior. However, party switchers are proportionately overrepresented in the data. We include all switchers, but only part of the nonswitchers. King, Keohane, and Verba (1994) note that this selection bias can cause biased parameter estimates. Fortunately, the parameters are not biased when logistic regression is used, as is the case in this study. Furthermore, an adjustment can be made to eliminate bias in the intercept as well. Consider that our situation is analogous to sampling in a medical study wherein a population of persons with a particular rare disease is compared with a large sample of persons in which the disease is not, or not yet, present. Agresti (1990) points out that these case-control studies are common in health-related applications. In our situation, without being pejorative, the "disease" we study is party switching by incumbent members of Congress, a historically rare but contemporarily important phenomenon.

The bias that results from pooling a small population with a large random sample for logistic regression analysis is restricted to the intercept of the model. Dwyer (1983) and Agresti (1990) show that logistic regression in case-control studies such as ours produces exactly the same estimated coefficients for the independent variables as does a standard logit model on a random sample. Agresti (1990, 127) further shows that to correct for bias in the constant, calculate

$$a^* = a + \log[P(A)/P(B)]$$

where, for our study, a^* is the adjusted constant, $P(A)$ is the probability of selecting party switchers, and $P(B)$ is the probability of selecting nonswitchers.

The two-stage random sampling procedure yields a sample of nonswitcher incumbents who represent all 50 states and each of the 36 years of the 1960–95 period. The nonswitcher sample contains 57.9 percent Democrats and 42.1 percent Republicans. House members comprise 78.7 percent of the nonswitcher sample, and senators make up 21.3 percent.

We use a logistic regression model to estimate the effects of several variables on the likelihood that an incumbent will switch parties. The underlying dependent variable is therefore the probability that an incumbent will switch parties. The observed dependent variable is whether the individual switched; switchers are coded as 1 and nonswitchers as 0.

Independent Variables: Goals and Constraints

We seek to capture three aspects of the reelection goal. First, a congressional incumbent might consider switching parties to avoid strong primary election competition. Party switching to avoid a tough and costly primary election contest could be an attractive option to members of Congress who also find themselves ideologically at odds with a majority of their party. This may have been the case, for example, with Representative Ogden Reid of New York. Reid, a liberal Republican House member, switched to the Democratic party in 1972 after consecutive conservative primary challenges had nearly cost him his seat.

We thus include a *Primary Election* variable in the model. This variable is the incumbent's vote percentage in the primary for the election immediately preceding the party switch or, for nonswitchers, the election immediately preceding the randomly selected year of congressional service. A large primary election victory should have a negative effect on the likelihood of switching. Other things being equal, a member who is relatively secure in gaining nomination would have little incentive to increase his or her uncertainty about making it through the first stage in the electoral process by switching parties.

For the general election, however, the picture may be different. The propensity to switch parties is likely enhanced if a legislator is unconstrained by party label. That is, if the incumbent wins despite the fate of fellow partisans in the constituency, he or she has a freer hand in making political decisions. A member of Congress who believes that constituents are voting for him or her because of personal attributes and attitudes rather than partisan affiliation will exhibit less hesitation to switch parties.

The variable *Presidential Constraint* is a measure of the legislator's independence from partisan constraints in the electoral arena. It is measured as the difference between the percentage of the two-party vote received by the congressional incumbent in the election before switching or before the year of service selected in the two-stage sampling process and the percentage of the two-party vote in the constituency received by the presidential candidate of the incumbent's party in the presidential election immediately before the switch or the year sampled. A high positive score on the constraint variable indicates that the incumbent senator or House member received a greater percentage of the general election vote than did his or her party's presidential candidate; the incumbent is thus unconstrained by the popularity of the party at the presidential level. This was the case, for example, with representative Bob Stump of Arizona before his switch to the Republican party. Stump won 64 percent of the votes as a Democrat in 1980 at the same time that incumbent Democratic president Jimmy Carter managed just 32 percent of the two-party presidential vote against Ronald Reagan. Stump switched parties and won reelection as a Republican in 1982 with 63 percent.

On the other hand, we interpret negative scores and scores near 0 on the constraint variable to mean that the legislator is relatively constrained by his or her current political party affiliation and therefore unlikely to switch parties.

Data for the primary election variable and the presidential constraint variable are from *America Votes* and *Congressional Quarterly's Guide to U.S. Elections.*

Finally, the dichotomous variable *Realignment* is included to help capture the effects of partisan realignment in the South. The southern realignment accelerated after Ronald Reagan's defeat of southern Democrat Jimmy Carter for the presidency in 1980. If realigning forces have been at work in producing party switches in the region, then this variable, coded as 1 for southern Democrats and 0 for Republicans and all other Democrats, will yield a positive regression coefficient.

Nearly all party switchers cite policy differences with their former party as a major consideration in the switch. Typical are comments in *Congressional Quarterly Weekly Report.* Democrat-to-Republican switcher Greg Laughlin of Texas stated that his conservative principles "are not in the agenda of the House Democratic leadership" (1995, 1894). Party switcher Nathan Deal was quoted (1995, 1084) as stating that his "conservative north Georgia principles are not shared by today's national Democratic party." Policy differences cut the other way as well. Representative Ogden Reid of New York, who switched to the Democratic party in 1972, said that "the Republican party is no longer in the mainstream of American life" (1972, 656).

We attempt to capture the degree of such policy differences by the variable *Party Unity,* measured as the party-unity score for votes in Congress. This number is the member's party-unity score, adjusted for absences, in *Congressional Quarterly Almanac* for the legislative year immediately preceding the party switch. For nonswitchers, party-unity scores are for the year before that randomly selected.

If members of Congress seek influence within the institution, they must be mindful of seniority. Senior members of a legislative body are less likely to switch political parties if switching entails losing seniority. The variable *Seniority* sums the number of years of service in the House or Senate at the time of the party switch or, for nonswitchers, at the year of congressional service sampled. We anticipate a negative relationship between institutional seniority and party switching in Congress. As a legislator gains seniority, especially in the majority party, he or she must consider the possible sacrifice of institutional power when switching parties. The importance of seniority is underscored by the fact that the Democrat-to-Republican party switchers in the 104th Congress were routinely allowed by the Republican leadership to retain some or all of their committee seniority.

Influence within the institution also comes with holding formal leadership positions. Congressional party switching should be less likely for individuals who, if they switched, would be forced to give up a leadership position. *Leadership* is defined as all partisan positions at or above the level of chief deputy whip, as well as caucus chairs, full committee and subcommittee chairs, and ranking members of committees and subcommittees. The variable is coded 1 for incumbents who held a leadership position before switching parties or, for nonswitchers, for the randomly selected year of congressional service, and 0 otherwise.

Other things being equal, members of Congress should be more likely to switch to the majority party. The benefits in terms of legislative power and influence are greater in the majority party because legislative committee and subcommittee chairs go only to members of the majority party. We measure the variable *Majority Party* as a dichotomy: 1 if in the majority at the time of the party switch and for all majority party nonswitchers and otherwise 0.

Finally, we take into account that the House and Senate have different rules, procedures, and traditions. These differences might affect a legislator's decision to switch parties. In particular, even a single minority party senator can slow or stop legislation. Minority party members in the Senate retain a great deal of power, whereas minority party members in the House are relatively powerless. For this reason we expect the indicator variable *Senate,* coded as 1 or 0, to have a negative effect on party switching.

Results and Analysis

Table 1 displays the results of the logistic regression and reports the coefficient estimate, standard error, and statistical significance level for each independent variable.

The sign of the *Primary Election* coefficient is negative, as expected, but the variable itself is not statistically significant. We take this finding to mean that few individuals in Congress switch parties because of fear of primary election defeat. Indeed, over the period studied, less than 2 percent of all House incumbents and slightly more than 5 percent of Senate incumbents seeking reelection lost in the primary.

The estimated coefficient for the *Presidential Constraint* variable is positive but fails to show statistical significance. We are impressed, however, with the fact that all party switchers over the past 36 years received a greater percentage of the two-party vote in their constituency for the election immediately before the switch than did the presidential candidate of their party. The mean constraint score for party switchers is 31.6, compared with a mean of 13.4 for nonswitchers.

The positive and statistically significant coefficient for the *Realignment* variable shows that most congressional party switching has been by southern Democrats. Of the 18 congressional party switchers studied, 13 are former Democrats from southern states.

The model confirms that high *Party Unity* scores make legislators less likely to switch parties. Although we have classified this variable as a policy variable, the measure itself encompasses underlying constituency effects as well. A House member's voting decision is based on a myriad of factors (Kingdon 1973), not least of which is his or her own policy predispositions and those of the constituency. Therefore, the party-unity score theoretically should be, and is, one of the best indicators of the likelihood of party switching.

The strength of the *Party Unity* variable is most easily seen in the high correlation with party switching ($r = +0.52$) and in the difference of means for the samples. The party switchers show a mean adjusted party-unity score for the year before switching of 45.7 compared with a mean party-unity score of 77.0 for the nonswitcher sample.

The estimated coefficient for institutional *Seniority* is negative but not statistically significant. The mean number of years served in the Senate or House at the time of the party switch is 7.3. Only 3 of the 18 party switchers had served 10 or more years before switching parties.

Seniority is often a key to attaining a party or committee leadership position. *Leadership* as defined in the model significantly reduces the probability of party switching. Only 3 of the 18 incumbent party switchers held a leadership position at the time of the switch, whereas 38.0 percent of the nonswitcher sample were party, committee, or subcommittee leaders.

TABLE 1.   Results of Logistic Regression Analysis of Congressional Party Switching

Independent variables	Estimated coefficient	Standard error	Significance
Reelection variables			
Primary election	−.02	.02	.51
Constraint	.04	.03	.23
Realignment	10.17	2.88	.00
Public policy variables			
Party unity	−.12	.03	.00
Influence variables			
Seniority	−.04	.08	.58
Leadership	−5.01	1.78	.00
Majority party	−7.83	2.21	.00
Senate	−3.43	1.66	.04
Constant (adjusted)	6.23		

	Predicted		
Observed	Party switcher	Nonswitcher	Correct
Party switcher	14	4	77.8%
Nonswitcher	2	193	99.0%
Overall			97.2%

The coefficient for *Majority Party* shows that members of the legislative majority are significantly less likely to switch parties than are members of the minority. For example, all seven party switches in the 104th Congress were by minority Democrats switching to the majority Republican party.

. Finally, the model shows that *Senate* members are significantly less likely to switch parties than are House members. Institutional factors that are generally of major importance to a career in the House—party unity, leadership positions, and majority party status—may be less important to senators. Senators can be influential legislators even in the absence of these factors and also have less need to switch parties for policy-making reasons.

Further analysis reveals differences between the party switchers in the 104th Congress and legislators who switched parties in earlier years. The incumbents who switched parties to become Republicans after the 1994 elections appear to have been somewhat less motivated by policy differences and more motivated by political opportunity than past congressional party switchers. The party switchers in the 104th Congress show a mean party-unity score of 62.3, and none scored less than 50 on this measure. In contrast, the mean party-unity score for those who switched parties in earlier years is 35.1, with 8 of the 11 scoring less than 50.0. To the extent that party-unity scores are also measures of policy compatibility, the party switchers in the 104th Congress were much closer to their former party than were the party switchers in earlier years.

The importance of policy differences with others in their party for the earlier switchers is illustrated by the fact that so many left the legislative majority to join the minority. All congressional incumbents in our study who left the Democratic party before the 1994 elections—from South Carolina Senator Strom Thurmond in 1964 to Florida Representative Bill Grant in 1989—gave up majority party status to join the minority. Each gave up potential institutional power in the majority party; it is likely that they did so at least in part because of ideological incompatibility and policy differences with the Democratic majority.

In contrast, the seven party switches in the 104th Congress permitted former Democrats to maintain or regain their majority party status. Though politically conservative as a group, none had displayed the severe ideological incompatibility with fellow Democrats that characterized many previous party switchers.

Conclusion

Our findings confirm that members of Congress switch political parties in pursuit of the same goals that Richard F. Fenno, Jr. identified in his study of committee behavior: reelection, influence within the institution, and good public policy. The cumulative effect of party switching over the past three decades has been Republican majorities in the House and Senate. Party switching by Democrats in Congress ceased after 1995, but their numbers permitted Republicans to retain congressional majorities in the 1996 and 1998 elections.

Republicans lost House seats in both 1996 and 1998, however, which left them with a scant majority in the 106th Congress and ended speculation about a continuing partisan realignment in their favor. Indeed, recent events can be interpreted to suggest that future party switching may benefit the Democratic party. Carolyn McCarthy of New York won election to the U.S. House of Representatives as a Democrat after switching parties in 1996. She was followed into the Democratic party less than a year later by two incumbent officeholders in New York: Debra Mazzarelli of the state assembly and Elizabeth McCaughey Ross, the lieutenant governor. Texas Democrats in 1998 elected party switcher Molly Beth Malcolm chair of the state party.

Whether party switching ultimately benefits one party or the other, it is likely to remain a relatively rare event among members of Congress. Holt (1967, 83) contrasts party switching in Congress with that in the British House of Commons; he notes that in British politics, "a major politician who changes his party allegiance can be found a new safe constituency should his previous electorate seem unlikely to follow him into the new party." American politicians, however, are tied to their home districts or states and must take their old supporters with them in any such adventure. Holt suggests that this fact alone accounts for the very small number of incumbents who have accomplished or even attempted a party switch.

Relatively rare events, however, can have major effects. Party switchers provided the margin for new House majorities in 1859 and again in 1995 and for new Senate majorities in 1861, 1955, and 1995. With the House majority now the smallest in more than 40 years, the potential for party switching by incumbents is of utmost importance to congressional parties and party leaders.

APPENDIX: CONGRESSIONAL INCUMBENT PARTY SWITCHERS, 1960–95

Strom Thurmond, South Carolina, switched to Republican party, 1964
Albert Watson, South Carolina, switched to Republican party, 1965
Ogden Reid, New York, switched to Democratic party, 1972
Donald Riegle, Michigan, switched to Democratic party, 1973
John Jarman, Oklahoma, switched to Republican party, 1975
Eugene Atkinson, Pennsylvania, switched to Republican party, 1981
Bob Stump, Arizona, switched to Republican party, 1981
Phil Gramm, Texas, switched to Republican party, 1983
Andy Ireland, Florida, switched to Republican party, 1984
Tommy Robinson, Arkansas, switched to Republican party, 1989

Bill Grant, Florida, switched to Republican party, 1989
Richard Shelby, Alabama, switched to Republican party, 1994
Ben Campbell, Colorado, switched to Republican party, 1995
Nathan Deal, Georgia, switched to Republican party, 1995
Greg Laughlin, Texas, switched to Republican party, 1995
Billy Tauzin, Louisiana, switched to Republican party, 1995
Jimmy Hayes, Louisiana, switched to Republican party, 1995
Mike Parker, Mississippi, switched to Republican party, 1995

REFERENCES

Agresti, Alan. 1990. *Categorical Data Analysis.* New York: Wiley.
Aldrich, John H. 1995. *Why Parties? The Origin and Transformation of Party Politics in America.* Chicago: University of Chicago Press.
Aldrich, John H., and William T. Bianco. 1992. "A Game-Theoretic Model of Party Affiliation of Candidates and Office Holders." *Mathematical and Computer Modeling.* 16 (8–9): 103–16.
Burnham, Walter Dean. 1995. "Realignment Lives: The 1994 Earthquake and Its Implications." In *The Clinton Presidency: First Appraisals,* ed. Colin Campbell and Bert A. Rockman. 363–391. Chatham, N.J.: Chatham House.
Canon, David T., and David J. Sousa. 1992. "Party System Change and Political Career Structures in the U.S. Congress." *Legislative Studies Quarterly* 17: 347–63
Caldwell, Christopher. 1995. "That Crazy Switchcraft." *The Weekly Standard* 6: 8–10.
Castle, David, and Patrick Fett. 1994. "Strategic Aspects of Party Switching among Congressional Candidates." Paper presented at the annual meeting of the Western Political Science Association, March, Albuquerque, N.M.
Clark, John A., John M. Bruce, John H. Kessel, and William G. Jacoby. 1991. "I'd Rather Switch than Fight: Lifelong Democrats and Converts to Republicanism among Campaign Activists." *American Journal of Political Science* 35: 577–97.
Dwyer, James H. 1983. *Statistical Models for the Social and Behavioral Sciences.* New York: Oxford University Press.
Dyer, James A., Arnold Vedlitz, and David B. Hill. 1988. "New Voters, Switchers, and Political Party Realignment in Texas." *Western Political Quarterly* 41: 155–67.
Erickson, Robert S., and Kent L. Tedin. 1981. "The 1928–1936 Partisan Realignment: The Case for the Conversion Hypothesis." *American Political Science Review* 75: 951–62.
Fenno, Richard F., Jr. 1973. *Congressmen in Committees.* Boston: Little, Brown.
Holt, James M. 1967. *Congressional Insurgents and the Party System, 1916–1919.* Cambridge: Harvard University Press.
King, Gary, and Gerald Benjamin. 1985. "The Stability of Party Identification among U.S. Senators and Representatives: 1789–1984." Paper presented at the annual meeting of the American Political Science Association, September, New Orleans, La.
King, Gary, Robert O. Keohane, and Sidney Verba. 1994. *Designing Social Inquiry: Scientific Inference in Qualitative Research.* Princeton: Princeton University Press.
Kingdon, John W. 1973. *Congressmen's Voting Decisions.* New York: Harper & Row.

Kweit, Mary Grisez. 1986. "Ideological Congruence of Party Switchers and Non-switchers: The Case of Party Activists." *American Journal of Political Science* 38: 184–96.

Lamis, Alexander. 1988. *The Two-Party South.* 2d ed. New York: Oxford University Press.

Nesbit, Dorothy Davidson. 1988. "Changing Partisanship among Southern Party Activists." *Journal of Politics* 50: 322–34.

Rothenberg, Stuart. 1985. *Party Switches: Interviews about Realignment and the Political Parties.* Washington, D.C.: Institute for Government and Politics of the Free Congress Research and Education Foundation.

Stone, Walter J. 1991. On Party Switching among Presidential Activists: What Do We Know? *American Journal of Political Science* 35: 598–607.

The Distribution of Pork Barrel Projects and Vote Buying in Congress

Diana Evans

The literature on distributive politics is dominated by the examination of legislative packages of discrete benefits for the districts of a majority of members of a legislature. In this classic picture of pork barrel politics, legislation consists strictly of a collection of dams, harbor dredging, sewage treatment, and similar projects. The sole purpose of bills of this type is the distribution of benefits to individual districts, and each legislator is assumed to want such a project for its electoral value, although each may or may not receive one. Nevertheless, a majority of members must receive a project, because a majority is required to pass the bill and members have an incentive to vote only for their own project.

However, distributive benefits, most commonly known as pork barrel projects, also are distributed for another purpose: legislative coalition leaders use them to purchase members' support for general interest bills. In this case, a certain number of legislators most likely already supports the bill on the basis of the widespread benefits it offers; if the bill lacks majority support, the leaders who wish to pass it can, in effect, buy a majority by adding pork barrel projects to the bill for a sufficient number of additional members. This use of distributive benefits has received some recognition but little systematic treatment in the literature (Ellwood and Patashnik 1993; Kingdon 1989, 100; Weingast 1994).

Yet evidence suggests that such a vote-buying strategy is successful. Leaders of legislative coalitions frequently have access to discrete benefits; when they use them to buy votes for general interest legislation, project recipients are indeed more likely to support the coalition leaders' positions than those who did not receive a project, all things equal (Evans 1994a). The leaders in question can be any public officials who seek to pass legislation: committee leaders, floor leaders, or the president. A vote-buying approach to passing general interest legislation then raises two related questions: First, by what overall coalitional strategy do legislative leaders award such projects? Second, how do they decide to which members to give the projects?

With regard to the overall coalitional strategy, there are two options: First, leaders can grant projects to a minority of members such that when added to those who support the bill on its merits, that number is sufficient to form a majority coalition for the bill. In this strategy, leaders exert tight control on the distribution of projects. Second, leaders can try to maximize support for the bill by giving to anyone who asks, in which case the tendency over time would be toward a supermajority of projects, far more than needed to pass the bill. If the latter is the case, control of project allocation is more diffuse and resides to a greater degree with rank-and-file members. Of course, both strategies rest on the calculation that the members who receive the projects will vote for the leadership position on the bill.

However, because legislation is not decided in isolation, it is likely that a minimal winning strategy would not be stable over a series of bills. If a committee's leaders followed such a strategy for one bill, they probably could not sustain it over subsequent similar bills, because minimal winning coalitions tend, in repeated play, to give way to universalistic coalitions (Axelrod 1981; Weingast 1979), as legislators seek to avoid the uncertainty of inclusion in bare majority coalitions. Of course, the mechanism here is likely to be different from that envisioned in the theoretical literature on the size of distributive coalitions. Unlike the pure distributive coalitions discussed in that literature, here the award of projects is not mediated among members but is used by leaders as a strategy to pass something else. Nevertheless, I argue in this study that once leaders have revealed a willingness to buy votes with projects, the control of project allocation begins to slip from their hands.

The second question addressed here concerns the specific allocation strategy that leaders follow as they determine how to distribute projects among individuals. The choice of strategy depends in part on leaders' access to information about members' true preferences concerning the bill without projects. Several allocation strategies are possible. First, leaders might give projects to members who otherwise would oppose the committee bill to buy their acquiescence. This approach is a direct means to attempt to add to the list of supporters of the bill, but the strategy is potentially risky for reasons described in a later section. Second, leaders can give projects to likely supporters of the bill and to those on the fence. Despite the apparent inefficiency of contributing to those who already favor the bill, it is a strategy political action committees (PACs) typically follow in their allocation decisions, which tend to contribute to members who are ideologically predisposed toward their interests and those with friendly voting records (Brown 1983; Evans 1988; Gopoian 1984; Handler and Mulkern 1982; Latus 1984; Wright 1985).[1] As Hall and Wayman (1990) have shown, such a strategy is more rational than it seems at first blush, for such contributions buy friendly legislators' active efforts to obtain favorable legislative treatment for the PAC when they might otherwise use their limited time to pursue other priorities. An analogous strategy might be followed by committee leaders, who give both to members of their committee and to nonmembers who are favorably predisposed anyway, in this case to protect the bill from hostile amendments and against a possible presidential veto. In addition, of course, they must give projects to fence-sitters, because their votes are essential to the formation of a majority coalition.

An alternative leadership strategy for awarding projects is more passive and therefore less targeted; in this case leaders wait for member requests and grant them, making clear that those who receive a project are expected to support the committee. Here the burden is on members to be sure they can give such support in return for a project. Clearly, leaders who use the passive strategy need less information about member preferences on the bill than those who give projects on the basis of members' likely support without one. Thus, the less information that is available, the more rational this approach is.

As will be seen, the coalitional and allocational strategies are related; that is, the size of the coalition depends at least in part on who controls the allocation of projects, leaders or rank-and-file members, which depends in turn on the availability to leaders of full information about member preferences on the legislation.

In addition to elaborating on the preceding strategic considerations, I examine empirically the process of project allocation on two general interest bills in the House of Representatives, both reauthorizations of the federal aid highway and urban mass transit programs. The bill passed in 1987 was the first 5-year highway reauthorization to offer pork barrel projects to a large number of members of the House in exchange for their support for the committee's position; the second is the next program reauthorization, which passed in 1991, by which time members of the House were aware that project awards were part of the new rules of the game on this legislation. The inclusion of special projects in these two bills offers an unusual opportunity to examine distributive project allocation on the first go-round and in repeated play on legislation on which pork barrel projects were exchanged for members' support for the bills to which they were attached. In the empirical analysis, committee leaders determine who will receive projects and that is the sense in which the term *leader* is used; however, distributive rewards can also be given by other leaders, including the president.

Distributive Politics and Project Allocation

A distributive policy is one for which benefits to one recipient can be changed without affecting the benefits to other recipients, the cost of which is paid by the general public through taxation. The question addressed here is the following: What coalitional strategy do leaders use when their primary purpose is not to pass a package of pork barrel projects but rather to pass a general benefit bill by adding pork to it? Do they give only to the needed minority or to a supermajority? The rational choice literature has framed the question of the size of distributive coalitions in terms of bills made up exclusively of individual projects and has debated the equilibrium size of such coalitions, posing the alternatives as minimal winning (Buchanan and Tullock 1962; Riker 1962; Riker and Ordeshook 1973) and universalistic (Barry 1965; Shepsle and Weingast 1981; Weingast 1979). Weingast argues that the desire for reelection leads legislators to adopt an institutional norm of universalism, which he defines as "the tendency to seek unanimous passage of distributive programs through the inclusion of a project for all legislators who want one" (1979, 249). This norm develops out of members' uncertainty that they will be included in any given minimum winning coalition; a norm of universalism obviously minimizes that uncertainty and maximizes the legislator's chances of getting an electorally beneficial project. Axelrod (1981) argues similarly but more generally that in a finite number of repetitions of the "prisoner's dilemma," individuals will not engage in the cooperation necessary for a universalistic coalition; however, if the game is repeated indefinitely, cooperation emerges, leading in Congress to the norm of reciprocity, the foundation of universalism.[2]

Coalition size has also been addressed theoretically in cases in which coalition leaders or lobbyists seek to buy votes for broader legislation, bills of the sort considered here. Denzau and Munger (1986) show that in the case of monetary contributions, interest groups are likely to give to members who are on the fence, not to supporters or opponents of the bill on which they have a preference; the result of that strategy is a minimal winning coalition. However, they do not take account of the important time-buying benefits of contributing to supporters (Hall and Wayman, 1990). Groseclose and Snyder examine theoretically the case in which two vote buyers are competing. They find that under a particular set of competitive assumptions, supermajorities are actually cheaper to buy than minimal winning coalitions, which makes oversized coalitions the usual result (Groseclose and Snyder 1996). However, although competitive vote buying probably occurs with some frequency among interest groups, empirically, vote buying by leaders frequently is one-sided. Groseclose and Snyder (1996, 304) note that in such cases, the result would be that derived by Denzau and Munger—that is, a minimal winning coalition. Yet they acknowledge additional reasons to give benefits to supermajorities, including vote buyers' uncertainty about legislators' preferences; in such cases, a supermajority of benefit recipients provides insurance that vote buyers will be able to achieve a voting majority in favor of their bill (1996, 311–12).

The empirical literature also has found that committees tend to allocate, if not to all members, then to oversized majorities in such areas as public works (Ferejohn 1974; Maass 1951; Owens and Wade 1984; Wilson 1986), appropriations (Fenno 1966), public lands (Fenno 1973), and tax policy (Manley 1970), among others, with particular distributional advantages to committee members. Similarly, to secure their budgets, bureaucrats give grants to legislators' districts; because they know they must ask for congressional support repeatedly, they make project grants so as to maximize that support (Arnold 1979).

Thus, except under narrow and frequently unrealistic conditions, arguments for oversized if not truly universal coalitions appear strong. However, in the situation analyzed here, a universalistic distributive coalition may not be necessary to accomplish the goals of project allocators, and under certain conditions a simple majority may not even be necessary. Indeed, in the most comprehensive empirical examination to date of the distribution of federal program spending, Stein and Bickers (1994b) found that such spending did not cover even a near majority of districts either within programs or within agencies. Similarly, when leaders use distributive projects to buy votes for general interest legislation, there is not necessarily a reason to expect even a majority of members to receive projects. However, as I discuss later in this essay, pressures toward universalism may grow from one bill to the next.

With respect to how benefits are allocated among members, particular attention has been paid to rivers and harbors legislation under the jurisdiction of the House Public Works and Transportation (now the Transportation and Infrastructure) Committee, the time-honored repository of pork. Because members are attracted to that committee for its constituency service opportunities (Smith and Deering 1990), one would expect them to take advantage of the chance to get the lion's share of benefits for their districts. Indeed, Ferejohn (1974) found such an allocational bias in favor of members of the Public Works Committee. Nevertheless, Murphy (1974) found that committee to be highly partisan and argued that rather than trusting the committee majority to allocate universally, both parties had agreed to formulas for the allocation of money in a number of programs; thus, spending allocations were bipartisan, a finding that extends to other program areas as well (Arnold 1979; Stein and Bickers 1994a; Wilson 1986). Additionally, in other program areas influential members of Congress, including members of the committees of jurisdiction, receive more benefits than others (e.g., Arnold 1979; Goss 1972; Owens and Wade 1984; Rich 1989).

As suggested earlier, where projects are awarded to purchase votes for a general interest bill, a committee's project allocation decisions are analogous to the contribution decisions made by PACs, which contribute to members who are presumed to be predisposed to support the committee's interests, members on the fence, and those in positions to have disproportionate influence on issues of interest to them. In the bureaucratic arena, Arnold argues that grants may also be given to the districts of congressional opponents to reduce their general benefit opposition to a program by improving the local benefit evaluation. Rather than winning those members' support, the award is designed to keep them from working against the program, while benefits to program supporters induce them to work for it (Arnold 1979, 56–58). However, with regard to campaign contributions, there is little evidence that a demobilizing strategy is effective (Hall and Wayman 1990).

Project Distribution Strategies

The highway legislation examined here is not distributive in the usual sense; the benefits were given out by formula and thus were not particularized for individual districts. Interviews with the participants indicated that the purpose of distributing projects to particular members was indeed to supplement existing support for the bill. By using such a strategy, under certain circumstances leaders need not give a project even to a bare majority of members. First, in the House they must bring the bill to the floor under a closed or modified open rule to prevent a free-for-all of amendments to add projects. Second, the committee leaders must be able to depend on at least some members to support the committee not only on the bill overall but also on amendments without receiving a project. Thus, the initiative is not entirely with rank-and-file members as it is under the simplest assumptions of the formal literature; instead, the committee leaders choose the shape of the coalition.

However, even if that approach is effective the first time it is used (perhaps especially then), noncommittee members, who feel like fools for "giving" their votes away on the previous bill, now have an incentive to try to take the initiative away from the committee; they thus conceal their true preferences and bargain for a project regardless of their support for the merits of the bill. It then becomes increasingly difficult for leaders to obtain accurate information about members' true preferences on the bill; concealment of preferences is a safe strategy unless members truly intend to withhold their votes and help to doom a bill that may offer other benefits to their districts or that they may favor for public policy reasons. Especially if the bill offers formula benefits to most members' districts, both sides then recognize the bluff for what it is, and the effort to hold the leaders up may fail. But the leaders want more than a simple affirmative vote on the bill. They want it to pass with as few hostile amendments as possible, and they want any presidential veto to be overridden. If amendments do not threaten the provisions about which rank-and-file members care, they may be willing to use their votes as bargaining chips with committee leaders. Indeed, on the two highway reauthorization bills examined here, such opportunities existed. On the 1987 bill, committee leaders wanted, among other things, to protect the 55 mph speed limit, which was under assault on a number of fronts. In 1991, the chair of the committee, Robert Roe, wanted a nickel increase in the gas tax and explicitly told members that support for the tax was the price of a district project. Thus, representatives credibly could threaten to vote with the opposition without endangering their formula benefits. In both cases, the leaders ultimately lost on these issues but not because project recipients did not support them.[3]

There is at least one possible objection to the expectation that projects will be allocated to a minority of members the first time a committee awards them. Once word gets out that leaders are buying votes, a large majority of members may seek to get in on the sale rather than waiting until the next bill. Thus, they might bargain from the beginning. From the perspective of committee leaders, the fact that they must come before the chamber repeatedly to pass legislation suggests some risk in following a minimal allocation strategy; that is, members who did not receive a project might conceivably retaliate on this bill or on subsequent legislation. Thus, even on the first bill in a sequence of awarding distributive projects, the committee could have an incentive to give projects to far more members than needed to form a majority for the bill.

Although such pressures toward universalism might develop during the passage of only one bill, time is nevertheless a limiting factor. That is, before the word gets out that votes are being bartered, there is likely to be a core of members willing to commit early to the committee's most cherished policy proposals; those members are ill positioned to bargain later, when they realize that they might have done so. Additionally, it takes time for members to get a feel for how freely the committee is willing to give out projects. Only after the committee reports the bill are other legislators likely to see who got projects. Only then will some realize that projects were given not only to the usual leaders but also to relative nobodies. By then it is too late to deal, especially if the bill comes to the floor under a restrictive rule that the committee now has a majority to pass. The upshot of all of this is that the first time a leader gives out distributive benefits to buy votes, he or she is likely to need to give them to a minority of members.

However, the next time the committee must bring similar legislation to the floor, members will be poised to demand a project and bargain accordingly: they will conceal their true preferences, especially if they are inclined to support the bill anyway. This time most members are likely to bargain for projects, and they will most likely be granted them, because the committee now cannot be certain that a majority would support the bill without them. Indeed, uncertainty about how members will vote could persuade leaders to give projects to a supermajority of members, thus reducing the risk of failure as much as possible. As accurate nose counting becomes impossible, bet hedging seems increasingly wise.

Nevertheless, when distributive benefits are attached to a general interest bill, a universalistic coalition, as opposed to a supermajority, is unlikely. A universalistic coalition is unlikely because the nondistributive provisions of the bill are likely to require some members to oppose it on ideological or constituency grounds, regardless of whether they receive a project. A benefit that goes only to part of the district may be insufficient compensation for a member's taking an ideologically dissonant position or one that is opposed by the majority of the district, because the net electoral impact of voting against the district or one's own record, even with a project, could be negative. Indeed, such members may not even seek a project, because they cannot promise to support the bill in return; as will be seen, failure to do so could doom the project.

My second concern in this study is how projects are allocated to individuals. As with the closely related question of the number of projects, individual allocation depends at least in part on the availability of accurate information on member preferences on the bill. Thus, the first step is for leaders to attempt to calculate the degree of support for the bill and its key provisions ex ante; if that number falls short of a majority, leaders must determine the minimum number of projects they must give (the process I just described). Then they must determine to whom those projects are to be awarded. To the extent that committee leaders control the allocation process, they have a choice of strategies that in themselves are not mutually exclusive. The most obvious is to attempt to add opponents to supporters by giving projects to those who otherwise would oppose the program. However, taken alone, this strategy is both naive and fraught with risk. First, as noted, the approach can only work with members who are not so opposed to the bill for constituency or other reasons that they must in any case vote against it or try to undermine it on amendments. The number of opponents whom this strategy can convert is thus limited. Second, giving to opponents and ignoring one's supporters risks persuading supporters to remind the committee not to take them for granted, perhaps by casting a vote in opposition to the committee's leaders on an amendment on one of their cherished positions.

A second and safer strategy is to give to supporters of the bill in an effort to win not only their loyalty on threatening amendments about which they might otherwise be indifferent but also to buy their active efforts in support of the committee position. By itself, this is an insufficient strategy if the committee's purpose is to compensate for a lack of majority support. However, if a majority of members is initially predisposed to support the bill, this strategy, however extravagant, can help to protect it. Such protection may come in the form of majority support for the committee's favored rule; failing that, it can save the committee from defeat on floor amendments. But if, as first envisioned, the committee lacks majority support for the bill, its leaders must give to someone in addition to probable supporters. Rather than giving projects to firm opponents, they are likely to look first to members who are most persuadable: those on the fence. A project can serve to convert an indifferent or conflicted member's calculated benefit from supporting the bill from zero to a net positive.

Thus, even the first time leaders use projects to buy votes, a purely efficient strategy of giving only to fence-sitters is not likely to be feasible. Support, particularly on a large, complex bill, is multifaceted. Some members who strongly support the bill's basic policy provisions on the merits may need inducements to support the coalition leaders' positions on some particulars;

otherwise, they may be persuaded that amendments that leaders see as hostile are innocuous or marginally positive. Thus, leaders likely will give projects to fence-sitters and supporters whose backing they calculate to be at risk on certain issues. Clearly, full information about member preferences is necessary for leaders to exercise this degree of control over project allocation. In such cases, we can expect a positive relationship between members' predicted overall support for the bill ex ante and their receipt of a project.[4]

Another, less systematic allocational approach is available to committee leaders. Rather than attempt to calculate members' likely support, they can take a more reactive posture by waiting for requests and granting them all with the clear mutual understanding that there is a quid pro quo: recipients are expected to support their benefactors on all important votes on the bill. In this approach, leaders reconcile themselves to the difficulties of acquiring accurate information and pursue a less active strategy of responding to requests rather than follow a carefully crafted strategy for the most efficient allocation of projects. The members who receive projects are to a much greater degree self-selected according to their ability to make good on their bargains, because those who betray their benefactors risk future retaliation. Although more expensive, this approach is the least risky for leaders, because it takes as given some degree of uncertainty about voting intentions and avoids antagonizing potential supporters with a refusal to grant a request for a project. The more members (especially nonleaders) who receive a project, the greater the potential for hostility among those who were refused; thus, the path of least resistance is granting projects to all who ask. If this strategy were used, there would be no relationship between members' expected support for the legislation and receipt of a project.

As this discussion implies, the size of the benefit-receiving coalition depends to some extent on who controls the allocation of projects. To the degree that leaders actively do so—which is most feasible when they have full information about members' true preferences—a minimal coalition is likely to result. In this case they will give only those projects necessary to round up existing support to a majority and to ensure the loyalty of their supporters on peripheral issues. On the other hand, when leaders lack full information about members' true preferences, they are likely to surrender, in effect, to member control over the allocation process and give to all of those who ask in return for a promise (enforceable by the leaders) to support leadership positions on the bill. The information available to leaders decreases due to members' concealment of their true preferences, which results from the spreading knowledge that the committee will bargain for votes with projects. This situation leads to increasing numbers of projects in subsequent bills backed by that committee (or leader), as even the most loyal supporters begin to bargain for projects along with everyone else but the strongest opponents. Initially, before it is clear to many that leaders will bargain in this way, information gathering may be relatively easy, as members bargain and commit on the central provisions of the bill. At this time, leaders can more accurately calculate how many projects they need to give and maintain some control over numbers. Once the project dealing becomes widely known, however, rank-and-file members begin to gain effective control over the allocation process, and the number of projects included in the bill balloons. Thus, the more information the leaders have, the smaller the number of projects in the bill, ceteris paribus; leaders are likely to have the most information the first time they use this approach.

Regardless of how projects are allocated to noncommittee members, those who are on the committee are expected to fare especially well. Those on a constituency-oriented committee such as Public Works are particularly likely to fare well with distributive benefits. In addition, chamber leaders and chairs of key committees and subcommittees also are likely advantaged. If the purpose of including such benefits is to buy the support needed to pass and protect the committee's version of the bill, the help of other key leaders is especially valuable. Indeed, on highway legislation before the 1987 bill, fewer than a dozen projects were awarded in any given authorization, and they went to leaders (Evans 1994b).

The literature provides little basis for expecting partisanship to be an important factor in determining who receives a project; as noted earlier, few studies have found partisanship to be a factor in project allocation. In the cases examined here, interviews with many participants indicated that the leaders of the Public Works and Transportation Committee wrote highway legislation in private, with a bipartisan consensus negotiated among the "Big Four," the chairs and ranking minority members of the full committee and the Surface Transportation Subcommittee.

Project Distribution on Highway Legislation

The 1987 highway and urban mass transit program reauthorization, the Surface Transportation and Uniform Relocation Assistance Act, actually passed initially in the previous Congress, in 1986, but failed in conference with the Senate and was carried over into the early months of the 100th Congress. It was an $88 billion, 5-year authorization, most of which went to completion of the interstate highway system and maintenance of the federal aid highway and urban mass transit systems. Only 2 percent of the total was designated for special projects, known as highway demonstration projects, to individual members. The second bill, the Intermodal Surface Transportation Infrastructure Act of 1991, reauthorized the highway and mass transit programs for 6 additional years at a cost of $151 billion. With the interstate system nearly complete, the 1991 bill significantly reoriented federal highway policy for the first time since the inception of the interstate program; it gave states far more flexibility to shift federal money from one transportation account to another and linked different transportation modes to increase the efficiency of the transportation system. This time, the legislation allocated 3.5 percent of the total to special project funding; the House version included 489 projects for 262 members, compared with 100 projects for 76 members in 1987. The maximum number granted in 1986 to any one member was 5; the maximum in 1991 was 15. And the 1991 total includes only projects that survived considerable cuts in member requests by the committee. Even so, 1991 saw a dramatic increase in the number of projects.

To discover the intentions of committee leaders and the process by which they awarded projects, in 1987, 1990, and 1994 I interviewed staff members for the House Public Works and Transportation Committee and its Surface Transportation Subcommittee. To obtain a more disinterested perspective, I also interviewed staff members on the Senate Environment and Public Works Committee and within the Federal Highway Administration. A congressional staffer provided the data on project recipients and costs.

The staff interviews indicate that the process involved in project distribution was indeed somewhat different on the two bills. In 1986, the members themselves initiated the requests for projects, but those who participated in the passage of the bill all said that the committee's leaders expected the support of project recipients. As one staff member said, "It's like the godfather: 'You came to me, but once I do you a favor, you have to be loyal.' The committee doesn't go out and say it's having a sale of demos; *you* go to the committee; . . . later, they call in their chits." By contrast, in 1991, the committee said it was having a sale of demonstration projects; as another staff member put it, they "sent out the word" that the committee was handing out demonstration projects. Even then some members evidently did not get the word that projects were available; one staffer said that some were added after members saw the projects in the markup bill and, realizing that they had nearly missed the boat, asked for one themselves. In 1991, as in 1986–87, committee leaders were explicit about the trade-off: those who received a project were expected to support the leadership, especially on their proposal (later killed in the Ways and Means Committee) for a nickel increase in the gas tax. Thus, the major difference between the process on the two authorizations appears to be the committee's deliberate adoption of the public "demo sale" strategy.

This change in the committee's approach (concurrent with a change in chairmen) was in part a result of the relatively large number of projects in the 1987 bill, which "gave members the green light" to press harder for projects for themselves the next time around, as one staffer said. The projects in the 1986 bill made it clear that a member did not have to be a leader to get one; even freshmen got them.

As expected, the number of highway demonstration projects grew dramatically between 1987 and 1991, from 100 for 76 members in 1987 to 489 for 262 members in 1991. Consistent with the expectations here, the percentage of members receiving a project went from a minority of less than 20 percent to a majority of 60 percent. The fundamental dynamics on the two bills were the same, however. Although the committee leaders did not solicit requests for demonstration projects in 1987, they certainly did not discourage requests; indeed, they exploited them. In the next section I examine the data more systematically with regard to who actually received projects.

Despite similarities in the project award process, the two bills came to the floor under different circumstances. In 1991, the rule under which the bill was considered was a highly restrictive one that allowed only 12 specific amendments out of more than 50 that had been proposed. That limitation was expected, because the committee is likely to try to prevent a free-for-all of project additions on the floor. By contrast, in 1986, when a bill that awarded projects on a wholesale basis was first debated in the House, the modified open rule was much more permissive; it disallowed only one specific amendment and left the bill open for all others. Despite the opportunity presented to add projects, members did not attempt to do so, even though relatively few of them received a project in that bill. It is not clear why members did not try to add projects on the floor when they had the chance. However, participants indicated that the bill was laboring under bad publicity and a threatened presidential veto as a result of the demonstration projects that were already in the bill. Even so, individual members were not clearly tied to those projects in the national media; the projects were described in the Public Works Committee report on the bill without a district number or member's name associated with any of them (House Committee on Public Works 1986). It is possible that members did not wish to be seen publicly dipping their fingers into the pork barrel, as they were more likely to be if they offered floor amendments to get a project.[5] Moreover, the committee could have and most likely would have taken such projects out in conference by citing negotiating needs; everyone would rightly have seen that tactic as retaliation by the committee. Indeed, staff members said that the committee removed projects as punishment for members who had defied the committee on other issues.

Data Analysis

The remaining question concerns which members received projects. The following analysis assesses the determinants of project allocation. The data alone do not allow us to discover directly the strategies that committee leaders used. It is possible, however, to determine whether the pattern of project allocation was consistent with a specific strategy. First, it was necessary to estimate the probability that a member would support the committee's positions on the bill without receiving a project. Second, I calculated the impact of expected support on the member's receipt of a project or projects using two-stage estimation techniques. This procedure simulates what committee leaders are thought to do as they decide to whom to award projects. Thus, there are in effect two endogenous variables: projects received and expected support for the leadership position. The project variable is measured in two ways. For each member, a dummy variable indicates whether he or she received a project; a second variable indicates how many projects the member received.

I estimated expected support for the committee position as follows: For each member, I calculated the percentage of recorded votes on which the member supported the position of the committee leaders on their eventual floor votes. The denominator was the number of votes on which the four committee leaders took a unified position as indicated by their recorded votes. To estimate the first-stage equation, the leadership support score was regressed (using OLS regression) on all of the exogenous variables in the model; I describe that model in the appendix. The results of the first-stage estimates are not of particular interest here; I do not report them in this essay but can provide them for interested readers. From the first-stage results, I calculated each member's probability of supporting the leadership without a project.

I examined the project allocation process using two measures of project distribution. I estimated the equations with a dichotomous left-hand variable, receipt of a project *(Project),* which takes the value of 1 if the member got a project and 0 if not. I also estimated the model using the number of projects given to the member *(N Projects).* The explanatory variables are the same in both cases. For the 1986–87 bill, it was necessary to pool data from the 99th and 100th Congresses, because three of the eight votes on the bill were taken in the 100th Congress. Thus, the data set consists of those members who served in both Congresses ($n = 381$). For the 1991 bill, the data set consists of all 435 members because they all had an opportunity to cast the five votes included here.

The *N Projects* model is as follows; it was estimated using two-stage least-squares (2SLS) regression:

$$N\ Projects = fn(Committee\ Support^*, Public\ Works, Leader, Donor)$$

I calculated *Committee Support* from the estimated parameters in the first-stage equations, which modeled members' actual votes on each bill, to create an instrument for members' expected level of support for the committee on the roll call votes taken on the bill. *Public Works* is a dummy variable that takes the value 1 if the member was on that committee in 1986 or 1991, when the projects were awarded. *Leader* takes a value of 1 if the member was one of the top party leadership or chaired or was ranking minority member of the Appropriations Committee, its transportation subcommittee, the Ways and Means Committee, or the Budget Committee; otherwise, *Leader* = 0. *Donor* is a dummy variable that, when it takes the value 1, indicates that the member represents a state that contributed more to the Highway Trust Fund in gas taxes than it got back in federal highway spending. *Donor* = 0 for members who represented donee states.

I estimated the impact of the explanatory variables on *Project* (this variable takes a value of 1 regardless of whether the member received 1 or 15 projects; it is 0 if the member received none) using a two-stage probit procedure developed by Rivers and Vuong (1988). The model is as follows:

$$Project = fn(Committee\ Support,\ Public\ Works,\ Leader,\ Donor,$$
$$CS\ Residual*)$$

The first stage is identical to that for the *N Projects* model; that is, member support for the committee position is regressed on all the exogenous variables, as described in the appendix. However, this technique differs from the usual 2SLS in its second-stage equation, which is estimated using probit analysis; it further differs by not requiring an instrument for the endogenous variable that appears on the right-hand side of the equation *(Committee Support)* but using the variable itself and including the residuals *(CS Residual)* from the first-stage model. The latter variable accounts for the variance in *Committee Support* that is not explained by the exogenous variables; such variance potentially includes the impact of receiving a demonstration project. Significance for the residual variable indicates endogeneity in the second stage; in that case, the *t*-statistics for the other parameter estimates must be evaluated conservatively (Rivers and Vuong 1988).

The results appear in tables 1 and 2. Table 1 reports the results for *Project*. First, it is clear that endogeneity is a problem in the 1991 equation only. The results indicate that a member's expected support for the committee's positions on neither bill played a significant role in the leaders' determination of who would receive a project; those parameter estimates failed to reach even a 0.05 level of significance, although the coefficients are positive. However, there was, as expected, a bias in favor of members of the committee in both years and in favor of leaders in 1986–87, when far fewer members received projects. Also in 1986–87, projects were less likely to go to members from donor states; these members had constituency-based reasons to oppose the highway program's formula allocations, which involved far more money than any number of demonstration projects. Such members would find it politically self-defeating to sell their votes on legislation that would result in a net revenue loss for their constituents.

Table 2 presents the results for *N Projects*. Although coefficients are positive and the *t*-statistics are slightly higher for *Committee Support,* they still fall short of statistical significance. However, members of the Public Works Committee were likely to get more projects than other members. No leadership bias exists in the number of projects (keep in mind that Public Works leaders are excluded from this variable). In these equations, donor state members were not particularly disadvantaged in the number of projects allocated in 1986, but they were in 1991, the reverse of the results for *Project*.[6]

TABLE 1.   Determinants of Project Allocation: Dichotomous Variable

	1987 bill	1991 bill
Committee support	.012	.004
	(1.602)	(1.36)
Public Works Committee	1.101*	1.674*
	(3.66)	(5.01)
Leader	.726**	.081
	(2.19)	(.27)
Donor	−1.649*	−.332
	(−2.21)	(−1.78)
CS Residual	.005	.008**
	(.67)	(2.05)
Intercept	−1.910*	−.101
	(−4.00)	(−.44)
R^2	.211	.121

Note: Numbers in parentheses are *t*-ratios.
$*p < .01$ $**p < .05$

TABLE 2.   Determinants of the Number of Projects Received

	1987 bill	1991 bill
Committee support	.004	.004
	(1.80)	(1.53)
Public Works	.635*	2.377*
	(5.71)	(11.38)
Leader	.222	.049
	(1.70)	(.15)
Donor	−.091	−.521*
	(−1.00)	(−2.62)
Intercept	−.096	.673*
	(−.66)	(2.83)
R^2	.187	.267

Note: Numbers in parentheses are *t*-ratios.
$*p < .01$

With the exception of *Donor,* the results are fairly consistent across dependent variables and estimation techniques. Members of the Public Works Committee are always favored. However, although the signs for *Committee Support* are in the expected direction, that variable is never significant; it comes closest in 1986–87, reaching the level of .073 for *N Projects.* Thus, the results do not support the inference that committee leaders follow a finely honed strategy of targeting members according to their likely support for the bill, in either a positive or a negative direction. Although they were somewhat more likely in 1986 to target projects to the top leaders of the House and to members of the money committees on which their programs partially depend, even that relationship disappeared in 1991. Additionally, they are not more likely to give to more supportive members to buy their time and energy or to give more to opponents to buy their inactivity if not their support. Of course, a nonlinear relationship may exist. However, alternative nonlinear specifications of the *Committee Support* variable were less successful than the linear version at detecting a relationship to project allocation.

Rather than targeting project awards in this way, the leaders of Public Works appear to have followed a reactive strategy as they determined who would receive a project once they had given projects to members of their own committee and, in 1986, to leaders. Although they were explicit about expecting the loyalty of those they favored with projects, they evidently were not particular about who received them. The burden thus was on project recipients to make sure they could fulfill the expected commitment before they requested a project or risk retaliation later. As noted previously, staff members who were interviewed on both bills alluded guardedly to such retaliation in a few cases.

Conclusions

A major question implicit in this analysis concerns control of the project allocation process. If the leaders of the committee were fully in control, we would likely have seen a clearer relationship between a member's probable support for the committee position ex ante and his or her receipt of a project because the committee devised and followed an explicit and presumably efficient allocation strategy. The only evidence, and it is slim, that such a deliberate process occurred appears in one of the equations for 1986–87. Indeed, on that bill one would have expected clearly to see such a strategy—that is, the first time the committee used distributive projects to buy votes. However, the weight of the evidence is on the side of member initiative and, in 1991, member control. In that year, a large majority of members received projects, and there is no evidence that their initial propensity to support the bill played any role at all. Given that the highway program distributes benefits in excess of tax outlays to the majority of states and congressional districts, it can hardly have been necessary to give projects to 262 members. However, the real issue for the committee was the proposed rule under which the bill was to be considered. That very restrictive rule would allow only 12 amendments out of the 53 that had been proposed to the Rules Committee. Opponents of the rule complained bitterly on the floor until the previous question was ordered by roll call vote. The rule, vociferously supported by the leaders of the Public Works Committee, won by a margin of 3:1. On a restrictive rule, members could bargain with their votes for a project and not worry about scuttling the program as a whole. And it is clear that between 1987 and 1991 the majority learned the game that the committee had decided to play.

Thus, the supermajority of members who received projects in 1991 is likely a result of the cat having been let out of the bag by the committee in 1986, when it revealed that votes would be bought. The committee took advantage of the resulting expectations by advertising the availability of projects in 1991 and demanding support for its position in return, thus treating the exploding demand for projects as an opportunity to secure its version of the legislation. That being the case, there is little basis for thinking that the demand for projects will not continue to grow. A Senate staff member who worked on the bill explained the growth in the number of projects as part of a broader change in the culture of Congress. Before the reforms of the 1970s and in the early years thereafter, there was enough discipline through the seniority system that the allocation of such projects could be restricted to the top leaders. After the dispersion of power, members had a greater sense of equality and exerted more pressure for individual projects in general interest bills. Only strong central leadership has the potential to stem such a tide.

APPENDIX

The exogenous variables expected to have an impact on members' degree of support for the leadership position on these bills are those usually employed in models of roll call voting; also included in the first-stage model are those exogenous variables expected to influence members' chances of receiving projects. The variables employed to explain members' support for the leadership are as follows: party (Republican = 1 and Democrat = 0); Conservative Coalition support score, purged of votes taken on these bills, with absences not counted as negative votes; a dummy variable that takes the value of 1 if the member sat on the Public Works and Transportation Committee and 0 otherwise; a dummy variable for leadership position, defined broadly as being in the top leadership of Congress or chair or ranking minority member of a committee of particular interest to the Public Works Committee (Appropriations and its transportation subcommittee, Ways and Means [which has jurisdiction for the gas tax], and the Budget Committee); seniority, which is the number of years the member had served as of 1986; and donor, a dummy variable indicating that the member represented a state that contributed more to the Highway Trust Fund through its gas taxes than it received in federal spending. For obvious reasons these members are expected to be less supportive of the highway program than those who receive more than they contribute.

Additionally, for the 1987 bill several PAC variables and two district variables were relevant. One amendment restricted the use of imported cement; thus the summed contributions of three cement industry PACs were included.[7] Another amendment would have reduced compensation to billboard owners for removal of their billboards from federal highways; thus contributions from the Outdoor Advertising Association were included. Because both votes were taken in 1986, contributions for the 1984 election were used. With respect to district variables, two issues were relevant. Two amendments and a rule dealt with the 55 mph speed limit; because there was pressure from western states to raise it, a dummy variable was included for states in the West.[8] If a member was from one of those states, that variable took a value of 1; otherwise it was 0. Additionally, two amendments would have stopped construction of the Los Angeles Metrorail system pending completion of a supplemental environmental impact statement; thus a dummy variable was included for members who represented the Los Angeles metropolitan area.

The OLS estimates produced adjusted R^2 values of 0.396 for 1986–87 and 0.490 for 1991. Significant variables in both models include party, Conservative Coalition score, membership on the Public Works Committee, and seniority. The dummy variable for donor state was significant in 1986–87.

NOTES

1. Denzau and Munger (1986) developed a theoretical model of interest group vote buying; in contrast to the findings of empirical studies, they conclude that groups pursue an apparently efficient strategy in which they make contributions only to those members who are on the fence for one reason or another. They do not contribute to those who would vote their way for constituency reasons, because the groups do not need to sway the votes of these members. However, their analysis ignores other reasons for giving to one's friends.

2. While acknowledging those results, Ferejohn, Fiorina, and McKelvey (1987) argue that under certain restrictive conditions, a legislature will pass a minimum winning set of the least expensive projects. However, their legislature has no committee structure and plays this distributive game only once, among other simplifying assumptions. Once a committee structure and the closed rule are introduced, they argue that the committee will construct a package that contains projects for a majority of its members and the least expensive proposals of enough other members to create a bare majority. However, it is unclear what happens here if members know that play is to be repeated, as they realistically do. That is, no standing committee reports one and only one bill; thus there may be pressure for universalism here as well.

3. For empirical evidence in the case of the 1987 bill see Evans (1994a).

4. We see in such cases that a supermajority allocation pattern is in fact a reasonable strategy for ensuring passage of the bill to which the projects are attached even when leaders have full information about member preferences. It is not, however, a nec-

essary strategy, because leaders can opt for one less costly in terms of the number of projects.

5. Later, of course, members go home and claim credit for their projects; however, they do so out of a national spotlight that can cast such projects as wasteful pork barrel spending.

6. The equations all were estimated with the member's party included as a variable. It had no effect, as was expected on the basis of both the literature on allocation patterns and the way that these bills were crafted. Hence, lacking a sound reason for including *Party*, the variable was dropped.

7. Included were contributions from the National Ready Mixed Concrete Association, the National Concrete Masonry Association, and the Portland Cement Association.

8. The states designated as western include all the West Coast states; the mountain states of Arizona, Colorado, Idaho, Montana, Nevada, New Mexico, Utah, and Wyoming; and the midwestern states of Iowa, Kansas, Minnesota, Missouri, Nebraska, North Dakota, and South Dakota. Alternative measures were tried in the model, but this one worked best.

REFERENCES

Arnold, Douglas. 1979. *Congress and the Bureaucracy: A Theory of Influence.* New Haven: Yale University Press.

Axelrod, Robert. 1981. "The Emergence of Cooperation among Egoists." *American Political Science Review* 75: 306–18.

Barry, Brian. 1965. *Political Argument.* New York: Humanities Press.

Brown, Kirk F. 1983. "Campaign Contributions and Congressional Voting." Paper presented at the 1983 annual meeting of the American Political Science Association, Chicago.

Buchanan, James M., and Gordon Tullock. 1962. *The Calculus of Consent.* Ann Arbor: University of Michigan Press.

Denzau, Arthur T., and Michael C. Munger. 1986. "Legislators and Interest Groups: How Unorganized Interests Get Represented." *American Political Science Review* 80: 89–106.

Ellwood, John W., and Eric M. Patashnik. 1993. "In Praise of Pork." *Public Interest* 110: 19–33.

Evans, Diana. 1988. "Oil PACs and Aggressive Contribution Strategies." *Journal of Politics* 50: 1047–56.

Evans, Diana. 1994a. "Policy and Pork: The Use of Pork Barrel Projects to Build Policy Coalitions in the House of Representatives." *American Journal of Political Science* 38: 894–917.

Evans, Diana. 1994b. "Reconciling Pork-Barrel Politics and National Transportation Policy: Highway Demonstration Projects." In *Who Makes Public Policy?,* ed. Robert S. Gilmour and Alexis A. Halley. Chatham, N.J.: Chatham House.

Fenno, Richard F., Jr. 1966. *Power of the Purse.* Boston: Little, Brown.

Fenno, Richard F., Jr. 1973. *Congressmen in Committees.* Boston: Little, Brown.

Ferejohn, John A. 1974. *Pork Barrel Politics.* Stanford: Stanford University Press.
Ferejohn, John A., Morris P. Fiorina, and Richard D. McKelvey. 1987. "Sophisticated Voting and Independence in the Distributive Political Setting." *American Journal of Political Science* 31: 169–93.
Gopoian, David. 1984. "What Makes PACs Tick? An Analysis of the Allocation Patterns of Economic Interest Groups" *American Journal of Political Science* 23: 259–81.
Goss, Carol. 1972. "Military Committee Membership and Defense Related Benefits in the House of Representatives." *Western Political Quarterly* 25: 215–33.
Groseclose, Tim, and James M. Snyder Jr. 1996. "Buying Supermajorities." *American Political Science Review* 90: 303–315.
Hall, Richard, and Frank W. Wayman. 1990. "Buying Time: Rational PACs and the Mobilization of Bias in Congressional Committees." *American Political Science Review* 84: 797–820.
Handler, Edward, and John R. Mulkern. 1982. *Business in Politics.* Lexington, Mass.: D. C. Heath.
House Committee on Public Works. 1986. *Surface Transportation and Uniform Relocation Assistance Act of 1986.* H.R. 99-665. Washington, D.C.: Government Printing Office.
Kingdon, John W. 1989. *Congressmen's Voting Decisions.* Ann Arbor: University of Michigan Press.
Latus, Margaret Ann. 1984. "Assessing Ideological PACs: From Outrage to Understanding." In *Money and Politics in the United States,* ed. Michael J. Malbin. Chatham, N.J.: Chatham House.
Maass, Arthur A. 1951. *Muddy Waters.* Cambridge: Harvard University Press.
Manley, John. 1970. *The Politics of Finance.* Boston: Little, Brown.
Murphy, James T. 1974. "Political Parties and the Porkbarrel: Party Conflict and Cooperation in House Public Works Committee Decision Making." *American Political Science Review* 68: 169–85.
Owens, John R., and Larry L. Wade. 1984. "Federal Spending in Congressional Districts." *Western Political Quarterly* 37: 404–23.
Rich, Michael J. 1989. "Distributive Politics and the Allocation of Federal Grants." *American Political Science Review* 83: 193–213.
Riker, William H. 1962. *The Theory of Political Coalitions.* New Haven: Yale University Press.
Riker, William H., and Peter C. Ordeshook. 1973. *An Introduction of Positive Political Theory.* Englewood Cliffs, N.J.: Prentice Hall.
Rivers, Douglas, and Quang H. Vuong. 1988. "Limited Information Estimators and Exogeneity Tests for Simultaneous Probit Models." *Journal of Econometrics* 39: 347–66.
Shepsle, Kenneth A., and Barry R. Weingast. 1981. "Political Preferences for the Pork Barrel." *American Journal of Political Science* 25: 96–111.
Smith, Steven S., and Christopher Deering. 1990. *Committees in Congress.* 2nd ed. Washington, D.C.: Congressional Quarterly Press.
Stein, Robert M., and Kenneth N. Bickers. 1994a. "Response to Barry Weingast's Reflections." *Political Research Quarterly* 47: 329–33.

Stein, Robert M., and Kenneth N. Bickers. 1994b. "Universalism and the Electoral Connection: A Test and Some Doubts." *Political Research Quarterly* 47: 195–317.

Weingast, Barry R. 1979. "A Rational Choice Perspective on Congressional Norms." *American Journal of Political Science* 23: 245–63.

Weingast, Barry R. 1994. "Reflections on Distributive Politics and Universalism." *Political Research Quarterly* 47: 319–27.

Wilson, Rick K. 1986. "An Empirical Test of Preferences for the Pork Barrel: District-Level Appropriations for Rivers and Harbors Legislation, 1889–1913." *American Journal of Political Science* 30: 729–54.

Wright, John R. 1985. "Contributions and Roll Calls: An Organizational Perspective." *American Political Science Review* 79: 400–414.

Congress, the President, and the Unrealized Bargaining Power of the Line-Item Veto: A Brief Note on a Short-Lived Law

Patrick J. Fett and Jeffrey S. Hill with Richard Delaney

Introduction

In some ways, the presidential line-item veto (LIV) was not an enormous change. As proposed, it was simply another attempt by Congress to control the budget by delegating authority from the legislative branch to the executive branch. It was hardly as important, for example, as the Budget and Accounting Act of 1921, which gave the president responsibility for writing the initial budget proposal. In both cases, Congress had good reason to delegate this power to the president, most notably the need to coordinate financial decisions in a way Congress had been unable to do by itself (Schick 1995, chap. 2). Moreover, delegation is not abdication. A large body of literature suggests Congress does not lose complete control over decisions it delegates to others (see, e.g., McCubbins and Schwartz 1984; Spence 1997; Weingast and Moran 1983). In the area of budgets, a review of virtually any fiscal year shows that the power to propose the budget is not control of the budget. Many presidents have learned to their dismay that Congress is very willing to modify or even ignore their budget proposals. Similarly, Congress could and did reverse the veto of specific line items (Towell 1998).

However, it would be a mistake to evaluate the impact of these acts simply by counting how often one branch prevailed over the other. As Neustadt (1990) suggests, the impact of formal powers goes beyond their immediate and obvious use. Although designed as technical budgeting tools, their major influence lies in altering the bargaining relationship between Congress and the president, increasing the advantages of the executive at the expense of the legislature. Thus, in the case of the 1921 Budgeting Act, the original intent was better coordination of revenues and expenditures. Its more important result was to make the president an active player in budget negotiations, set the agenda for debate with his proposal, and significantly increase overall presidential influence.

The LIV must be examined in the same way as the 1921 Budgeting Act—both as a budgeting tool and as a bargaining tool. Viewed as a means of budget control, the brief history of the LIV was unimpressive. Part of its failure was due to a lack of experience, which time would no doubt have cured. But it probably would never have lived up to the expectations of its proponents. As a bargaining tool, however, the LIV had great potential to alter the congressional-presidential relationship. Presidents could have used it in three different ways:

1. As a direct influence on the final budget, presidents would have much more ability to insist on the preservation of their initial budgeting proposal.
2. As an indirect influence on authorization legislation, presidents could threaten future punishment of those who opposed their current proposals.
3. As a direct influence, presidents could kill legislation by obstructing the deals necessary to pass a bill.

As we shall show, this last influence is the more significant one because it means the LIV could have had the unintended effect of blocking authorizing legislation as well as the appropriations legislation for which it was intended.

The LIV as a Budgeting Tool

The LIV was sold to the public as a tool to excise inappropriate pork barrel projects and tax expenditures and thus increase government efficiency and balance the budget. As one columnist wrote, "Any pork-barrel waste that the president doesn't deep-six becomes his personal albatross for all eternity" (Chapman 1997, 25). But President Clinton's brief experience with the LIV showed one person's pork barrel waste is another person's good public policy. Defining *waste* is an inherently subjective process. Although there may be some glaring examples of wasteful or inappropriate expenditures, one person's "inappropriate boondoggle" is another's "necessary, regional need" (Towell 1998). Moreover, experience in the states suggests that the LIV would have had little effect on the overall budget deficit or surplus. Numerous studies of state budgets have found no relationship between the LIV and budgetary control (see, e.g., Abney and Lauth 1985; Berch 1992; Joyce and Reischauer 1997; Nice 1988). Although conclusive inferences are not possible, the brief history of the LIV is consistent with these findings about state government LIVs.

The LIV as a Bargaining Tool

The life span of the LIV was not long enough to develop any shifts in the bargaining relationships between Congress and the president, but we will show that there was enormous potential to do so. The LIV could have enhanced presidential influence over Congress by allowing presidents to threaten all types of legislation. These threats would have been exercised as a direct threat to appropriations by using the LIV to veto specific items and earmarks, as an indirect threat to authorizing legislation by using the LIV to punish opponents, and as a direct threat to authorizing legislation by inhibiting the formation of legislative coalitions.

As a Direct Influence on Appropriations

The LIV's major impact on appropriations would have been in budget negotiations. Armed with the ability to kill specific spending proposals, the president would have an enhanced ability to prevail in budget negotiations with Congress. At the minimum, a president could have cut the spending he opposed and left spending he supported. But the threat of this power would have been more important than its use. Presidents would have been able to deal from a greater position of strength by offering not to veto specific congressional priorities in return for the preservation of specific presidential priorities. Over time, funds would have been directed away from where congressional majorities wanted them to go and left in projects supported by presidents (Fisher 1993, 45). Appropriation legislation would more closely resemble the president's initial budget proposal to Congress. This kind of partisan budget cutting is well documented in the state government literature (see, e.g., Gosling 1986; Nice 1988) and is most often found when the executive office and legislature are controlled by different parties (Abney and Lauth 1985). Thus, rather than simply being a means to control spending, the LIV would have become a tool by which a president could further decrease Congress's control of the budget.

As an Indirect Influence on Authorizing Legislation

The LIV provided presidents with a bargaining tool that they could have used outside of budget negotiations. Of course, the LIV could not have been used to veto a section of an authorizations bill. But it would have allowed presidents to punish people who passed bills over their opposition. Legislators who refused to support a presidential initiative would be threatened with the loss of pork barrel projects in their district. In this way, the effect of the LIV would not be limited to fiscal legislation. It would also give the president a weapon to use to preserve policy in authorizing legislation. Retribution of this kind has always been a part of the president's arsenal, but the LIV would have expanded it. For example, presidents can deny federal discretionary grants or spending to a member's district. Such a move raises the cost of opposition to the president, but a member may be willing to accept this cost. Similarly, a president can use the whole bill veto to kill a legislator's project, but legislators know that they can craft omnibus legislation to avoid this threat. As long as the president favors the net impact of the omnibus bill, a veto would not be triggered by the inclusion of policies the president opposes. By eliminating the effectiveness of this strategy, the LIV would have increased the potency of presidential threats and decreased a legislator's ability to avoid them. Indeed, many state governors had already used the LIV in this fashion. Former Senator Dale Bumpers reported he used it "to get legislators in line" when he was a governor (Taylor 1996, 866).

Probably, the LIV would not have seen widespread use as a punishment. Instead, it more likely would have been used to vote trade, allowing some projects to remain while putting others on the chopping block. In either case, the LIV would seldom be exercised but used more as a threat to give legislators more incentive to work closely with the executive branch (Joyce and Reischauer 1997).[1]

As a Direct Influence on Authorizing Legislation

The LIV could have done more than indirectly affect the passage of nonfiscal legislation. A resourceful president could have used it to eliminate authorizing legislation he opposed. The LIV could not, of course, have directly eliminated the authorization legislation. Instead, it would have worked by eliminating the side payments that make legislation possible. Indeed, this use is where the LIV had the greatest potential to upset the balance of legislative-executive negotiations.

This potential use of the LIV can be understood by examining how legislative coalitions can be built. Side payments in the form of individual pork barrel projects are often an important part of coalition building. The passage of a great deal of legislation often involves transition rules and individual projects used by legislators to buy votes or head off opposition. Indeed, supporting coalitions would often not be possible without these side payments. If the president could eliminate the side deals necessary to the creation of the coalition, then the policy opposed by the president would fail.

We can see how side payments work with reference to figure 1. The figure represents a hypothetical five-person legislature that is addressing two issues, X and Y. Each point labeled 1 through 5 represents the ideal point of the individual legislator. The current policy is represented by point sq. The closed curves drawn around each ideal point and through sq represent the policies that the legislator would prefer to the current policy. The different shapes of these curves, ellipses or circles, indicate the relative importance of each issue. The elliptical indifference curves of legislators 4 and 5 indicate that the issue on the horizontal axis, X, is more important to them than the issue on the vertical axis, Y. (For simplicity, we omit the elliptical indifference curves of legislators 1 and 2.) The horizontal dimension, X, represents an issue important to all five members of the legislature. The circular curve of legislator 3 shows that the issues are of *equal* importance to her district. In this way, we have represented the

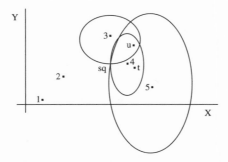

Fig. 1.   Building Coalitions: Changes on Y as a Sidepayment to Legislator 3

preferences of the legislators over a national issue, *X,* and a regional issue, *Y.* Nothing would automatically cause legislators to tie these two issues together in any debate.

We show two possible changes to the status quo that a legislator who has agenda control would introduce; for the purposes of illustration, we use legislator 4. These possible changes are points *t* and *u*. Point *t* portrays a change only in the national issue, *X.* Because the two issues are not usually considered together, this is the kind of change that would generally be introduced. This shift represents an improvement in *X* for legislators 4 and 5 but not for anyone else. The figure clearly shows that this proposal would lose.

The importance of side payments such as pork barrel projects is evident when considering proposal *u*. Without changing the new proposal's position on *X,* an agenda setter can also propose a shift in *Y* favorable to legislator 3, who will now support the change from *sq* to *u*.

This long description of figure 1 represents the well-known legislative practice of logrolling. That logrolling and pork barrel projects are important to the passage of substantive legislation is nothing new. Presidents are well aware of the need to make deals and have significant resources for it. They can already promise campaign help, grants, and federal contracts. Serving as chief legislator and party leader, they can play the role of the agenda setter referred to in the discussion on figure 1. Presidents can use their influence informally to reward allies with pork barrel projects by encouraging congressional party leaders to support the side payment. Or, as head of the executive branch, presidents can reward allies with discretionary grants and contracts. They can also use their personal popularity to threaten or reward legislators by "going public," thus enticing them to support any changes.

But all of these resources are finite or fragile and may not be readily available to a president. For example, when different parties control Congress and the executive branch, the president may not be able to deliver a side payment that involves a legislative amendment. The leaders of Congress would have no incentive to follow the requests of the opposition party's president. Grants and spending contracts would still be useful in such cases, but these items are not as readily available in an era of budget cutting. A president could still attempt to influence passage by going public, but again this strategy has its limitations. A popular president can appeal to the public only a limited number of times, and the option is unavailable to an unpopular executive. In short, the president's ability to ensure passage of a bill can be severely constrained. Moreover, although all of these influences work to convince legislators to support presidential initiatives, none of them can be easily used to kill legislation the president opposes. A president has the ability to veto an entire bill, but this move can be fought by using omnibus legislation.

The advantage of the LIV is that it can overcome all of these constraints, especially the last one. Consider again the change from sq to u in figure 1, but assume that the president (not pictured) opposes the change in X. He could veto the bill and prevent the change. Legislators could then counter the move by constructing an omnibus bill with enough of the president's favored programs in it to prevent the president from vetoing it. Grudgingly, the president would be forced to allow the bill to pass and policy would change to u.[2] With the LIV, however, the president can prevent the change in X.

But what if the side deal had not been a tax expenditure or a pork barrel project? The LIV did not allow the veto of authorizing legislation. However, even when opposing nonfiscal legislation, the LIV can still be used to prevent logrolling. The president would need only let it be known he would veto any funding for the change in Y. The program, with changes on both issues, could still pass Congress, and the president could still sign the legislation, but the change opposed by the president would not subsequently receive any appropriations. Any net benefit legislator 3 expected to receive would be eliminated. If legislator 3 is aware of the president's commitment to prevent funding of logrolling, then there is no longer any incentive for the legislator to vote for the move from sq. The proposed legislative change would be dead. Thus, even though the LIV did not give the president the ability to kill nonfiscal legislation, it would have allowed the president to defeat policies he disliked by eliminating the financial side deals necessary for passage. The president may not have been able to veto the change in authorizations policy, but he could undermine its supporting coalition.

For the president, an added benefit of killing a bill this way is its stealth qualities. If the change in X was popular, a president could not have opposed it without risking public displeasure. With the LIV, the president could have opposed it without this public disapproval because he would not have needed to announce his opposition to the change in X. Congressional leaders could have tried to go public themselves to let the voters know what the president was actually doing, but the specifics of the president's tactics would have been difficult to explain simply and concisely. Moreover, the president would then have countered that he was not actively opposing the change in X, only the side payments included in the legislation, and would sign a bill that did not contain these other provisions. Of course, the side deals would not have been included in the bill if passage without them was possible. The LIV could not block all nonfiscal legislation. If there were no logrolling of this kind, then it could not have worked in the described way. But it would have been possible to use the LIV in enough cases to make it a powerful and wide-ranging weapon.

Clearly, the previous scenario portrays a massive change in the relationship between Congress and the president. Given this new power, a president could have forced negotiations that otherwise would not have occurred; Congress could not have used omnibus bills to frustrate presidential vetoes or to avoid negotiation and compromise with the president. Legislators would have been forced to make a president an even more active participant in the crafting of legislation, and the president's subsequent ability to control the legislature's agenda would have been vastly increased.

Perhaps the most important part of the previous hypothetical example is what it does not describe. It mentions nothing about the president's support in Congress or among the voters. It mentions nothing about the state of the budget and the funds available to the president. Unlike other tools used in congressional-executive bargaining, the LIV would not have depended on presidential popularity, available grant money, or party support in Congress. As long as his opponents could not have mustered a cohesive two-thirds majority to override his veto, a minority party president who was poor and unpopular would still have had significant bargaining power. The significance of the LIV was that it was robust; it did not depend on any of these more ephemeral sources of informal presidential power. It was a tool that could have been used strongly by even a weak president.

Conclusion

Much of what determines a president's success is not under his control. For example, some research suggests that the president's ability to influence legislative outcomes depends on the number of partisans he has in Congress, the amount of ideological compatibility he has with legislators, and his popularity overall and within the individual districts (see Bond and Fleisher 1990). However, the power and effect of the LIV did not depend on any of these factors. It could have been used successfully if the president did not have partisan or ideological majorities in the House or Senate, if the president won election by a small margin, or if the president was personally unpopular. The robustness of the LIV was even more significant when considering it could have been used outside of fiscal decisions and thus injected the president into negotiations on authorization legislation. Neustadt (1990) showed that the president's informal powers often determine his success in the policy arena. Under these circumstances so much depends on the ability of the individual officeholder and his staff. The LIV would have placed an extremely powerful tool in the arsenal of an astute president. The dynamics of congressional-presidential bargaining would have been changed dramatically, to the detriment of Congress.

NOTES

We first developed the concepts in this essay a few months before Patrick Fett's death. We presented an earlier version of this paper at the 1997 annual meeting of the American Political Science Association, August 28–31, Washington, D.C.

1. During the short history of the LIV, the Clinton administration made at least one attempt to use the LIV to vote trade. During negotiations on the fiscal year 1998 defense spending bill, Office of Management and Budget Director Franklin D. Raines offered to forgo the use of the LIV in exchange for the funding of the administration's priorities. According to the staff director of the House Appropriations Committee, James W. Dyer, the threat was dismissed (Taylor 1998). Whether the threat could have been used more effectively in the future is, of course, something we will never know.

2. This kind of omnibus legislation would be portrayed as a multidimensional figure whose overall policies would be preferred to the original status quo.

REFERENCES

Abney, Glenn, and Thomas Lauth. 1985. "The Line-Item Veto in the States: An Instrument of Fiscal Control or an Instrument of Partisanship?" *Public Administration Review* 45: 372–77.

Berch, Neil. 1992. "The Item Veto in the States: An Analysis of the Effects over Time." *Social Science Journal* 29: 335–46.

Bond, Jon R., and Richard Fleisher. 1990. *Presidents and Legislators.* Chicago: University of Chicago Press.

Chapman, Stephen. 1997. "Line-item Veto Could Crimp Big Government." *Chicago Tribune,* August 21, sec. 1, p. 25.

Fisher, Louis. 1993. "Should Congress Grant the President Line Item Veto or Expanded Rescission Authority—Con." *Congressional Digest* 72 (February): 45, 47, 49, 51.

Gosling, James J. 1986. "Wisconsin Item-Veto Lessons." *Public Administration Review* 46: 292–99.

Joyce, Philip G., and Robert D. Reischauer. 1997. "The Federal Line-Item Veto: What Is It and What Will It Do?" *Public Administration Review* 57: 95–104.

McCubbins, Mathew D., and Thomas Schwartz. 1984. "Congressional Oversight Overlooked: Police Patrols versus Fire Alarms." *American Journal of Political Science* 28: 164–79.

Nice, David C. 1988. "The Item Veto and Expenditure Restraint." *Journal of Politics* 50 (2): 487–98.

Neustadt, Richard E. 1990. *Presidential Power: the Politics of Leadership from Roosevelt to Reagan.* New York: Free Press.

Schick, Allen. 1995. *The Federal Budget: Politics, Process, Policy.* Washington, D.C.: Brookings Institution Press.

Spence, David B. 1997. "Agency Policy Making and Political Control: Modeling Away the Delegation Problem." *Journal of Public Administration Research and Theory* 7: 199–219.

Taylor, Andrew. 1996. "Congress Hands President a Budgetary Scalpel." *Congressional Quarterly Weekly Report,* March 30, 864–67.

Taylor, Andrew. 1998. "Few in Congress Grieve as Justices Give Line-Item Veto the Ax." *Congressional Quarterly Weekly Report,* June 27, 1747–49.

Towell, Pat. 1998. "$287 Million in Projects Restored to 1998 Bill." *Congressional Quarterly Weekly Report,* February 28, 506.

Weingast, Barry R., and Mark J. Moran. 1983. "Bureaucratic Discretion or Congressional Control? Regulatory Policymaking by the Federal Trade Commission." *Journal of Political Economy* 91: 765–800.

Contributors

John H. Aldrich is the Pfizer-Pratt University Professor of Political Science at Duke University. He has written on American politics, especially on political parties, elections, and Congress, both contemporaneously and historically. He is currently studying political behavior in various democracies.

Steven J. Balla is Assistant Professor of Political Science at The George Washington University. His research and teaching focus on American political institutions and public policy, including legislative-executive relations, state politics, health policy, and formal and empirical methods. His research has appeared in *American Political Science Review*, *American Politics Quarterly*, *Journal of Health Politics, Policy and Law*, *Journal of Law, Economics and Organization*, and *Journal of Public Administration Research and Theory*.

William T. Bianco is Associate Professor of Political Science at the Pennsylvania State University. His research interests are in Congress, legislative politics, and representation.

David Castle is Professor of Political Science at Lamar University. His published work has appeared in *American Politics Quarterly*, *American Review of Politics*, *Presidential Studies Quarterly*, and other journals.

Christine DeGregorio is Associate Professor in the School of Public Affairs at American University. Her research examines the interdependencies among three key participants in the lawmaking process: officeholders, staff, and lobbyists on Capitol Hill. She is the author of *Networks of Champions*.

Richard Delaney received his bachelor's degree from Northeastern Illinois University. His participation in this volume grew out of research he did for an independent study project.

Diana Evans is Professor of Political Science at Trinity College, Hartford, Connecticut. Her current research concerns the use of pork barrel projects by congressional leaders to win votes for broad public policy concerns.

Patrick J. Fett (1959–1996) was associate professor of political science at the University of Memphis. His primary research interest was the interactions of Congress and the president and can be found in the *Journal of Politics*, *Congress and the Presidency, PS: Political Science and Politics*, and *Legislative Studies Quarterly*. The Midwest Political Science Association's Patrick J. Fett Award was created in his memory.

Richard Forgette is Associate Professor of Political Science at Miami University (Oxford, Ohio). His primary teaching and research interests are in legislative politics and public policy. He was the 1996–97 APSA Steiger Congressional Fellow. He has published articles in the *Journal of Politics* and *Legislative Studies Quarterly* and is the author of the book *The Power of the Purse Strings* (1992).

Linda L. Fowler is Director of the Nelson A. Rockefeller Center and Professor of Government at Dartmouth College and holds the Frank Reagan Chair in Policy Studies. The author of two books on candidate recruitment in congressional elections and numerous articles on a variety of topics in American politics, Fowler is currently at work on a study of how voters learn in the New Hampshire primary and a book on the role of attentive publics in the policy process.

Brian Frederking is an Assistant Professor of Political Science at McKendree College. Recent publications include *Resolving Security Dilemmas: A Constructivist Interpretation of the INF Treaty* and articles in *International Studies Quarterly* and *International Politics*.

Jeffrey S. Hill is Associate Professor of Political Science at Northeastern Illinois University. His primary research interest is how public policy is influenced by the interactions of the separate institutions of government, particularly Congress and the executive branch. His work includes articles in *American Journal of Political Science, Journal of Politics, Journal of Law, Economics and Organization, Journal of Theoretical Politics,* and *Legislative Studies Quarterly.*

Bryan W. Marshall is Assistant Professor of Political Science at the University of Missouri, St. Louis. His areas of interest include American politics and quantitative methods. He is currently engaged in research on the appropriations process and congressional-executive relations.

Brandon C. Prins is Assistant Professor of Political Science at the University of New Orleans. His current research interests include American and comparative foreign policy, interstate conflict, and congressional-executive relations. He has recently published articles in *Journal of Peace Research, International Studies Quarterly,* and *Congress and the Presidency.*

David W. Rohde is University Distinguished Professor of Political Science and Director of the Political Institutions and Public Choice Program at Michigan State University. He has been editor of the *American Journal of Political Science* and the chair of the Legislative Studies Section of the APSA. He has written books and articles on various aspects of American national politics.

Wendy J. Schiller is Associate Professor in the Department of Political Science at Brown University. Her research focuses on individual Senate behavior and its relation to representation. She also studies the effects of bicameralism on interest group coalition building.

Kenneth Shepsle is the George Markham Professor of Government at Harvard University. His research concerns Congress, parliamentary politics, positive political theory, and, most recently, intergenerational politics.

Barbara Sinclair is Marvin Hoffenberg Professor of American Politics at UCLA. Her publications include articles in the *American Political Science Review, American Journal of Political Science, Journal of Politics,* and *Legislative Studies Quarterly* and several books, including *The Transformation of the U.S. Senate* (1989), winner of the Richard F. Fenno Prize for the outstanding book published in 1989 in legislative studies awarded by the Legislative Studies Section of the American Political Science Association and of the D. B. Hardeman Prize for the outstanding book on the U.S. Congress published in 1989–90 awarded by the L.B.J. Foundation.

John R. Wright, Professor of Political Science at the Ohio State University, specializes in American politics, with emphasis on interest groups and their relations with Congress, the Supreme Court, and the federal bureaucracy. He is author of *Interest Groups and Congress: Lobbying, Contributions, and Influence* as well as numerous articles in the *American Political Science Review, American Journal of Political Science, Journal of Politics,* and other leading scholarly journals. His current research investigates the activities of interest groups in the federal bureaucracy.

Index